Breaking Down the Digital Walls

SUNY series, Education and Culture:
Critical Factors in the Formation of
Character and Community in American Life

Eugene F. Provenzo Jr. and Paul Farber, Editors

BREAKING DOWN THE DIGITAL WALLS

Learning to Teach in a Post-Modem World

R. W. Burniske and Lowell Monke

with a Foreword by Jonas F. Soltis

State University of New York Press

Published by
State University of New York Press, Albany

For information, address State University of New York Press,
State University Plaza, Albany, N.Y., 12246

Production by Michael Haggett
Marketing by Patrick Durocher

Library of Congress Cataloging-in-Publication Data
Burniske, R. W., 1960 –
    Breaking down the digital walls : learning to teach in a post-modem world /
R. W. Burniske and Lowell Monke; with a foreword by Jonas F. Soltis.
        p. cm. — (SUNY series, education and culture)
    Includes bibliographical references (p.) and index.
    ISBN 0 –7914– 4753 –7 (hc : acid free) — ISBN 0 –7914– 4754 –5 (pb : acid free)
    1. Education—Data processing. 2. Internet (Computer network) in education.
3. Teaching. I. Monke, Lowell, 1949 –   II. Title. III. Series.
LB1028.43 .B89 2000
371.33'4—dc21   00-02788

10 9 8 7 6 5 4 3 2 1

We dedicate this book to the most important teachers in our lives: Nick and Penny Burniske and Melvin and Phyllis Monke.

CONTENTS

FOREWORD

Everyone senses the pervasiveness and radical nature of the electronic revolution going on in the world today. We talk of the earth becoming a "global village" spanned by "information highways" and the bringing about of the "homogenization of cultures." In a mere fifty years the computer has come from being a huge vacuum tube filled machine that counts, adds, subtracts, divides, multiplies, and stores information to a desktop and even a laptop wizard of communication, visualization, entertainment, and work station.

Every educator, from those old timers still unsure if they can master and use this new "machine" to those younger ones for whom the computer was an integral part of their home life and schooling, all know that the computer will (if it hasn't already) become a major tool of teaching and learning and a ubiquitous feature of daily life in the twenty-first century.

But what are its optimal educational uses? How can it best serve the most desirable aims of education? Is it just a tool that all students will need to learn how to use to make a living or can it also serve as a pedagogical vehicle for shaping human lives and sensible, sensitive persons?

In this book, in a way most accessible to both young and old educators or policymakers, Burniske and Monke address these fundamental questions about the role of education in the "post-modem" world. In a most absorbing and enchanting way, they perform this task by telling us a story, their own story of how two teacher-colleagues half a world apart struggled to make computing and communication work toward the ends of developing critical thinking, genuine dialogue, and global understanding in their classrooms.

Everyone knows that computers can serve students as vast stores of information and provide them with opportunities to chat and share ideas with other students almost anywhere on the globe. This makes academic resources available to all and opportunities for communication transcend local boundaries. But what of academic discussion, critical thinking, and argument in the best sense of the word—that is, openness to new and different ideas, the careful weighing of evidence, and the trusting of reason to persuade in the mutual search for meaning, truth, and well-being?

Through the development of a number of curricular projects linking classrooms in Malaysia, Japan, Iowa, South Africa, England et al., Burniske and

Monke show us how they wrestled not only with the technical problems of using the Internet, but, more important, with the practical and philosophical questions of how to serve their higher pedagogical purposes of nurturing genuine communication, dialogue, and argument. They thoughtfully offer well-measured appraisals of their successes as well as their failures so that we can learn from both.

Theirs is an exemplary joint authorship, not in one voice but in two. Alternating the writing of chapters, they speak to each other as well as to the reader. They both write clearly, engagingly, and sincerely. They share a sound philosophical view of what ought to be the broad and basic educational aims of using the Internet in school: dialogue, dialectic, and open-minded inquiry. They write to a nontechnical audience and invite real and productive thought by teachers and administrators and policymakers about how to use the "information highway" to go well beyond the mere accessing of information. They even treat "netiquette" and the responsibilities of teachers and students using the Internet to communicate with others. They do all this with amazing verve and sophistication from the real context of their own collaborative teaching experiences. Their international school experience also adds a persuasive global dimension to their work. At heart, they are *real* teachers and have much to teach us all.

This is a most welcome addition to the contemporary literature about computers and schooling. It should help to raise our thinking and talk to a new level of sophistication and high-mindedness as we try to link the best educational aims of the past to the present and future of the electronic revolution.

Jonas F. Soltis
William Heard Kilpatrick Professor Emeritus
Philosophy and Education
Teachers College, Columbia University

ACKNOWLEDGMENTS

A good book is the best of friends, the same today and forever.
Tupper (1980, 539)

Were it not for good friends, this book wouldn't exist. Their wit and wisdom are woven into the fabric of this text along with years of moral support. I could not have met the challenges of teaching and writing without the encouragement and camaraderie of George Shadroui, Max Steele, John O'Brien, Lowell Monke, Tom Lardner, Jorge and Kathy Capello, Tom and Marilyn Hopkins, Jean Guy Gelinas and Lynn Surette. I am similarly indebted to the students at Cairo American College, Deerfield Academy, Academia Cotopaxi, the International School of Kuala Lumpur and the University of Texas who have been an integral part of my education. Their voices, and the lessons we learned together, helped shape this narrative and give it meaning. In addition, I've been blessed by the contributions of students and teachers at schools around the world who participated in the global, telecollaborative projects described in this book. If not for their extraordinary courage and collegial spirit I could not have experimented with online learning activities, nor discovered the challenges of teaching in a post-modem world.

I am grateful to those who helped nurture this project, from its inception to final publication. A fellowship from the University of Texas provided support for the initial composition. The editors of *Teacher* Magazine and *Phi Delta Kappan* offered thoughtful criticism and editorial assistance with their publication of selected excerpts. Jonas Soltis gave generously of his time and spirit, encouraging publication through his enthusiastic endorsement at a critical moment. The manuscript's reviewers, Patrick Dickson and Irene Ward, provided careful readings and insightful critiques. Priscilla Ross and her staff at SUNY renewed our faith in publishers, demonstrating a humane sensibility from start to finish. And while the flaws remain my own, the strengths of this book are certainly greater thanks to the generous critiques and thoughtful reactions that my work received from Lester Faigley, Peg Syverson, Linda Ferreira-Buckley, Judith Lindfors, Davida Charney, Terry Sullivan, John Slatin and Judi Harris.

Ultimately, though, I owe the greatest thanks to my wife, Jackie, and our sons, Justin and Christopher, for giving me the time, space, and inspiration to write this book. I can only hope this returns a small portion of the pride and joy that they have given me.

—R. W. B.
Austin, Texas

No one deserves my thanks more than R. W. "Buddy" Burniske, whose enormous energy and clear vision guided us through many difficult times in writing this book. I want to join him in thanking all the good folks at SUNY for their faith in our work and the graceful manner in which they led us through the publishing process.

I can't imagine this project ever being completed without the unwavering academic and personal support of Jackie Blount, or the insights and friendship of David Owen, Robert Hollinger and Eric Abbott at Iowa State University. The Des Moines Public Schools are havens for so many remarkably dedicated educators it is difficult to single out just a few, but I am most indebted to Bob Davitt, who brought me to Central Campus and gave me the kind of trust, freedom and protection few teachers experience. I thank Mike Schaffer, Jean Ellerhoff, Phil Parks and Pat Ramsey for their willingness to jump into the uncharted waters of telecollaboration with me. And, like Buddy, I want to express my appreciation to the students there and at schools all around the world who I suspect taught me far more than I taught them.

I want to thank Steve Talbott for persistently encouraging me to write and for first publishing "The Web and the Plow" in NETFUTURE. Versions of that essay subsequently appeared in both Orion and Teacher Magazine. I owe a great deal to Val Setzer, who first showed me a different way to look at technology; to Phil Walsh for trying to keep me from losing sight of everything else; to my sister, Judy Watts, whose stability and loyalty provided a much needed touchstone during my years of wandering; and to Kim Bush, whose great friendship and long conversations on our treks in the Andes I kept in mind as I tried to explain my ideas in this book.

I tend to be ruled by inertia. If I had not married such an adventuresome woman I never would have encountered the unique people and rich experiences overseas that led to this book. Julie pulled me along to Ecuador, and gave her wholehearted support to this project in spite of all of my efforts to undermine it. Whatever I have managed here is nothing compared to her accomplishment of running her own business, taking care of our two very active boys and dealing with my mental absence as I tried to finish my dissertation and this book in the same year. For her support, and the patience of Benjamin and Mitchell, I am forever grateful.

—L.M.
Des Moines, Iowa

Before I built a wall I'd ask to know
What I was walling in or walling out,
And to whom I was like to give offense.
Something there is that doesn't love a wall,
That wants it down.

Robert Frost, *Mending Wall*

Breaking Down the Digital Walls

1

The Manabi Hut

R. W. Burniske

Without dialogue there is no communication, and without communication there can be no true education. Paulo Freire (1997, 73–74)

Our collaboration began inside a thatched hut in the Andes.

The year was 1987, and Lowell Monke and I were colleagues at an international school in Quito, the Ecuadorian capital situated 9,000 feet above sea level in "the Avenue of Volcanoes." Lowell taught mathematics and computer science, while I taught English and U.S. History. Our respective disciplines might well have kept us apart, as academic departments often divide faculty within schools. What's more, Lowell was in the final year of his contract, preparing for repatriation to his home state of Iowa, while I was a new teacher from Massachusetts trying to find a niche in a foreign school and culture. It would have been easy for us to slip past each other, our paths crossing briefly while we headed in opposite directions, our work and studies grounded in what some consider opposite realms. However, we shared a few common experiences, including farm life and fading athleticism, along with an enduring bond: affection for ideas and people who cared about them, people with the courage to examine their convictions.

There was also the matter of amoebas.

Ecuador, though blessed with wondrous geography, is cursed with microscopic parasites eager to meet *gringos* lacking intestinal fortitude. Lowell and I were pure *gringo* in this regard, which meant that when a new eating establishment opened near Academia Cotopaxi and one found it possible to lunch there without acquiring amoebic dysentery, well, one did that—on a daily basis. That is what led this odd couple, one teacher from the Sciences and the other from Humanities, across *Avenida Naciones Unidas,* past the shopping complex that proved a harbinger of things to come, and through a narrow passageway to the small, round hut situated on a quiet, residential street behind the mall. The food was simple, but consistently good and healthy. The owners specialized in seafood from "Manabi," an area along the Pacific coast of Ecuador. Our daily regimen consisted of fried fish, lentils, banana chips, and incessant argument. As *rico* as the food may have been, it eventually became an excuse for the even richer discussions. So began my lunches with Lowell, as close to Wallace Shawn's dinner with Andre as anything I've ever known, and every bit as rewarding (Shawn 1982).

We were, like many teachers in mid-career, struggling to keep the faith, cognizant of limitations within ourselves and our academic disciplines. Those limitations made us hunger for something more satisfying and holistic. We'd grown weary of "administrivia" and the petty politics of colleagues jockeying for positions within existing hierarchies; we'd also lost patience with clichés, the oft-recited, seldom examined, school maxims concerning pedagogy and pupils. Education had become a series of strategies and bumper stickers, the work of technicians who espoused one gimmick after another at workshops, confident that their techniques were the panacea for what ails today's schools. What of the art in teaching, though? What of all those questions for which we didn't have answers (or at least satisfying ones)? Where should one turn when a planning book full of strategies and tactics collided with questions that the latest workshop didn't address?

If nothing else, "The Manabi Hut," as it came to be known, was a quiet haven from the lunacy of a school situated in the footpath of the national soccer stadium, the flight path of Quito's international airport, and the worn path of more students than it had space to accommodate. Within that school we heard the disputes of self-righteous individuals with superficial answers to everything from the physical plant to the class schedule, yet little to camouflage the self-interest that informed their views. The Manabi Hut, meanwhile, presented a forum, a place for the exploration of ideas, often beginning with a question we could not resolve, extending from one lunch to the next. Lowell enjoyed my comments on literature, particularly the fault I found with students who resisted it, while I appreciated his critiques of the computer, and the inability of students and faculty to perform elementary functions with it. Typically, we supported positions that confirmed our views and dismissed those challenging them.

With time, though, we allowed our guard to fall, exposing the doubt that is an integral part of one's faith. While seated at our table in Manabi, we found ourselves crawling from one side of it to the other, defending our colleague's discipline and students against simplistic critiques. This effort to play devil's advocate allowed us the novelty of trading places, exchanging a seat in the Humanities for one in the Sciences, or vice versa, adopting views of the Other for a time without forfeiting the rights to our original seat. We were new to this game, groping our way intuitively toward an understanding of how to play it. As I look back, however, I realize that those discussions confirmed the observations of a philosopher who tried describing "the mathematical and the intuitive mind" as well as an inherent irony of argument:

In disputes we like to see the clash of opinion, but not at all to contemplate truth when found. To observe it with pleasure, we have to see it emerge out of strife. So in the passions, there is pleasure in seeing the collision of two contraries, but when one acquires the mastery it becomes brutality. We never seek things for themselves, but for the search. (Pascal 1958, 38)

Our discussions helped us reach an important destination: the point at which we tired of our own rhetoric. We were reluctant to make the next step, confessing ignorance or uncertainty, especially when friends joined us and we reverted to the clash of opinions rather than the pursuit of truth. To cross the next threshold we needed to shed our vanities, those parts of ourselves that clung to the desire for victory at the expense of truth. Only later, away from the theater of The Manabi Hut, in the absence of our passions and pride, did we quietly digest food and thought, conceding that our counterpart was right about a certain matter. Well, perhaps. This begged an obvious, though troublesome, question: How could we inspire students to engage in open-minded inquiry when we barely had the capacity for it ourselves?

The Indispensable Opposition

Eventually, we realized the particular themes of our discussions weren't as important as their aim. Contained within our dialogues were learning opportunities rarely discovered in the school environment. To seek truth or "think out loud" in a faculty meeting would invite ridicule. The preoccupation in that environment is political persuasion, particularly when administrators arrange meetings like a press conference rather than a forum for discussion. Nonetheless, as the academic year drew to a close Lowell and I shed previous defense mechanisms, initiating new inquiries with little more than, "You know, I was just wondering why . . ." Though we didn't speak of it at the time, we understood the trust implicit in that phrase, for we make such gestures only when we believe the listener will meet us with equal wonder.

Eventually, our lunch sessions helped us construct more satisfying answers through the paradoxical idea of "supportive opposition," the presentation of an antithesis that helps refine another's argument rather than destroy it (Kinneavy 1980). This liberated us from the one-upsmanship of competitive debates, transforming confrontations into collaborations. Nevertheless, we occasionally clashed, disagreeing with such passion that neighboring diners had to wonder if we were friends or foes. Perhaps we were both, but that seemed inevitable for people trying to discover truth. Politely accepting platitudes or nodding at unexamined beliefs wouldn't serve our purpose. We needed to do more than tolerate opposing viewpoints; we had to find ways to encourage them, for reasons that the historian Walter Lippman had articulated upon the eve of war:

> The opposition is indispensable. A good statesman, like any other sensible human being, always learns more from his opponents than from his fervent supports. For his supporters will push him to disaster unless his opponents show him where the dangers are. So if he is wise he will often pray to be delivered from his friends, because they will ruin him. But, though it hurts, he ought also to pray never to be left without opponents; for they keep him on the path of reason and good sense. (1984, 501)

We were on the verge of adapting Lippman's philosophy, like two alchemists combining the foes' aggression with the friends' empathy, when our lunches came to an end. In June 1988, Lowell and his family returned to North America; I traveled with my family to Great Britain and graduate work in Renaissance drama. My summer's study would reveal the method to the madness of our verbal skirmishes as well as the flaws of pedagogical approaches I had inherited from mentors. The simplicity of this insight was maddening, and within it lay the seed for telecollaborative projects, a topic that Lowell and I had never broached during all those lunches. It was the idea of *dialectical discourse,* a practice that is "characteristically oral and dialogual, not written and monologual" (Kinneavy 1980, 187). It informs much of our work, from personal correspondence to telecollaborative projects, but while it was a common expression of seventeenth-century drama, this concept may seem foreign to twenty-first century students.

The Drama of Dialectics

Though it seems an odd request in a book about telecollaborative learning, imagine traveling back in time, not just a decade or two, but four hundred years, to the start of the seventeenth century and the country that gave birth to the United States of America. The sights and sounds of a terribly foreign culture would greet and bewilder a time-traveler. However, stepping out of our own time and place—approximating the experience that Lowell and I enjoyed as expatriate teachers in Ecuador—helps us see our contemporary situation more clearly. What's more, by looking backward at the peculiarities of a culture that shaped the English language and American identity we may help ourselves envision the future of online culture and telecollaborative learning, which would undoubtedly strike our ancestors as equally strange and foreign.

Upon arrival in a village outside London in the year 1600, the vibrant sights, sounds, and smells might overwhelm us. However, as our senses adjust we begin to notice what's "missing" from this new environment. While we see more trees, animals, and pedestrians, we also notice an absence of motor vehicles, telephone lines, and TV antennas. Quite soon, we realize that the presence of certain things doesn't affect us as profoundly as the absence of others, particularly the absence of modern media. There is no Internet, no television, no radio, no telephone, and almost no books or print publications. Where do these people turn for news and information, or print and electronic entertainment? The primary broadcast medium is spoken language, though it sounds quite different from modern English. Nevertheless, that language, and the stories it conveys, shapes this culture and society. Nothing proves this more emphatically than a trip to a London theater.

Indeed, there is plenty of news and information, as well as entertainment, in the British theater of 1600. All walks of society gather within this public space to exchange news and information, tell stories, and enjoy the entertainment of bear-baiting, juggling, fencing, and various other activities—including professional drama (Gurr 1987). Here again, the modern visitor notices what's missing. There are no female actresses, for instance, and few special effects. Some stages are equipped with trap doors and a few quaint, primitive devices. However, the lack of special effects compels some of the most extraordinary poetry and prose ever written, because the primary means of delivering "news and information"—while entertaining, inspiring, and moving an audience—is *language*. As a result, playwrights of that time period had to think of language as their medium, one that not only communicated lofty thoughts, but also advanced the plot. In the absence of modern lighting, for example, one of Shakespeare's characters must tell us "the morn in russet mantle clad / Walks o'er the dew of yon high estward hill" (Shakespeare 1969a, 935). In other words, "Look, the sun is coming up!"

I call attention to this because it reveals how far we've traveled since 1600, particularly with respect to media and communication. At the turn of the seventeenth century, language was the primary means through which dramas could define character, create suspense, prompt laughter, provoke tears, and describe universal conflicts. The playhouses of London furnished a marvelous medium for communication, giving expression to human comedies and tragedies, histories and romances. However, some of these expressions would disappoint modern visitors, particularly those seeking resolution to conflicts. For while its elaborate language and dramatic presentations engaged the audience's thought and emotions, this art form, particularly as it matured, often resisted the impulse to resolve deep tensions. Love did not *always* conquer Envy; if it did, Othello would overcome Iago and live happily ever after with his wife. Nor did virtue *always* get the better of vice, for if it did we might never witness a tragedy—or discover painful truths.

Perhaps this is the most important discovery for a modern visitor to the seventeenth-century theater: the lack of "closure" in dramatic performances. What caused this trend? Why did playwrights of the latter Elizabethan and (with King James' coronation in 1603) "Jacobean" period engage in something so contrary to the standard fare of twenty-first-century television and film? What lessons might we learn from this tolerance of dramatic tensions? If nothing else, these dramas help us realize that the emergence of media since the turn of the seventeenth century has enabled new ways of *telling* stories, but not necessarily better stories. Just ask the Hollywood producers who turn to Shakespeare for scripts. Unfortunately, cinematic productions seldom prove faithful to these dramas, for a preoccupation with visual style dilutes their narrative substance. What's more, they often compromise the spirit of Renaissance drama by forcing resolutions where none were intended, forgetting that the playwright's work gave life to *dialectics,* a dialogue seeking truth.

In it, characters confront problems, seek ways to resolve them, and try to convince one another that they have resolved them. But they themselves are simply fictional hypotheses that function as the author's instruments of inquiry. They are his means of examining with sensitivity questions that are of continuing concern. (Altman 1978, 105)

This is essential for the modern audience trying to understand these dramas—or follow the argument of this book. We may engage emotionally with characters, but must, like the playwright, remain detached enough to reason, mature enough to accept ambiguity and tension. This feat requires a sophisticated control of anxieties, born as they are of conflicting forces within us. The desire to resolve, the Jacobean dramatist believed, was often the desire to destroy, since it did violence to the dialectics that exist in the natural world. The art of Renaissance drama invites the audience to balance passion against reason while watching the writer's "instruments of inquiry" struggle with "continuing concerns." This explains why eleven of Shakespeare's thirty-seven plays end without conclusion, and why Prospero invites his former enemies, the men who usurped him, to step into his "poor cell" for a night of "discourse" at the end of *The Tempest* (Shakespeare 1969b).

However, imagine the plight of a classroom teacher trying to explain such noble gestures to adolescents at the start of the twenty-first century. Not only is Shakespeare's language foreign, but so is the idea of "the rarer virtue" that Prospero demonstrates, the profound empathy and understanding that he extends to people who not only opposed him, but left him and his infant daughter to die at sea. How many of us are capable of forgiving such adversaries, valorizing empathy more than revenge? For all our technological progress in the intervening centuries, popular Western culture often celebrates simplistic, violent conclusions to complex problems. How does one argue with the opposition, or engage in dialectics, when there is so little support for reason, compassion, or under-standing? How do we teach adolescents to think critically when their culture is saturated with images of people who shoot guns first, and think later—if they think at all?

Whether conducting a classroom discussion, a Model United Nations' simu-lation, or a global telecollaboration, educators ask students to entertain "con-tinuing concerns" that simultaneously excite passion and stimulate reason. This is remarkably challenging, however, for students uninitiated to the world and self, particularly if they are impatient with ambiguity and unaware of the diffi-culties involved in trying to define the "self." My studies of Renaissance drama provided an important, historical perspective, describing the sixteenth century as a critical turning point, a time of

increased self-consciousness about the fashioning of human identity as a manipulable, artful process. Such self-consciousness had been widely spread among the elite in the classical world, but Christianity brought a growing suspicion of man's power to shape identity: "Hands off yourself," Augustine declared. "Try to build up yourself and you build a ruin." (Greenblatt 1980, 2)

Here at the start of the twenty-first century online interactions present new challenges to self-fashioning. As Sherry Turkle has observed, the "imperative to self-knowledge has always been at the heart of philosophical inquiry" but that imperative acquires even greater urgency for adolescents who "struggle to make meaning from our lives on the screen" (1995, 269). Prior to the Renaissance, re-ligious dogma discouraged meddling with the self, but today cyberspace presents challenges to the very notion of "self." Indeed, the postmodern view "questions the existence of a rational, coherent self and the ability of the self to have privileged insight into its own processes" (Faigley 1992, 111). This should concern anyone involved with telecomputing, because online activities compli-cate the issue of identity for adolescents. Students must "read" others, inter-preting who they are and what their words mean at a time in their lives when they themselves are trying to discover a personal voice and identity. Often, they define themselves by opposing "the Other," anyone they perceive as hostile or threatening, but what are the consequences for a generation that participates in such online behavior? Although they may think it a harmless diversion, just a game of words and wit, they are developing discourse practices and a world-view that contradict the spirit of collaboration. How far removed is this from our Renaissance ancestors, who defined themselves in relation to a "threatening Other" who "must be discovered or invented in order to be attacked and de-stroyed" (Greenblatt 1980, 9)?

The student of Renaissance drama understands the consequences of this im-pulse: self-destruction. The protagonist's desire for revenge, and the resolution of conflict by silencing the "opposition," precipitates the death of Hamlet, Othello, Lear, Macbeth, and more. Yet how many twenty-first-century students, ignorant of such dramas and metaphysical concerns, understand this phenomenon? Might their ignorance subvert dialectical discourse online, prompting verbal assaults that destroy educational opportunities? Could the disrespect bred in Internet "chat rooms" sabotage telecollaboration, causing the premature dismissal of opposing viewpoints? There are no "plug and play" solutions to such problems. Rather, they require careful attention to discursive habits, a reorientation that encourages students to embrace the opposition as a supporter rather than an antagonist. How do we help them understand this paradox? Perhaps an architectural analogy will help.

To an architect, the strength and reliability of a wooden bridge depends as much upon opposition as it does the integrity of materials. The wooden bridge of the seventeenth century featured crossbeams exerting equal and opposing force upon one another. The frame could only support weight with the maintenance of these opposing forces; to remove the crossbeams would collapse the bridge. Similarly, to remove opposition from an individual would remove the restraint preventing that individual's fall, morally and spiritually, and isolate him from the truth. These principles, when applied to society, call for opposition to sustain order. To prevent chaos and disaster the individual must confront opposition without trying to destroy it. The Elizabethan and Jacobean dramas help us realize, ultimately, that opposition restrains self-destructive passions. While we're encouraged to sympathize with the characters, we are not expected to resolve the greater tensions that fashion better human beings.

For obvious reasons, these dramas require an audience that accepts ambiguity and tension. Their creators dedicated themselves to the exploration of complex forces and ideas; their theaters celebrated the pursuit of truth, not power. In their paradoxical way, the plays demand engagement and detachment, urging us to suspend judgments and resolutions, for if we hasten to end problems we will politicize issues that transcend politics, pursuing Power where we ought to seek Truth. If dramas, and dialectics, conclude, it is because we, the audience, force them to do so. However, our reward is a misguided embrace of facile "solutions" to complex problems. What these dramas argue for, what Lowell Monke and I propose for educational telecollaboration, is an acceptance of opposition that creates the "salutary anxiety" necessary for learning (Greenblatt, 1980). Without that tension we spoil our intellectual odysseys, arriving at premature conclusions. However, our shortcomings will be exposed when the Caroline curtain falls upon the stage. For while we may enjoy the momentary catharsis that fiction supplies—Hamlet's virtue conquering his foes' vice—the conflict between opposing forces will resume outside the theater (and classroom), presenting far less conclusive endings to dialectical dramas.

The Lion and the Man

This brings us back to the twenty-first century, and public discourse about tele-collaboration in the classroom. Above all, Lowell and I wish to join this discussion as teachers. We cannot speak on behalf of all classroom practitioners, but by starting from our experiments with telecollaborative learning we hope to stimulate a conversation that *must include* teachers—not just researchers, administrators, and policymakers. Since classroom teachers are often pushed to the periphery of such discussions, the first step is to make room at the table, letting those with an alternative viewpoint speak before the dominant discourse overwhelms them. An ancient fable reminds us why this is significant:

A Man and a Lion were discussing the relative strength of men and lions in general. The Man contended that he and his fellows were stronger than lions by reason of their greater intelligence. "Come now with me," he cried, "and I will soon prove that I am right." So he took him into the public gardens and showed him a statue of Hercules overcoming the Lion and tearing his mouth in two. "That is all very well," said the Lion, "but proves nothing, for it was a man who made the statue."
   Moral: We can easily represent things as we wish them to be. (Jacobs 1984, 50)

Aesop's Man is alive and well at the start of the twenty-first century, holding forth in discussions concerning computers in education. We've heard this Technological Man in presidential rhetoric that championed the Information Age, state and federal proposals for infrastructure expenditures, and educational research prophesying the triumph of computer literacy over traditional "letteracy" (Papert 1996). In each instance, Technological Man has portrayed the computer as a *smart* machine that will deliver us from the evils of ignorance and fulfill our dreams of technological utopianism. Persuasive though he may be, we must not allow this Man to silence Aesop's Lion. Educators have experienced enough reform movements to know that today's technological panacea may become tomorrow's placebo. Indeed, we ought to receive the rhetoric of Technological Man with a healthy bit of skepticism. While he extols the virtues of telecomputing, reciting a clichéd chorus of hopeful possibilities, he may forget to deduct 'Net losses from the 'Net gains that fully describe the 'Net effect of telecollaboration in the classroom.

This book, a collaborative effort, represents things as we have found them, not as we have wished them to be, while introducing telecollaboration to our classrooms. This does not, however, mean that we cheer for the Lion to overwhelm Man's argument by roaring "Refuse it" (Birkerts 1994). The Lion, and his pride of latter-day Luddites, would have us dismiss computer technology, admonishing listeners to prostrate themselves before Nature's altar. For all their nostalgic appeal, however, such pastoral yearnings repress the human impulse to shape the world. They also deny a fundamental truth. Our infatuation with human creations rivals our affection for Nature. Those creations, whether technological or artistic expressions, spring from the desire to imagine and construct a different world (Bronowski 1973; Frye 1964). While technology often introduces new problems even as it solves old ones, we cannot erase our signature upon the Faustian pact signed when *homo sapiens* first cleared a space to build shelters and cultivate gardens. Thus, we are forced to accommodate conflicting desires, our ambivalence evident in advertisements depicting Technological Man reclining upon a pristine, tropical beach with his cellular phone and laptop computer nearby.

Neither the beach nor the Man will recover their prelapsarian state, nor will the cell phone or laptop disappear. Together, they give expression to the dialectical tensions that define our moment in history. The primary aim of this book, informed by the same principles that have guided our work as telecollaborative educators, is to inspire healthy, dialectical discourse, an exploratory discourse rooted in the belief that "truth was found in dialogue" (Kinneavy 1980, 187). By allowing both the Man and the Lion to have their say, we hope to temper the hype and hysteria that frequently attend discussions of computers in education. Unless restrained, our passions may overwhelm the opposing viewpoints necessary for developing effective pedagogical practices, prompting the hasty adoption of bad innovations. Such actions demonstrate the educator's ability to adapt and survive professionally, but they neglect the fundamental need for pedagogical experimentation and invention.

We began *Breaking Down the Digital Walls,* and the telecollaborative projects it describes, with a desire to interrogate educational telecomputing, subjecting it to rigorous inquiry. By doing so, we hoped to shed light on contemporary efforts to introduce computer technology to classrooms, drawing attention to oft-neglected issues. In its 1999 report, the National Center for Education Statistics announced that Internet access in K–12 schools had increased from 35% in 1994 to 89% in 1998 (NCES 1999). However, extraordinary investments in infrastructure have failed to stimulate comparable investments in educators, the people who will be held accountable if this experiment fails. Recent studies on state, national, and international levels reveal a paucity of "teacher training," a term that one national U.S. survey broadly conceived as only "nine hours of training in educational technology" while admitting the results of their study "tell us nothing about the quality of these professional development efforts" (Wolk 1997, 41).

Such neglect betrays a misguided faith in technology to stimulate learning. Educators charged with the integration of new technology frequently employ variations of traditional pedagogy, borrowing methods from activities such as correspondence courses, which stressed the "delivery" of material for distance learning. This is hardly a recipe for educational progress. Rather, it invites the transfer of teaching methods from one medium to another, dressing inadequate pedagogy in electronic robes while pretending alterations are unnecessary. This tendency manifests itself in a number of ways, but perhaps one of the most telling is the embrace of misleading terminology.

The use of networked computers to send or retrieve information qualifies as a "telecomputing" activity, but genuine interaction is required for "telecommunication." To take the work to a more sophisticated level, enabling students separated by distance to "share the labors" of research and inquiry would require what has become known as "telecollaboration." However, as our experience will demonstrate, this proves far more difficult than many people admit. What's more, we lose important distinctions if we think of these terms as interchangeable, embracing the idea that any use of networked computers is at once a telecomputing activity that inspires telecommunication and a robust, telecollaborative community. While this is a convenient way to represent things, and a temptation for educators and entrepreneurs who prosper from the Internet gold rush, it proves counterproductive to the diffusion of effective, educational innovations.

Research has demonstrated that only 2.5% of a given population fulfills the role of "innovators," while roughly 13% prove to be "early adopters" of new innovations (Rogers 1995). This is especially significant when we consider how little is known about the efficacy of telecollaborative activities and what exactly "goes on" inside them. What do the students do? What do they learn? How can we measure that learning? What pedagogical practices ought to be encouraged? Which should be discouraged? Certainly, computer technology introduces new possibilities, but it also introduces new problems and responsibilities. It is incumbent upon all members of a social group, therefore, to test an innovation before embracing it. This underscores the importance of our historical moment, since the educational telecomputing paradigms and praxis we endorse today will determine the diffusion of innovations tomorrow.

Unfortunately, contemporary emphasis of educational "outcomes" often distracts us from student reading, writing, and research practices. As a result, the processes involved suffer relative neglect. While espousing constructivist principles, advocating the *ideas* of "telecollaboration" and "global classrooms," educators and policymakers have assumed that certain activities will automatically occur once schools are connected to the network infrastructure. Of primary importance, as electronic mail and the World Wide Web lose their novelty, is discussion of classroom experiences by classroom practitioners. That conviction has motivated the action research that Lowell and I have conducted for nearly a decade, prompting numerous trials, and even more errors, with telecollaborative activities. More than anything, we've tried to inspire critical thinking, helping students interrogate information and assess the credibility of sources they encountered online. Initially, that prompted us to consider the ramifications of project designs.

In developing a taxonomy for educational telecollaborative activities, Judi Harris has identified three primary genres: interpersonal exchanges, information collections and analyses, and problem-solving projects (1998). Despite researchers' admonitions, early adopters of these paradigms have frequently settled upon "keypal exchanges" (interpersonal exchanges) and "scavenger hunts" (information collections); unfortunately, keypal exchanges often suffer poor reciprocity and superficial inquiry (Levin 1989) while scavenger hunts lead students into the cul-de-sac of "infotainment" where information is confused with knowledge. What's more, the third paradigm, that of problem-based learning, suffers a disappointing reductionism when students seek premature resolution of complex problems rather than resisting closure to extend their inquiry. Without realizing it, therefore, the inexperienced teacher who hopes to create a "telecollaborative" project might achieve little more than "telecomputing" if the project's design emphasizes information collection without demanding analysis or problem-solving; meanwhile, we settle for recreational forms of "telecommunication" if we allow "interpersonal exchanges" to become self-indulgent discussions of social lives.

Given these limitations, and the potential for "paradigm paralysis," a most compelling question arises. How might we design *and* facilitate telecollaborative projects that encourage students to ask questions rather than embrace superficial answers that become "inert ideas" (Whitehead 1929)? If we approach this with a dialectical spirit, then we must find a way to satisfy both Hirsch's idea of a memory *schema* developed through a "core curriculum" and Sizer's demand for better "habits of mind" (Hirsch 1987; Sizer 1996). For online activities to promote learning, they should encourage student research that assists the development of a mental schema while providing opportunities to interrogate information, transforming data into knowledge through socially constructed meaning (Duffy 1996). In other words, we need to emphasize both the process and product of telecollaborative learning, thinking of ways to help students graduate from simple "telecomputing" activities to more challenging forms of "telecommunication" that culminate in truly "interactive" learning activities.

I won't dispute the potential for meaningful interaction among students separated by time and geography, yet connected by computer networks. However, I would argue against feeble definitions of "interactivity," because educational discourse suffers whenever we confuse the click of a hyptertext link or post of a discussion forum message with genuine interaction. What we must accomplish is the quantum leap from potential to reality. Without that leap telecollaborative activities frequently creep toward the extremes of the "keypal exchange" or "scavenger hunts" that offer diversion, but fall short of the educational objectives we set for our students. Ultimately, we must inspire students to move beyond the "presented problems" of traditional exercises, in which the teacher generates the questions and students offer "correct" answers, to exercises that encourage the investigation of their own "discovered" and "created" questions (Getzels 1982).

The resulting activity, we have discovered, is a telecollaborative paradigm that is both dialectical and dramatic in nature. This book serves as an introduction to those dialectics and the dramas they engender. We invite readers into an exploratory discourse rather than a demonstrative one, applying ancient methods to decipher modern riddles (Altman 1978). To participate, one needs little more than intellectual curiosity seasoned with patience and persistence. We shall explore issues that telecollaborative experiments have prompted, resisting facile conclusions while investigating the universal concerns of classroom practitioners around the world. We take it as an article of faith that the truth is located within dialogue, and that our purpose is to help ourselves and other educators engage in a more meaningful discussion of educational telecollaboration. That can only be achieved, however, through critical inquiry interested in creating and discovering more thoughtful questions rather than embracing simplistic answers.

I must admit that certain risks influence the form, if not the purpose, of this exploration. As we all know, many educational technology texts are obsolete by the time they reach educators. Consider, for example, the "How-to" books dedicated to obsolete software applications that are presently collecting dust on bookshelves. The computer industry's pace and the dynamic quality of the World Wide Web defy the writer of "How-to" books, for their contribution is neither lasting nor definitive. Therefore, we need texts of a different kind, ones that blend theory and practice, so that even if hardware and software change by the time a manuscript goes to press the philosophy underpinning the book remains valid. Lowell and I think of this as a "Why-to" book, a hybrid for educators who wish to understand logistics without sacrificing philosophical concerns, yet expect theoretical musings to speak directly to classroom pragmatics. Our line of inquiry extends from "myth and wonder to rumor, to division of topic, to belief, to conjecture, and finally to serious thought" (Kinneavy 1980, 165). This is as it should be, for the rush to "integrate technology" often prevents careful scrutiny of the myths and rumors it promotes, precluding serious conjecture and thoughtful discussion.

As educators, we must continually pause for reflection, simultaneously exploring and articulating the knowledge that is implicit in our actions (Schon 1995). Failing that, our efforts will simply reinforce impoverished definitions and inadequate pedagogy. Perhaps the best way to avoid that fate is to ask two fundamantal questions before initiating a telecollaborative project: "What will my students gain from this? What might they lose?" This is, indeed, the crux of our dialogue—the dialectical tension that compels more than superficial success stories or knee-jerk dismissals.

Two Hemispheres, One Brain

As globe-trotting teachers, Lowell Monke and I have sustained our discussion of continuing concerns across four continents. By August 1992, we found ourselves half a world apart; Lowell settling in Des Moines, Iowa, while I moved to Kuala Lumpur, Malaysia. Our conventional, "snail mail" correspondence was lethargic, but our desire for dialectics undiminished, so when the computer coordinator at the International School of Kuala Lumpur mentioned his interest in experimenting with electronic mail I volunteered to help. In early 1993, Lowell and I began *Project Utopia,* with students in Kuala Lumpur and Iowa exchanging ideas for a fictional utopia via primitive telecommunications link. Within a year, I had a private e-mail account. Predictably, I sent my first e-mail message to Lowell. Since then, we've exchanged thoughts on an almost daily basis, reviving dialectics through asynchronous conversation. The humanities teacher would send his message while the computer teacher slept in the antipodes; the computer teacher replied, furthering discussion by sending questions and counterarguments via satellite to the slumbering humanities teacher on his side of the Pacific.

We became, in effect, two hemispheres of a sleepless brain, one continually pondering the rhetorical situations in which it found itself. The Western hemisphere, suffering a plutocratic government masquerading as North American democracy, confronted an information explosion with more television, radio, video, and Internet access than it could absorb; the Eastern hemisphere, meanwhile, witness to a benign dictatorship masquerading as Asian democracy, confronted government censorship of print and electronic media, a "blacking out" of images that "outrage the modesty" of citizens or portray the government unfavorably. This rhetorical situation, and the dialectical tension it describes, has inspired several telecollaborative experiments and endless e-mail discussions since 1993.

From their inception to their design, dissemination to coordination, our projects have relied upon telecollaboration and dialectics. However, they seldom reinforce the polarized rhetoric one hears about online learning. For while the hype claims every use of the Internet results in "computer-enhanced pedagogy" the hysteria tells us to refuse it. The best resistance to such extremism is open-ended inquiry, a dialogue that continues to ponder new possibilities while wrestling with the myriad problems encountered online. Through it all, Lowell and I have managed to rendezvous only three times since this work began. Thus, the Internet has served as our primary medium for communication, enabling us to plan and coordinate educational projects and undertake our most ambitious telecollaborative effort to date: writing this book.

Perhaps none of this qualifies us to judge the net effect of telecollaboration in the classroom. However, it should provide assurance that we'll deliver something more than theory and far less than hype. We draw upon practical experience to raise significant questions, and inspire discussions without forcing others to take sides or resolve the tension that ensues. We've asked our students to do the same, cajoling them to consider opposing views rather than allowing preconceptions and competitive instincts to limit their pursuit of truth. As any teacher of adolescents can tell you, however, this is not easy. Nonetheless, despite its elusive nature—in classrooms as well as online—we believe dialectical exchanges among students and teachers offer the best learning opportunities. We offer this book in that spirit, inviting readers to argue with us, pursuing truth through the kind of discourse that is missing from simplistic telecomputing activities. After all, to invent better paradigms for educational telecomputing we must include multiple perspectives and complex interactions within a community that embraces the indispensable opposition.

Obviously, this places the technical concerns of hardware and software in the background. We prefer to discuss pedagogical issues and philosophical concerns, taking turns with the narrative to convey both the form and content of our work. At the end of this chapter I will fall silent and Lowell will speak, revealing the dialectical nature of this book's composition and narrative. This presents challenges for the reader who prefers a simple thesis and conventional narrative. However, those who find truth in dialogue will understand why we've approached the narrative in this fashion, leaving certain questions unanswered and several threads exposed, rather than silencing ourselves with superficial answers or the liquidation of our individual voices. Experience with the Internet, as well as encounters with Renaissance dramatists, has taught us to resist the self-immolating rush to resolution. As a result, our exchanges often find us taking opposite sides of the table, with the humanities teacher arguing for new possibilities within the rhetorical spaces created online while the computer teacher cautions against its seductions and limitations.

Clearly, we are two authors in search of a patient reader, someone willing to reflect upon contradictory experiences and assertions without demanding resolution. This runs counter to modern culture, which often valorizes the speed of telecommunications without pausing to consider its vices. Educators must resist this temptation, however, for if we value efficiency and speed more than civility and understanding, what hope is there for healthy dialectics in cyberspace? We must slow down to help ourselves, and our students, find ways to make sense out of these exchanges and the information they convey. This is where the network technology cannot help us, for it privileges speed over contemplation. No new software application will serve us as well as the experience of seasoned correspondents who understand the consequences of heated exchanges. How do we help students engage in dialectics when they lack emotional maturity, contextual understanding, and composition skills? How can we encourage them to "argue" respectfully when their correspondent is a disembodied voice, a faceless individual they cannot see blush from embarrassment or rage while reading e-mail?

These are good questions, certainly, and they deserve our attention. Indeed, they are key to breaking through the stubborn walls—of commerce, curricula, and clichés—that prevent the discovery of a more satisfying truth. We promise, therefore, not to dodge difficult issues, glorifying "'Net gains" while neglecting "'Net losses." Nor will we pretend that telecollaboration is simply a matter of acquiring Internet access. What's more, we empathize with readers encountering our words for the first time as much as we empathize with students and teachers who are new to telecollaborative learning. Imagine what students feel while seated before a computer screen composing words that will be broadcast to a global audience? They address strangers in countries they've never visited and try to articulate their thoughts when they don't really know who they are or how their prose voice sounds to others. Indeed, we *should* empathize, and we must be realistic about the challenges this type of activity presents. After more than a decade of talking across tables and computer lines, Lowell and I still "misread" each other from time to time. It's disappointing to find an "emoticon" necessary for one's counterpart to catch an ironic e-mail inflexion. However, such moments help us discover our own limitations and reach a deeper understanding of "the Other" and the media through which we communicate.

Finally, we're mindful of the confusion caused by having more than two parties engaged in a dialectical discussion. Do the dynamics of an electronic mailing list explode that idea altogether? Is there such a thing as a tri-lectic? Poly-lectic? Is it possible to cultivate truly interactive relationships in online discussions that provide little opportunity for "mutual interruptibility" (Stone 1996)? These questions are especially pertinent for students who have yet to learn the importance of "looking at" and "looking through" media (Bolter 1991; Lanham 1993). Imagine the consequences for those who devote so much time to "looking at" their words and images on a computer screen that they neglect "looking through" this medium to the human beings at the other end of the line? We need a way to pull students from the screen and help them listen to their counterparts, lest we sacrifice the "indispensable opposition" required for self-knowledge and self-fashioning.

One way to do this is to invite people into a print version of The Manabi Hut, where they may eavesdrop upon our dialogue and use it to question their own views of telecollaboration in the classroom. The original Manabi Hut, it's worth noting, grew from humble origins to great popularity in short time. Within a few years it was one of the most popular lunchtime haunts in Quito. Then, just as suddenly, it was gone. There's a cautionary tale in this, one that speaks to the current infatuation with cyberspace and neglect of the hidden prices we pay for 'Net gains. Educators may wish to use the Internet to pursue truth rather than disseminate trivia or propaganda, but this is no simple feat.

Distance learning paradigms dedicated to the "delivery" of material rather than dialectical exchange have established unfortunate precedents. What's more, the extraordinary expenditures on technology coupled with the relative paucity of professional development opportunities for teachers hold little promise for innovative practices. We need to explore new paradigms for educational pedagogy, but without sacrificing the dialectics that compel students—and teachers—to do more than send and retrieve data.

So, welcome to our little hut. Pull up a chair. Join our table. You're welcome to pitch in whenever you like, so long as you seek the truth. "We can easily represent things as we wish them to be," but it's more satisfying to present them as they truly are, believing there *is* a truth out there, not just solipsistic waves passing through the 'Net. If it's politics you desire, an opportunity to manipulate people to serve your own interests, we'd kindly request that you have a seat at another table. Don't take that personally. It's just that we're tired of those who, like the Man in Aesop's fable, wish to "spin" the tale to suit their needs, beckoning the naive listener with glib promises ("Come now with me and I will soon prove that I am right"). There's room for everyone in The Manabi Hut, but this table's reserved for those seeking truth—and wisdom. If you don't mind, we'd prefer to let both the Lion and the Man speak, while restraining the lying man from senseless roaring.

2

The Web and the Plow

Lowell Monke

*In my experience and observations, computers, unlike other tools, seem to
produce the best results when users have an antagonistic attitude towards them.*
Jaron Lanier, developer of the first virtual reality device (1995, 68)

Aesop's lion is perhaps a bit too noble an image for me, coming as I do from a
part of the world famed more for raising pigs. Yet, until half a century ago rural
America had its own noble beast, the workhorse, which for centuries evoked
such a powerful image that it eventually provided the standard—horsepower—
by which its mechanical successors are still measured. I would like to begin our
exploration of the role of computer telecollaboration in education by invoking
that image once again in a somewhat different way.

My father grew up on an Iowa farm at a time when the fieldwork was still
done with horses. He has often told me how much he enjoyed working with the
teams his father owned, but a big part of that satisfaction seems to have come
from his ability to sweettalk, bully, and sometimes bluff those often uncoopera-
tive beasts to do his bidding. No doubt, if we substituted horses for computers in
Jaron Lanier's observation my dad would wholeheartedly agree. In reminiscing,
his biggest chuckle always comes when he recalls how his younger brother, Virgil, struggled to develop the strength and determination to bend the will of
those powerful animals to the needs of the farm. The horses were none too kind
to him, apparently, especially when they "smelled the barn" at the end of a hot
day in the fields. Dad tells of watching them flying across the pasture for home at
full gallop, equipment careening along behind, with little Virgil clutching the
reins, trying to stay on the seat, hoping only to somehow steer clear of disaster.

The image of my uncle hurtling along behind headstrong charges often
comes to mind when I work with computers. Even though I teach students how
to use computer technology, I often sense that rather than being the master of it

I am merely holding on as it rampages along out of any real human control. This seems especially true of computer telecommunication. The educational community has been heavily bombarded with hype about "the information superhighway." But in practice the connections are often unreliable, the interfaces unintuitive, the documentation unintelligible, the information unfindable, and more and more the waits unendurable. And when we do get the systems working, the technology itself changes so fast that we never feel fully confident about what we are doing. We often sense that we are just clutching the reins, trying to stay on a wagon being swept along by technological forces that have "smelled the barn" and are racing us through the field toward a destination not really of our own making.

A Computer Teacher's Doubts

Eight years ago, when R. W. (whom everyone calls Buddy) and I designed our first telecollaborative project, I was just beginning to question the uncritical enthusiasm that was swirling around educational computing. Somehow, the solutions being offered by the computer revolution didn't seem to address the issues that lay at the heart of our educational system. Sure, the computer promises to provide my students with an endless supply of information, but what good will that do if they can't make sense of it? It promises to help my students express their ideas better, but what good will that do if they don't have any ideas to express? It promises to help them develop marketable skills for a technological society, but how valuable is that if they have never developed the good judgment needed to give direction to that society, or their own lives?

The key question for me was this: How is computer technology going to help my students develop those inner qualities, such as insight, creativity, and good judgment, which education at its best has always sought to inspire? To put it another way, Is there a way to harness the power of computer technology to serve my students' search for meaning in their learning and in their lives?

This question is scarcely asked these days, much less answered (it certainly doesn't go over big at educational computing conferences). Maybe it's because the answer can't be found through creating a new course and buying a textbook to cover it. Or maybe it's because it is too hard to imagine developing objectives that would give us measurable outcomes (hmm . . . let's see: John scored 85% on wisdom, Jane got 87%). Or maybe these issues are just irrelevant to our pragmatic, vocation-oriented approach to education today. Whatever the reasons, I think they are shortsighted, for practical as well as philosophical reasons. Let me give you one brief example to illustrate why.

During one of our early projects—*The Media Matter*—a student (I'll call him Peter) came up to me to ask about the analysis he was to do concerning TV news. One of the questions we wanted the students to consider was whether the source seemed to have a liberal or conservative bias. Peter asked me, "What do 'liberal' and 'conservative' mean?" Good question (try answering it), except that I could see from the vacancy signs flashing in his eyes that this was not a matter of clarification but total ignorance. The meanings of these words weren't vague—they didn't exist. Here was an eighteen-year-old-man, qualified, or at least physically and legally capable, of voting in elections and, as I soon discovered, he had not the slightest inkling of the meaning of those two terms.

What sense does this young man make of the political discourse going on around him (this is Iowa, after all, where presidential candidates know hog farmers, and some hogs, by their first names)? To say he merely lacks information is to both misunderstand the deficiency of his thinking and stretch the meaning of "information" beyond recognition. He admitted to having encountered the terms many times. What he was missing was something more fundamental. He was lacking *comprehension* of the great (and not so great) ideas of our culture that could give meaning to the information that passed through his eyes and ears. Somehow he never got initiated into the conversations that define our culture.

Unfortunately, in my twenty years of teaching I have encountered many students who have exhibited this condition. It is such an endemic problem in U.S. education that a multitude of remedies have been offered by reformers—from the development of Sizer's (1996) process-based "habits of mind" to the rote memorization of lists to attain E. D. Hirsch's (1987) "Cultural Literacy." The problem wouldn't really warrant special mention here except that by the standards of those educational reformers pushing high-tech solutions Peter was actually well-educated. His math and English skills were good. He was already technologically proficient; he was taking the most advanced computer class the school district offered. He could whip you up a magazine layout, create a formula-filled spreadsheet, or design a relational database. Name your destination on the information superhighway and he could get you there—just don't ask him to explain what he found when he arrived. When he graduated that spring he was ready for work or college. But was he ready to be part of his community? Was his community ready for him to be part of it? How much had his extensive computer education prepared him for entry into community life? How much had it distracted him from preparing for that life?

The Character of Technology

Philosophers from Plato (1952) to Postman (1993) have noted that new technologies of any kind are always mixed blessings. Their obvious benefits are always accompanied by not-so-obvious, and often unpleasant, side effects. When the automobile replaced the horse and buggy, no one contemplated that one of the side effects would be cities fouled by air pollution (Winner 1977). Neil Postman cites another example that is perhaps more closely related to our discussion.

When Gutenberg announced that he could manufacture books . . . he did not imagine that his invention would undermine the authority of the Catholic Church. And yet, less than eighty years later, Martin Luther was, in effect, claiming that with the word of God available in every home, Christians did not require the papacy to interpret it for them. (1988a, 151)

Whether this was a benefit to society or a detriment I have no intention of getting into. But certainly it was a side effect that Gutenberg, a devout Catholic, did not anticipate.

These side effects were not immediately recognized. As Jacques Ellul argues, the negative effects of a new technology tend to be "long-term and are felt only with experience" (1990, 73). This quality, perhaps as much as anything, keeps us from seeing clearly the double-edged character of new technologies.

Postman has concluded that technologies are ecological; that is, their introduction sends out ripples that rearrange relationships throughout the system (Innis 1951; Postman 1993). Regardless of the technologies' intended uses, they also work at a deeper, personal level, influencing, though not fully determining, the way we act, the way we think, the way we view the world (Borgmann 1984). If I drive a car to school in the morning, rather than, say, riding a bike, the use of the car influences not only the speed and comfort with which I get there—my main purposes for using it—but it also insulates me from contact with nature and people. It also provides little exercise. Riding a bike exposes me to the possibility of skidding across the pavement on my nose at 15 mph, but it stimulates my circulation and makes few demands on energy resources (other than my own). It also gives me a chance to hear the birds sing and at least exchange greetings with fellow riders and pedestrians. Each time I choose a tool to use, certain values get amplified while others get reduced (Bowers 1988; Ihde 1990). These values, in turn, tend to both reflect and influence my entire worldview.

The computer is one of the most powerful worldview-influencers. While we are working on it, it works on us, chipping here, smoothing there, molding our expansive minds to fit its powerful but much narrower capabilities. Because its operation is based solely on the highly abstract thinking process called logic, it amplifies this one aspect of our cognition. Because it is purely instrumental it amplifies what is utilitarian. But these amplifications—among others—come at the expense of other ways of thinking and knowing, such as intuition, physical contact, and the entire gamut of emotional and spiritual experience. As social critic Theodore Roszak says, "We do not bring the full resources of self to the computer" (1986, 71).

Perhaps this is why Jaron Lanier recognizes a certain antagonism toward the computer among its more creative users. We *should* feel a sense of dis-ease when forced to operate in an environment that so limits our human capacities. Technology critic Steve Talbott asserts in considering the one-sidedness of computer "intelligence" that it is critical that we struggle to bring the computer within the full spectrum of human intelligence rather than vice versa. "The more intelligence, the more independent life, the machine possesses, the more urgently I must strive with it in order to bend it to my own purposes" (1995, 131). As Talbott goes on to observe, that so many of us don't even notice this need indicates a growing imbalance in the development of our own human capacities.

Certainly a primary purpose of education is to develop all of our human capacities—"the full resources of self." Thus, it seems to me that we need to be very careful about employing devices that limit the exercise of all those resources. The more we rely on such devices, the less full and robust and diverse the development of our students' ways of knowing is likely to be. Looked at in this way, telecomputing—indeed, the computer itself—can be seen as an inappropriate tool for some ages and educational endeavors. I say this not to condemn all uses of the computer in the classroom, but to point out what I believe is a major responsibility that goes with it.

What the Computer Leaves Out

This responsibility requires that we think about how telecomputing might restructure the learning environment, both through our conscious efforts and through the more subtle ecological transformation I just discussed. Langdon Winner, one of the most important thinkers about technology today, suggests that in all sectors of society we must try to understand "the many ways in which technologies provide structure for human activity" (1986, 6). This is just what Buddy is trying to get us to do, I think, when he stresses in Chapter 1 that we think about what will be lost by the use of computer technology as much as we think about what will be gained. If we look closely, we may find that some of the things we are giving up are the opportunities to develop the very qualities whose absence in our students is most worrisome to us. To illustrate this let me revisit the farm. I do this, by the way, not out of a nostalgic love of "the good old days." I couldn't get off the farm fast enough. Thanks to frigid winter days spent scooping manure out of hog houses at a time when "sputniks" were being shot into space, the romantic images that guided my childhood came from over my head, not below my feet. Today I feel a personal sense of "dialectical tension" in my attitude toward those years, but I return to farming here because it offers some helpful parallels between the technological transformation of agriculture in

America and what is happening in education, which seems to be at the beginning of a similar transformation.

While I was growing up my dad rented a farm that bordered one owned by an old fellow named Louis Prien. Louie was a relic. He was probably the last holdout in our area against the shift from horsepower to tractor power. My dad liked to say Louie was as stubborn as the mules he drove through his fields. Louie wouldn't, or couldn't, adapt to changing times. He got left behind by progress.

Those of us who knew Louie certainly didn't look upon him as some meditative ascetic; he was given more to cursing than philosophizing. But through his lonely persistence he did provide a constant reminder of what progress took away from farming. Mechanization, which sits us high above the soil and runs us across much more of it at a much faster speed, somehow also alters our psychological relationship to it. Land becomes a resource from which we extract as much profit as possible. Likewise, the hundreds or thousands of livestock we can run through our feedlots become viewed primarily as products. Our crops and our animals are essentially means to an end, which is profit.

As I look back now it is clear that for Louie the soil, the livestock, the work were the ends as well as the means. It was as impossible to separate him from his land as it would have been to separate his land from the creek that ran through it. He knew each animal he owned, probably by name. Working with all of it, bringing it to life year after year is what gave meaning to his life.

My dad understood this even though he never articulated it and may not have been able to. He may also have understood in his bones that increased mechanization was prying loose his sense of belonging to the land. I suspect this (along with the normal irritation caused by a know-it-all teenage son) was probably the thorn that was digging under his skin when he chastised me with uncharacteristic sharpness one day for making fun of how slowly Louie and his mules moved through the fields. My dad was a bridge between worlds, and though he accepted the benefits and demands of the new one he could still appreciate what the old world offered—and wasn't at all pleased that his son could not.

What does all of this have to do with computers and education? There are at least a couple of important lessons to be learned, I think. The most important may be that in choosing the computer we are not simply making a choice based on one tool being better for a job than another. The computer, like the tractor, carries some pretty hefty psychological and cultural baggage along with it. Employing it without concern for the weight of that baggage may result in some important educational values being unintentionally left behind.

Here is one example. Quiet contemplation was once held up to students as a key cognitive process needed to digest received knowledge, understand personal experiences, and develop ideas; all of which, with practice, can help the student make meaning of the world. The computer's capabilities lie primarily in accessing and manipulating information. As I learned from my encounter with Peter, great skill with the tool that manages information doesn't guarantee comprehension of that information. As Roszak points out, there is a real danger in confusing access to mountains of information with the real meat of learning. "An excess of information may actually crowd out ideas, leaving the mind (young minds especially) distracted by sterile, disconnected facts, lost among the shapeless heaps of data" (1986, 88). As the computer's role in education expands and it lowers the floodgates to data, will the wisdom that grows out of making meaning from experience and ideas give way to the accumulation of information as the highest goal of our schools? Will quiet contemplation give way to "hyper" 'Net-surfing as the most esteemed intellectual process? Will we at some point find ourselves asking, along with T. S. Eliot, "Where is the wisdom lost in knowledge? Where is the knowledge lost in information?" (1963, 147).

Unfortunately, we seem to be headed in that direction. Indeed, we have been moving that way for a long time. But the computer seems to have intensified and accelerated that movement. Listen to those pushing computers at the schools and you will hear "information" spoken almost as a mantra. Look at the packaged telecommunications projects and you will see that the vast majority involve the collection and sharing of data. There is, of course, a place for this kind of activity. But in leaning heavily on computers for learning, we risk altering, without conscious intent, what we mean by education, and finding, to our surprise, that we have come to the same position as my dad, shaking our heads over students who can't even comprehend what has been lost.

A second lesson we could learn from Louie Prien is that the computer, like the tractor, tends to distance us from what we are learning. This may seem a strange statement, considering the ability of the computer to facilitate communication between students on opposite sides of the world. But the "distance" I am talking about has to do not with physical distance but rather the cognitive distance from firsthand experience. Dramatist Max Frisch defined technology as "the knack of so arranging the world that we do not experience it" (quoted in Postman 1995, 10). Philosopher Albert Borgmann observes that we live in a society filled with commodities—packaged objects whose production process is hidden from us by the many technologies employed to create them. He goes on to contend that "commodities and their consumption constitute the professed goal of the technological enterprise" (1984, 48) and that "commodities are more fully available if the supporting machinery is less obtrusive, i.e., more concealed and reliable" (1984, 116). What both he and Frisch are calling our attention to is the way in which modern technology conceals from us a vast array of relationships between ourselves and the fundamental processes and objects that lie beneath the things we encounter in our lives. Roszak seems to be applying this view to educational computing when he observes that placing a computer between the child and the subject "puts more distance between intention and result" (1986, xxxvi). Just as trading the mules for a tractor increases the distance between the farmer and an intimate knowledge of the soil, the more complex the eductional technology is, the farther removed we find ourselves from the object of study.

The trade-off involved with this distancing may actually be beneficial when studying something as inaccessible as the surface of Mars. But what if the subject is trees? The best the computer can do is teach the student about trees, through images and text—abstract symbols, decontextualized and cast on a two-dimensional screen. Contrast this with the way small children normally come to know trees—by peeling its bark, climbing among its branches, sitting under its shade, jumping into its piled-up leaves. Just as important, these first-hand experiences are enveloped by feelings and associations—muscles being used, sun warming the skin, blossoms scenting the air—none of which the computer even approximates.

This is exactly what Roszak is talking about when he says we don't bring all the resources of self to the computer. It is what Frisch was talking about when he said technology keeps us from experiencing the world. It is the enormous qualitative difference between learning about something and learning from something. It is a sorry fact that our schools are already largely commodicized (Apple 1990). As such, they do very little to facilitate this latter kind of highly contextual learning; perhaps if they did, the computer wouldn't look so attractive in comparison.

The computer can get us lots of information about lots of things. But in extracting, and abstracting, the essential information, it filters out the rich context that direct experience provides. One of the problems that is encountered in using telecommunications for education is that while it broadens the students' knowledge by bringing them the accounts of other people's experiences, it cannot deepen it the way firsthand experience can. In our contemplation of tele-collaborative learning, therefore, we should consider not only the physical distance that is collapsed by this medium, but the cognitive distance that is expanded by it. Sitting high atop the computer, students may be able to survey thousands, millions of acres of knowledge, but only if those students forgo taking the time to sink their hands deep and long into the educational soil that lies right at their feet.

All of this is merely to emphasize that computers bring certain values to the educational table. These values will amplify certain kinds of learning while ignoring or even discouraging others. Among other things, the computer encourages an appreciation for efficiency, measurability, objectivity, rationality, progress, and the accumulation and manipulation of data, lots of data. These are all traits noted by both computer advocates and their critics. But what promoters never talk about is what is not inherently encouraged by the computer, and is, therefore, less valued in using it than those cited above. Here is a short list:

- The pursuit of truth.
- The comprehension of complex ideas.
- The generation of one's own ideas.
- The discovery of meaning.
- The use of good judgment.
- The exercise of emotional maturity.
- The development of wisdom.

These are precisely the qualities that Buddy and I believe should be the fundamental goals of education—and the computer itself does nothing to enhance them. It is sad but perhaps not surprising that in more than a decade of listening to vendors, business liaisons, administrators, technology consultants, and "futurists" exude over the benefits of using computers in the classroom I have rarely heard any of them mention these profoundly human goals. Indeed, for each of these qualities a substitute seems to have arisen: for the pursuit of truth, the pursuit of skills; for the comprehension of complex ideas, the compilation of them; for the generation of one's own ideas, the slick packaging of others'; for the discovery of meaning, the search for resources; for the exercise of emotional maturity, the diminished challenge of disembodied relationships (often dehumanized further into "networking"); for the development of wisdom, the achievement of success. What is troubling here is not that these latter qualities are included in our educational objectives, but that in the rush to computerize learning the concern for the former has virtually disappeared.

What Humans Must Bring to the Computer

I've given the computer a good bashing, so I must hasten to clarify that I am not blaming the computer for our educational woes. Our schools' blossoming love affair with computer technology is merely an indication of our society's long evolving willingness to reduce learning to that which is material, mechanical, and measurable, and which promotes an essentially economic view of life (Callahan 1962; Tyack 1974). The computer happens to be particularly well suited to this limited view of learning. That does not make it irredeemable, but for those of us with more holistic learning goals it presents us with a tremendous challenge to bend it to our educational will. Thus, as schools scramble to join in the online festivities it seems even more crucial that we understand what the computer leaves out of learning, so that we stand a better chance of recognizing what we human beings (teachers in particular) must bring to the telecomputing banquet. Because the computer actually tends to distract us from the pursuit of the higher goals of education, the need for a teacher who can keep a focus on them becomes more critical. One of the most important roles for the teacher in the high tech classroom is to compensate for the computer's mechanistic tendencies; to assure that all "resources of self" are brought into the learning process. It is a task that can only be performed by a caring, thoughtful human being dedicated to elevating the inner life of each individual child.

It seems to me that this is one new teaching role we have to accept. Certainly it should be a major concern in any telecomputing activity. Computer technology is rapidly becoming a major ingredient of education in this country. We can't turn education over to computers but we can't turn our backs on them either. History has a lesson for us here, if we accept Marshall McLuhan's interpretation of it:

If we persist in a conventional approach to these developments our traditional culture will be swept aside as scholasticism was in the 16th century. Had the Schoolmen with their complex oral culture understood the Gutenberg technology, they could have created a new synthesis of written and oral education, instead of bowing out of the picture and allowing the merely visual page to take over the educational enterprise. The oral Schoolmen did not meet the new visual challenge of print, and the resulting expansion or explosion of Gutenberg technology was in many respects an impoverishment of the culture. (1964, 75)

Somehow we have to find a way to create this new synthesis, in which all modes of learning are honored and given an appropriate place. But it should be clear by now that I do not think this is as easy as giving each child a computer and an e-mail address. As McLuhan implies, embarking on such a course would, in all too many respects, lead to an impoverishment of our educational culture, and, no doubt, our culture in general.

What I have been trying to hammer home is that using computer technology in education is hard work; not in the sense of getting the machinery to work or the kids "talking" to one another across the oceans and mountains and prairies; that's really the easy part. The hard work is finding ways to get the technology to help us nurture our students' attempts to reach their own highest human potential. With the perplexing task of integrating computer technology with print and oral traditions before us, now is hardly the time for the teacher to step aside and become "the guide on the side" to please the wide-eyed technophiles. The responsibility we have for preserving what is dear to us from the old as well as discovering what is truly beneficial in the new is enormous, and not something to be left to chance encounters in cyberspace.

A new synthesis of education. This is really what Buddy and I have been attempting for the past decade. It is the harnessing of a new powerhouse to the educational plow, not to replace the old familiar workhorses, but to enhance and extend their reach when it serves human purposes. Educational telecollaboration is, for us, not just a matter of how to get the machines and students communicating with each other. It is not just a technical activity. It is, rather, an enterprise governed by the search for opportunities for student growth. At times we have been surprised at the depth of human understanding that the computer has facilitated. At other times we have had to work very hard to keep the technology from choking it. But always, we have tried to expand the capabilities of our young students' minds and hearts, rather than expand the use of the computer for the sake of being at the "cutting edge." Indeed, I see as one of the key responsibilities of classroom teachers the protection of the interests of the children in their care against the commercial/technological alliance that too often cares more about education as a market than as a servant of children's needs. This is not to say we should resist all change to education. Our system of education has been in desperate need of radical change for decades. But if schools are going to be part of the educational revolution, the change has to emerge from the classroom, not the boardroom, not the houses of Congress, and certainly not from cyberspace. It has to be led by teachers who care about the lives of each of their students, not policymakers focusing on the economic competitiveness of the nation. This is the common drive, the one transcendent goal that Buddy and I have always agreed on, and which has been the glue that has held our dialectic together over the years.

The Challenge and the Hope

For innovative teachers seeking ways to effect that change, computer telecommunication is an attractive environment. It is still a frontier (though a rapidly fading one, I fear), one of the few areas in which the individual classroom teacher can work creatively, outside the constantly tightening restrictions imposed by curriculum supervisors, mass-produced texts, and standardized testing. There is still room for pioneers in cyberspace, and the temptation is strong to leap toward it as a new and liberating means of learning. Indeed, it is precisely this potential for getting outside the normal factory-like compartmentalization of high school curriculum that motivated Buddy and me to look at the 'Net as a means of putting into action some of the ideas we had batted around in The Manabi Hut. Our original excitement has matured (I hope that is the proper term for it) into the cautious enthusiasm that we bring to our work today. Education is changing, new visions are emerging, of which, for better or worse, the computer is an integral part. For a while yet, we have the opportunity, and therefore the responsibility, to try to bend these new workhorses to our will, our human purposes. This is where the challenge lies. And this is where antagonism can be mated with enthusiasm. Meeting the challenge posed by these machines, directing them along the course we believe is best, offers an incredible mind-stretching opportunity not only for us as teachers but for our students as well.

In the pages that follow we will take a look at the attempts we have made to stretch our students' minds with the aid of the Internet. We present them as models for contemplation, not emulation. In no way do we want to give the impression that ours is the only way to telecollaborate. Moreover, pioneering gives you the chance to explore new terrain, but it also provides opportunities to make mistakes. We have made our share and will try to present them as honestly as our successes, for as Mike Rose puts it (and every good teacher knows), "Error marks the place where education begins" (Rose 1989, 189). We certainly have been educated by our work in telecollaboration, and hope that education will continue as others reflect on our analysis of it. We hope you will approach our work with the same critical eye we cast on the work of those who came before us: Do these projects carry the potential to move students nearer the educational goals we have embraced? Have we been able to benefit from the use of the technology while compensating adequately for its dehumanizing qualities? What are the weaknesses, the strengths in our approach to using this medium of communication? These are all questions we keep asking ourselves and in presenting this as a dialogue between the two of us, we are indeed inviting you into The Manabi Hut to join in the conversation. It is a conversation about a new exploration, full of surprises, satisfactions and disappointments, rewards and dangers.

We believe it is our responsibility as educators to lead that exploration critically, always concerned about what we are giving up as well as what we might gain—searching for the synthesis that McLuhan advocated. Only if we approach the computer and the 'Net in this antagonistic but determined way will we avoid becoming the teaching equivalent of my poor uncle Virgil. With the welfare of our students at stake it is not enough for educators to merely ride contentedly along on the technological bandwagon. That course will inevitably turn us into technicians and education into mere training. If we want to truly enrich and ennoble the lives of our students, then we each have to grab the reins and force these new dynamos to work for us in ways that once again elevate the human purposes of education.

3

Don't Start the Evolution Without Me

R. W. Burniske

> ... *that series of inventions by which man from age to age has remade his environment is a different kind of evolution—not biological, but cultural evolution.*   Jacob Bronowski (1973, 19–20)

Now that we've described who we are, how our collaboration began, and the philosophy that informed our design of telecollaborative projects, it's time to discuss the projects themselves. This chapter focuses upon my situation as a teacher in Malaysia, establishing the sense of place necessary for a reader to understand the rhetorical context from which I speak. As you will see, the dialectical tension that shaped our collaboration was heightened by the stark contrast between the physical, political and social environments in which Lowell and I worked.

Subsequently, I offer a brief history of our telecollaboration, providing a thumbnail sketch of each project to help the reader follow our work's trajectory. This should supply the necessary background for subsequent chapters, helping the reader participate more fully in our dialogue. What's more, it underscores the evolutionary character of telecollaborative learning and the importance of continually reflecting upon the design and implementation of individual projects.

Censoring the Censors

Kuala Lumpur, Malaysia

For the uninitiated, the name conjures exotic images, but today's Kuala Lumpur cares more about real estate development than cultural exotica. It aspires to be yet another city that never sleeps, and the noise of incessant construction helps fulfill that ambition. In the mid-1990s, two crews competed while constructing the Petronas Towers, which were then the two highest structures in the world. Sunsets, when the polluted haze allowed, revealed a skyline punctuated with hydraulic cranes; condos and shopping malls sprouted like mushrooms. "KL," as the locals call it, became a nightmarish vision of the future: an unopposed government manipulating the populace through state-controlled news media while ignoring the environmental degradation caused by myopic development. In October 1995, one government news agency reported that the thick haze shrouding Kuala Lumpur was "due to poor air quality." Ironically, the haze was so dense that we could not see the Petronas Towers, nearing completion less than five miles from our school campus. A midday rainstorm cleared the air temporarily, followed by the official story: forest fires in Sumatra and Kaliman- tan were the cause of these recurrent shrouds. Each new telling of this tale en- ables Kuala Lumpur's citizens to postpone necessary action, suffering the delu- sion that they are not responsible for their toxic environment.

Meanwhile, the International School of Kuala Lumpur (ISKL), located in the former tin mining town of Ampang, reflects the frenetic change and devel- opment of the greater metropolitan area. In less than a decade Kuala Lumpur transformed ISKL from a country day to suburban and soon-to-be inner city school. To illustrate how forcibly external cultures permeate school cultures, ISKL responded to these developments by doubling its enrollment (840 to 1690), building a new elementary school campus in the suburb of Melawati (six miles away), and adding a new wing to its Ampang campus (ISKL 1995). This sudden growth, coupled with extraordinary prosperity, helped ISKL build a reputation as one of the finest international schools in the world, serving a multinational business and diplomatic community. By the mid-1990s, the en- tire school was connected—from offices to classrooms, libraries to lounges—by a state-of-the-art computer network.

These tangible changes give concrete definition to the notion of future shock. Yet, think of all the intangibles, the subtle alterations that affect what El- liott Eisner has dubbed the *implicit* and *null* curriculum of a school (1985). The implicit curriculum consists of everything that the school teaches indirectly through assemblies, dress codes, detentions, and the like; the null curriculum refers to neglected subjects, such as automotive repair, woodworking, and home economics. Often, what a school omits from its curriculum—or fails to consider as a contributor to its *ethos*—is just as important as what it self- consciously includes in the *explicit* curriculum. Therefore, the kind of "progress" I've described is equivocal. A school cannot undergo such rapid change without altering its ethos. ISKL forfeited the intimacy of a small school for the competitiveness of a large one. The introduction of an electronic bulle- tin board service, designed to network two campuses, increased the frenzy more than efficiency. Most significantly, the incessant "busy-ness" of both the city and school gave rise to a celebration of extracurricular activities at the expense of academic rigor. In fact, such activities were no longer "extras," but promoted as "co-curricular activities" vital to the school's mission.

Consequently, the culture of the mall displaced the culture of the library, breeding a "videocentric" environment ideal for watching television, not a "logocentric" one conducive to reading, writing, and reflection. The library cannot compete with the mall, for the noise of the latter devours the silence of the former. When asked where they liked to read one student replied: "You can't read on this campus. There are too many distractions. I read at home." To exacerbate matters, students and faculty were frequently excused from classes for school-sponsored activities such as athletic competitions with international schools in Southeast Asia. The first sacrifice at the Altar of Activity is classroom continuity, followed closely by genuine debate over the merits of "extracurricular" activities. How should the classroom teacher respond when a jello-eating contest is considered a "co-curricular activity" worthy of preempting academic courses? In other words, how does the classroom teacher celebrate the "life of the mind" in a culture enamored with physical activity? How do we integrate telecollaboration into such schools without turning it into yet another "activity" rather than an occasion for critical thinking?

I was hoping to discuss such issues, but the school environment presented few opportunities for open-ended discourse. The school administration followed the lead of local officials: setting a strict agenda (curriculum), controlling the media (school publications) and suppressing dissent (the faculty meeting as press conference). As a result, the faculty seldom dared challenge the status quo, fearful of reprisals from an administration that knew it had the upper hand. Local teachers were afraid of jeopardizing their privileged status while the expatriates, who lacked a teachers' union, were frequently reminded of the many applicants standing in line at international recruiting fairs looking for job openings. None of this nurtured dialectics; rather, it revealed how much ISKL had become a "product" of both its constituency and environment. Nonetheless, if the administration's "pedagogy" stifled problematic questions and genuine discourse in faculty meetings what might it foster in classrooms?

My initiation to Malay-styled censorship began in 1992, when *The Economist* ran a cover story on censorship through the ages. The article featured photographs of Venus de Milo and the David to demonstrate how draconian government censorship of artwork had *once* been ("Censors" 1992); ironically, Malay censors applied a black, felt-tip marker to Venus's breasts and David's genitalia. They did this on every copy before issuing them to newsstands. To this day, government censors grind their felt-tip markers to the nub on the likes of a Vogue cover girl's *derriere,* a Cosmopolitan woman's cleavage, or any other image that "outrages the modesty" of Malaysian citizens. Meanwhile, the electronic media are not spared this "blacking out" of physical cleavage or editorial passage. When

Steven Spielberg objected to the release of *Schindler's List* in censored form, for example, the film was promptly banned from Malaysian movie theaters.

Imagine a humanities teacher in this environment merging with traffic on the Infobahn, conducting online research on "censorship" or joining an environmental newsgroup. Now imagine my students, in 1992, being asked to discuss their utopian visions of a more perfect society via telecommunication with students in Des Moines, Iowa. That was like asking the Iban of Borneo to imagine talking with members of a nearby longhouse without taking a canoe ride. Yet, that's the kind of change that occurred within my classroom. As a result, the Internet helped me censor the censors, all who would manipulate information for their own political gain. In Malaysia, it was often difficult to find people brave enough to venture an opposing viewpoint. And that is what the Internet meant to me during my four-year stint in that country: opposing or, at the very least, alternative viewpoints. Before locating the entrance ramp to the Infobahn I felt as isolated as the Iban of Sarawak, but by the time I departed, in June 1996, the Internet had made it possible to engage in dialectics rather than embrace the official story. More important, it helped students look beyond conventional media to learn about their world, interrogating information, and its sources, while learning how to use a computer as a rhetorical tool instead of a computational device (Lanham 1993).

Project Utopia (February–March 1993)

I had been hired to teach English in the International Baccalaureate (IB) program. While similar to the Advanced Placement (AP) program, the IB is more prescriptive, and students do not always enroll of their own volition. Since many European universities refuse to recognize international school diplomas as official transcripts, demanding the IB diploma instead, students planning to matriculate at those institutions have little choice. One of the core requirements for students in both Higher and Subsidiary Level English is the study of "World Literature," defined as texts not originally written in English (Organisation 1998). Unfortunately, my predecessors at ISKL, new to the IB program, had selected North American literature to fulfill this requirement, primarily because it had "always" been a fixture of the 11th grade English curriculum. When I objected, suggesting this could jeopardize the students' IB diplomas, a cold, tropical wind blew in from the high school administration. The cold front remained stationary until May of that year, when a fax from IB headquarters reprimanded the ISKL English department and presented an official warning.

All of which leads to an emphatic point: creators of telecollaborative projects in K–12 schools must find ways to work within preexisting curricula. Like most newly hired faculty members, I had little say in the curriculum I inherited.

My teaching experience and graduate study, rather than empowering personal initiative, were primarily dues paid for the privilege of working in a reputable school that defined "professionalism" as a pledge of allegiance to its Curriculum. In my second day of orientation I was handed an outline stipulating the texts I would teach and the order in which I would teach them. It was understood that all students of English, at every grade level, would take common exams in their respective classes. Thus, it was essential that all teachers "be on the same page," towing the lines of convention rather than crossing them with innovations.

Nevertheless, as the first semester evolved, and my disenchantment with the school environment grew, it was obvious something had to change. Studying *The Great Gatsby, The Crucible,* and *The Handmaid's Tale* as "world literature"—in a program dominated by British and American authors—felt like old-fashioned colonialism. My students, the privileged expatriate children of the international business and diplomatic communities, were shuttled from palatial residences behind walls to an elitist school behind more walls, mixing with people of the same socioeconomic background. They didn't see much need for dialectics, nor did they think their curriculum deficient. So as that first semester came to an end—and I suffered through piles of lifeless prose written for exams that were all too common—I began planning a study of Margaret Atwood's novel, *The Handmaid's Tale.*

My initial plans for this study, which would begin after the December holidays, were shaped by a simple question: "What if students explored the idea of utopia in both fiction and history, then created their own utopian community and exchanged their designs with other classes?" While turning those thoughts over I received a letter from Lowell Monke. It was a newsy, family letter, the kind former colleagues exchange in hopes of "catching up" with each other. It concluded with a postscript that Lowell had probably written as an afterthought: "Let me know if you'd like to try connecting our classes for a telecommunications experiment." I wrote a quick reply, describing my situation and what I wanted to do in the coming semester. Lowell thought he could find someone in his school's English Department who might be interested. A month later he did; I sent his colleague a fax to sketch out my intentions:

For what it's worth, here's what we've done on this end: Began with a reading of Atwood's novel, *The Handmaid's Tale.* That led to discussion of utopia/dystopia. Then, four "study communes" researched separate utopias. Commune #1 looked into actual utopian societies from history (Oneida, Shakers, kibbutzim, etc.). Communes #2, 3, 4 were focused on fictional utopias, considering visions ranging from *Animal Farm* to *Fahrenheit 451, Brave New World* to *Lost Horizon, Looking Backward* to *1984.* Oral reports presented information that included an overview of the utopias' genesis, laws/customs/ punishments, and strengths/weaknesses.

Please don't feel compelled to do what I've just described. I'm simply trying to describe an approach. The preparation time could be shortened considerably. To save time you could read Vonnegut's "Harrison Bergeron" or Le Guin's "The Ones Who Walk Away from Omelas." They're short, accessible stories that stimulate good discussion on the theme. A day or two in the library could fix them up with regard to actual utopias—if you feel it necessary—but I'll leave that to you.

About my students: English 11, regular section. Diverse group. Most of them are ESL kids, so this will be a good challenge for them. They're well traveled, but English skills need polish.

Revised Schedule—I appreciate your need for time. How about if we aim for an exchange in about two weeks? Say February 17? Too soon? You tell me. I can stretch things out a bit more, but having already stalled a bit (to allow the technicians to work on logistics and Lowell to locate you) I can't take the project too far into March. Here's what I'm thinking right now.

To simplify matters it makes sense to limit the document to 4–5 pages. That will force students to write the concise, sparkling prose we crave.

If we split them into groups, then they can specialize in one area and respond to their counterparts' offering. Each group is limited to a 1-page (*single-spaced*) document.

Here's the tough part. How to cover all areas of a society in four groups! I've been stuck on this for a week. So I did the sensible thing: asked the kids. They formed the following groups to address the fundamental concerns. Where one places a subtopic such as "industry" or "transportation" will depend upon the values of the utopia.

1. GOVERNMENTAL BRANCH—How is government to be created and organized? What will be the principal laws and how will they be enforced? Police force? Military?

2. ENVIRONMENTAL BRANCH—How will ecosystems be maintained/protected? How is pollution to be controlled? Waste management? Medical concerns? AIDS? Disease . . .

3. EDUCATIONAL/SOCIAL BRANCH—How will people be educated? What family structures will exist? How will information be disseminated? Special customs? Holidays?

4. ECONOMIC BRANCH—How will work and goods be divided? How will business with the outside world be handled? Describe commerce within the utopia.

The first exchange should present the bare essentials. An introductory page, identifying the utopia by name, geographical setting (they've agreed to Earth, 1993, but we're still arguing about a more specific venue), and an "overview" of customs could precede "branch" reports. This gives us two weeks for rough drafts, full group discussions, revision, etc. before the exchange. We could fax each other on February 15 to say whether or not the timing is OK.

OK? Let's not worry about step #2 yet (questions/responses to the utopias). That seems premature, and wishful. If my earlier plan seemed reasonable, then we can aim that way, but let's hold off on dates and such. Please, SHOUT if any of this sounds too confining, or if you wish to alter terminology, the approach or ANYTHING else . . . (let's be utopian collaborators, after all).

Step #1—create Utopia. 1 page/group. 4–5 pages total. Due: Feb. 17. Acceptable? Please advise . . . once again, thanks for your courage!

Surprisingly, we managed four "exchanges" of these reports, using a primitive telecommunications link that enabled connection to an electronic bulletin board at Central Academy in Des Moines, Iowa. There, we would deposit our file into Lowell's account and retrieve Iowa's report. Though limited to these brief reports, without benefit of follow-up discussion, my students were fascinated by what these exchanges signaled for the future of communication. More important, they learned the benefit of limiting the length and number of transactions as well as working in small groups to facilitate discussions. Meanwhile, Lowell and I discovered there was a lot of work to be done, in both design and facilitation, before participants could enjoy a rich, healthy discourse.

South African Elections '94 Internet Project (April–May 1994)

Despite its limitations, *Project Utopia* succeeded in one very real way: it helped me perforate the walls of censorship and institutional myopia pressing in upon us. Unfortunately, there would be no further experiments that year. ISKL did not have an electronic mail system as yet, and the cost of those exchanges—glorified long-distance phone calls from our computer in Malaysia to Lowell's in Iowa—was prohibitive. Nonetheless, I couldn't help wondering how we might conduct more ambitious telecollaborative studies. *Project Utopia* had inspired a few constructive discussions, but many of them dissipated as students' imaginations, liberated from real-world concerns, took flight. While I didn't wish to dampen their enthusiasm or their creativity, I did hope for more substantial dialectics. The key to this, I was convinced, was shifting from the contrived fiction of a "school project" to the more authentic concerns of current events.

In November 1993, I was following yet another prescribed curriculum: the twelfth grade IB Subsidiary course. Newly revised to introduce more world literature, the course included the short stories of Nadine Gordimer, South Africa's Nobel prize-winning author. While reading the Introduction to her *Selected Stories,* an anthology of her work from the 1950s, 1960s, and 1970s, I was struck by Gordimer's reflections:

What I am saying is that I see many of these stories *could not have been written* later or earlier than they were. If I could have juggled them around in the contents list of this collection without that being evident, they would have been false in some way important to me as a writer. What I am also saying, then, is that in a certain sense a writer is "selected" by his subject—his subject being *the consciousness* of his own era. (Gordimer, 1975, 14–15)

Embedded in this passage was a departure from our syllabus—and the seed for a telecollaborative project. The Republic of South Africa had just announced plans for its first democratic elections in April 1994. By then I was supposed to be reviewing for IB exams with a small group of twelfth grade students while marching the majority, who chose not to take the exams, through a familiar rite of passage: the senior research paper. I wondered if we could revisit Gordimer's stories in April and ask South Africans what they thought of them. Were they still relevant, universal stories, or would the transition to a democratic government make them feel like obsolete, historical artifacts? I had never sent or received an e-mail message, nor did I know anyone who had attempted what I envisioned, but the starting point was my own imagination. To concern myself with the technical issues would merely blur the vision necessary to launch a project. Which is not to say that I wouldn't need technical assistance, just that my initial concern was the destination, not the means of transportation.

In January 1994, Dan LoCascio, the computer coordinator at ISKL, informed me that he had set up a primitive electronic mail system, connecting a modem to one computer in the faculty work area adjacent to the high school computer labs. The faculty area was a narrow room with half a dozen Macintosh computers, monochrome Classic IIs and LC IIIs, arranged along the outer wall. LoCascio was eager to test the system and asked if I'd like to give it a try. I sent my first message via electronic mail that afternoon to the only person I knew with an e-mail address: Lowell Monke. I don't recall the text of that message, but I'll never forget the sensation that Lowell's reply brought the following day: the one-way street of a computer screen had turned into a two-way avenue.

More than the technological leap it signified, this transformation startled me because of its potential impact upon human communication. As an expatriate educator in Egypt, Ecuador, and Malaysia I had suffered more than a few trials with international postal services. The computer had served as a glorified typewriter, allowing my wife and me to compose family newsletters with simple graphics and various font styles, but the letters it helped us produce remained vulnerable to international postal services. With the arrival of electronic mail, however, the computer was no longer a dull, plastic box with wires dangling behind it; rather, it had become a communication device with people at the other end of the wires, people whose "snail mail" letters often took months to reach me, but who could now correspond within hours, perhaps even minutes, at minimal cost. For an expatriate who appreciated letters enough to store them in old shoeboxes and ship them from one continent to the next, *this* was profound and exciting news.

Over the next few months Lowell and I had almost daily contact, sharing personal anecdotes and catching up on lost time, but also wrestling with the design of a project focused on the South African elections. Lowell was teaching computer application courses at the time, but had a few colleagues that he thought would be interested in participating. I drafted several project designs, all of which seemed unwieldy and chaotic. Lowell shredded them, finding one flaw after another, until I wanted to throttle him. How could we structure it, I wondered, so that this didn't become a trivial exchange of data or a glorified chat room? I wasn't afraid of violating our curriculum or forfeiting control in the classroom. Instead, I worried about orchestrating a high-tech diversion that pandered to adolescents. The encroachment of extracurricular activities upon the classroom has prompted an unfortunate loss of balance and purpose. As a result, teachers suffer far too many concessions to "edutainment," activities that encourage a breadth of superficial experience at the expense of deep, sustained thought. The last thing Lowell and I wanted was to further *that* trend.

Our initial challenge, therefore, was to create a structure that encouraged healthy dialectical tension, a framework that would support both formal, academic work and informal, topical discussions. We wanted, in essence, to create a project for students that would allow them to learn from one another through dialectical exchanges similar to the ones that Lowell and I had enjoyed over the years. All of our wrangling drew Lowell and I closer, prompting one of the most important events in our telecollaborative careers. Lowell and his wife, who had attended a conference in Hong Kong that February, decided to pay us a visit while "in the neighborhood." This would be one of only three face-to-face meetings Lowell and I would have over the next eight years. In the course of that weekend we settled upon a design similar to *Project Utopia,* calling for weekly exchanges of special category reports, though inviting daily e-mail as well. Our next challenge was figuring out a way to sort the mail and distribute it to all participants.

Lowell departed before we'd resolved that issue, and I moved on to query several international schools, asking if they could participate in the *South African Elections '94 Internet Project.* An impressive title, certainly, but it felt more like a dream, one inspired by the people of South Africa, and Nelson Mandela in particular. Schools were slow to reply to my faxed queries. Some did not have access to Internet Service Providers or suffered an unreliable connection; many declined due to curricular concerns. "A combination of vacation and mock IB exams will dominate the students' schedules in the coming weeks," observed an administrator at the International School of Kenya. "Once the IB mocks are finished we will be in review for the actual examinations." Such responses were discouraging, and revealing, but it seemed absurd to let an historic moment, a "teachable moment" of this magnitude, pass without making more of it in one's classroom. I couldn't imagine even the most tradition-bound educators petitioning South Africa's Independent Electoral Commission to postpone elections so that they wouldn't coincide with International Baccalaureate and Advanced Placement exams. Thus, we had to find ways to integrate this event, and emerging technology, into our academic calendars and professional lives.

Despite all the challenges, our first exchange of student documents took place on April 12, 1994. Students in Kuala Lumpur, Des Moines, and The Hague submitted the first reports to the project's "listserver," an electronic mailing list that automatically distributed contributions to all who subscribed. The project asked students to consider South Africa's elections from the perspective of the country in which they resided. Students worked in groups as experts in one of five areas: (1) History, (2) Arts & Literature, (3) The Media, (4) Political/International Relations, and (5) the Local Scene. After researching their country's relationship with South Africa through their category's filter, each group prepared a "one-page" document for weekly transmissions via the listserver.

These efforts were rewarded during South Africa's election week when, for the first time, South African students joined the project. A miracle? Perhaps not for those living in freer, democratic states, but what of students in South Africa who had never corresponded with peers overseas before? What of South African educators who had suffered the censorship of apartheid? Consider, too, the students in Malaysia who, despite their government's daily ritual of media manipulation, were suddenly privy to uncensored reports from people in South Africa, Europe, and North America. Perhaps this helps one understand what a miraculous, and powerful, educational tool this technology can be. As one of my students observed in his evaluation of the project:

I live thousands of miles from Holland, South Africa, and Iowa, and yet was able to share in an event that gives hope for the world. My greatest personal thrill was corresponding with someone my age in South Africa. I was talking with someone who lived the elections.

What's important to notice here is that the student wasn't enthralled with technology. While he was aware that computers and the Internet made this project possible, the boxes and wires of telecollaboration were simply a means to an inspiring, and educational, end. The miracles we witnessed grew out of the human spirit—from Nelson Mandela's will to the South Africans' hope, and the good faith of all who contributed to the project. The technology was, indeed, a marvel to me, but consider how limited it was, particularly from the vantage point of what now exists. I had access to electronic mail through a computer located in the faculty work room adjacent to a computer lab. All of the e-mail messages had to pass through my personal account. Each day I would download files onto a diskette, sort them by subject using the Eudora mail reader, then distribute the messages to the respective research groups. Their responses would simply reverse the process, with a flurry of diskettes loading files onto one computer's hard drive in my classroom. I would then transfer the files to a diskette, transport them to the faculty room, and submit them to the project listserver through my e-mail account.

As taxing as this may sound, the chief obstacle for many participants was not technological, but curricular. Each of the participating schools outside South Africa was torn between this singular opportunity and the obligation to prepare students for external examinations. Just days after Nelson Mandela's election, amid remarkable online discussions, Iowa sounded the first alarm. When his colleague, history teacher Mike Schaffer, was forced to withdraw students from the project, Lowell offered a sad commentary upon the yoke of traditional curricula:

Date: Wed, 4 May 1994
Subject: Damn tests

Problems at the Academy. I'm afraid Mike has had to scale back the contribution of his students just at the time when some deep reflection is warranted. He has pushed up against the AP test schedule about as hard as he could. But this after school, small group project became such a consuming affair for his seniors that he ended up dedicating a lot of class time to it right at the time he usually gets them ready for the tests (I believe this class takes two separate tests—they compress two courses into one). Now he is up against it. Most of his students take two or three other AP tests, starting this week and they have not been able to follow through with their work on SA, but it is not at all a matter of losing interest. As Mike mentioned the other day [. . .] the students who have been involved with this told him they were really disappointed that they had to pull back for AP exams because they just now feel that they know something about South Africa and want to continue to share that knowledge and learn more.

Despite such developments, *The South African Elections '94 Internet Project* was an extraordinary experience, offering students in the antipodes a chance to participate vicariously in an historic moment. My students learned far more about conventional news media, both local and international, by comparing its reports with eyewitness accounts from their Internet correspondents. While publications like *USA Today, Newsweek,* and *The International Herald-Tribune* splashed images of rioters and bus burnings upon their pages, we were corresponding with people who felt tension, but saw little violence within their communities. They painted a less sensational, but far more personal, portrait of their beloved country. One of the best examples of this was Paul Sainsbury, a student at St. Andrews' College in Grahamstown, South Africa, who volunteered to keep a journal during the election week and submit daily entries to the project mailing list. He described everything from the voting queues in his town to the television reports on South African television. One of my students, a keen observer of the media, asked Sainsbury if the Malaysian prime minister's visit with Nelson Mandela, in the midst of the elections, was as big a "media event" in South Africa as Malaysia's state-run newspaper, *The New Straits Times,* claimed. Sainsbury offered an electronic shrug; he found no mention of the Malaysian prime minister in South Africa's media that week.

As creators and coordinators, Lowell and I doubted we would ever equal the excitement of this project. It's not often that one can anticipate an "historic moment" of this magnitude and help students participate in it. However, we continued to learn a good deal about how to "think through" the technology of a computer network. The listserver resolved the problem of dissemination, certainly, though there were embarrassing moments when personal messages, meant for a private audience, were submitted to the public forum of a mailing list. What's more, the influx of e-mail, from students, teachers and would-be "lurkers" around the world grew at an alarming rate. We needed more time for reflection between category reports; one week was simply not enough to digest the reports, write follow-up e-mail, and prepare yet another report. Telecollaboration presented itself like a hydra-headed problem; no sooner had we lopped off one problematic head than two more sprouted.

In chapter 4, Lowell will comment upon the concerns that this project raised from his vantage point on the other side of the world. For now, I'll close by saying that we seemed to have stumbled upon a promising structure. The "expert clusters" were an especially good innovation, inspiring collaboration within our local classrooms, mitigating the chaos of telecollaboration, and improving the reciprocity among students trying to follow current events while corresponding with peers around the world. It's important to remember, after all, that we had to sustain research and online conversations despite our students' frequent absence from classes due to curricular and extracurricular activities.

The Nadine Gordimer Short Story Project (September–October 1994)

The South African Elections '94 Internet Project was an enlightening and transformative experience. It suggested that something profound was happening "out there," yet I wondered if this were a harbinger of things to come or an experience that defied replication. The answer to that question is probably "yes," but following my initiation to cyberspace, and communion with South Africa, one thing was certain: my conception of what constitutes a "class," a "syllabus," or even "pedagogy" would never be quite the same. I wanted to continue experimenting with this medium, to challenge myself while opening my classroom to the world, rather than letting Malaysian officials or high school administrators dictate the parameters. One consequence of this was the hastily designed *Nadine Gordimer Short Story Project* at the start of the following school year.

I was teaching a group of advanced tenth grade students in a pre-IB course called "Introduction to Literary Analysis." Free of the higher level's prescriptions, I wanted to see how much lead time one really needed to set up a telecollaborative project and whether it would succeed without having "an ace in the hole" like Lowell Monke at the other end. Was it possible to cast the 'Net and locate partners less than a month before a project's start? Could we arrange a productive dialogue without students on both ends submitting formal reports? I put out a call for participation on several educational mailing lists, including "Schoolza," the South African educators' list that I had employed during the elections' project, and declared a general aim:

To discuss selected short stories by Nadine Gordimer, encouraging students to become more critical readers and writers. In addition to sharing observations with respect to the conventional concerns of the short story (point of view, character, conflict, theme, etc.) we would also like to discuss the relevance of these stories in a post-apartheid South Africa. Are these timeless, universal stories or historical documents which rely more upon a specific time and place than universal theme?

To provide structure, as well as limit the chaos of e-mail correspondence, students would specialize in one of the following categories: (1) Point of View/Character; (2) Setting; (3) Conflict/Resolution ; (4) Writing Style/Figurative Language; and (5) Theme. Each of these expert groups produced a report of 250 words for every story, providing:

1. Brief analysis of the respective element of the story.

2. At least three "Why" questions (to excite further questions and analysis).

We studied two stories each week, starting with Gordimer's fiction of the 1950s before proceeding to the 1960s and 1970s. A school in Japan subscribed to the listserver and deposited a report. Unfortunately, they couldn't find a copy of the anthology we were using, nor could we find theirs. Students found it difficult to pursue a discussion without the common ground of a shared story. Faced with the challenge of faxing each other stories, or scanning them to send as e-mail attachments—time-consuming practices that neither I nor my counterpart in Japan could afford—our dialogue came to a premature end.

Correspondence with South Africa, meanwhile, proved sporadic. We attracted several individuals, but no school groups. My students grew weary of sending out reports or messages that were subsequently neglected. Reciprocity was clearly a big issue, particularly when students were trying "to excite further questions and analysis" but receiving no replies. Despite its failings—or perhaps because of them—I learned three valuable lessons from this project: first, telecollaborators should remember to KISS (Keep It Simple, Stupid); second, it's essential that one find a committed partner and school to sustain dialectical discourse; and third, one month is not sufficient "lead time" for a telecollaborative project that aspires to create an online community of inquiry. How was I to know, after all those years living inside the box that was my sequestered classroom, that South African schools followed a southern hemisphere calendar? By the time we reached October they were preparing for final exams and I was beginning to realize there was far more to telecollaboration than access to the

Internet. Painful though it was, this experience proved crucial to the evolution of my thinking about telecollaborative projects, informing the design and facilitation of what followed.

Great Expectations (March–May 1995)

The 1994–95 academic year witnessed profound changes in the computer facilities at the International School of Kuala Lumpur. The increased number of faculty e-mail users forced the creation of a second Internet station in the faculty work room, but with a staff of one hundred on the Ampang campus there was often a lengthy queue. Consequently, at the end of the first semester the school established an electronic bulletin board service and private e-mail accounts that students and teachers could access anywhere on campus through a local area network. Meanwhile, the privileged few who possessed a modem and stable phone line could also gain dial-up access from home. Once more, new technology presented new possibilities, but also introduced new challenges and responsibilities. How might one use an electronic bulletin board for instructional purpose? What concerns should one address with students before launching such a project? Like many teachers, I had not received training for such work, nor were there any colleagues who might offer guidance, since none of them had attempted anything like this before. I would have to improvise, making it up as I went along. Such is the case when schools invest in hardware and software, but devote scant attention and resources to the professional development of teachers.

Given the developments at ISKL I wanted to explore the possibilities for a computer network to serve a local community, perhaps forging new relationships across the curriculum and age groups. I also wanted to address a fundamental problem that the Gordimer project exposed: how to stimulate and sustain dialogues through a telecollaborative effort. Clearly, a thoughtful project design wasn't enough to ensure reciprocity, but by placing student dialogue at the foreground, and emphasizing its importance throughout the project, perhaps we would improve the quality and consistency of the online discussions.

During my second and third years at the International School of Kuala Lumpur I taught the International Baccalaureate's Higher Level English course, a two-year program culminating in oral and written examinations. The IB Higher Level English course had four components: "World Literature" (which includes two essays for external assessment); "Detailed Study" (the focus of a formal oral examination); "School's Free Choice" (used for "internal" assessment) and "Groups of Works" (a study of genre for written examinations). To fulfill the Groups of Works requirement, ISKL had selected texts listed within the Art of the Novel category, designing an eclectic mix with Charles Dickens's

Great Expectations, Henry James's *The Portrait of a Lady,* Joseph Conrad's *Heart of Darkness,* Manuel Puig's *Kiss of a Spider Woman,* and Margaret Atwood's *The Handmaid's Tale.*

To season this heavy diet of prose and stimulate discussion I asked students to keep a journal, documenting their individual "reading style," the reading habits and idiosyncracies that had evolved over the years. Some had never thought about this topic before, though they could describe habitual reading environments: in bed late at night, on the school bus, a hammock, et cetera. However, they understood the significance of a reading style as soon as we began weekly "read-aloud" sessions of *Great Expectations.* For this, we gathered in a circle and took turns reading, each person offering an oral interpretation of one paragraph, regardless of length, before the next in the circle took a turn. We continued in this fashion until we reached the asterisk denoting the end of Dickens's original 1861 installments. I did not allow students to take the novel out of class, and admonished them not to read ahead in a personal copy of the book; my intention, after all, was to approximate the experience of Dickens's first readers, who had to wait for the next installment of the novel to be published before they could find out what happened next. This stimulated discussion of how reading practices shape our experience and understanding of a text. Several students noted that, for the first time, they were cognizant of *how* they were reading as well as *what* they were reading.

When March arrived and we were barely midway through the novel, I was forced to distribute copies and ask the students to finish in modern fashion: two weeks' time. I also asked them to write journal entries, comparing their experience of group read-aloud sessions with silent, private readings. Most of the students preferred the former, recalling how characters sprung to life when we enacted the text (for instance, when Pip attended Miss Havisham's birthday celebration, we read the installment gathered in a tight circle on the floor, lights off, passing a candle from one reader to the next). Others observed how the passage of time in their own lives more closely approximated Pip's maturation in the text. Where we previously needed a month to read four installments that described two years in Pip's life, the readers were suddenly able to "cover" two years in one evening. Our discussion of time and reading styles made the students and myself wonder if the acceleration of change, so noticeable in Kuala Lumpur, and the distractions of modern society, so prevalent in the school environment of ISKL, had made the novel an "endangered species" of literature.

With the arrival of March, the IB/AP teacher confronts yet another conundrum: how can one simultaneously complete the course material, achieve a sense of closure, and begin review for the external examinations? Like many teachers, I was convinced that my students deserved a fuller appreciation for the "Art of the Novel." Yes, we had read the prescribed texts, discussed them, investigated the background of respective authors, and written journal entries and essays, but something was still lacking. Somehow, I wanted to "show" my students what I had been "telling" them about novels. I wanted them to dive beneath the surface of the texts—beneath the experience of active readers even—to a place of knowledge and understanding reserved for practitioners of the art. I reflected on Charles Dickens's serial publication once more, marveling at his fertile imagination and extraordinary resolve. I asked the students if they thought such a feat could be accomplished in this era. One of them, a budding cyberpunk, said he not only thought it could, but that he imagined it was already happening somewhere on the Internet.

Perhaps it was, but I couldn't find evidence of it while searching the Internet from my home in Ampang. So I began designing *Great Expectations—Electronic Novellas in the Making,* a project that would turn each of my students into a latter-day Dickens. We would use the school's electronic BBS to publish five weekly installments of the students' original novellas. For the first time I could establish shared accounts for groups logging into the system with a common name and password. This compelled discussion of "'Netiquette" and the need to respect access privileges. It also raised the issue of reciprocity once more, forcing me to admit my limitations as a classroom teacher facilitating a telecollaborative project. How would I respond to thirty students writing 1,000-word novella installments every week? How might I disseminate copies of this work without causing a meltdown in the school's photocopying room? This is where electronic publishing proved itself an ally.

After initiating the twelfth grade authors to the school's BBS through shared accounts, I set up three more accounts for their critics, tenth grade students in my "Introduction to Literary Analysis" course. The ILA scholars, pre-IB students in most cases, were conducting their own study of the novel, devoting the spring term to Thomas Hardy's *Tess of the D'Urbervilles.* Thus, they were a well-primed audience for "novellas-in-progress." Each tenth grade student drew one twelfth grade author's name from a hat, and had the choice of a second author on their own. This guaranteed every twelfth grade author at least one reader; popular reaction to the novellas would dictate how many additional responses an author received. The critics were required to write a full-page critique for both authors, analyzing the prose as well as plot, character, and theme. These letters were to be handwritten and submitted for my perusal before delivery to the authors.

In this fashion we mixed old and new forms of written communication. While the authors employed twentieth-century telecommunications for serial publication, the critics emulated nineteenth-century correspondents, handwriting their critiques and sealing them with wax or playful postage stamps. I instructed the critics to encourage their authors while arguing aesthetic sensibilities, aiming for a mutually rewarding experience. The authors had an appreciative, though critical, audience to help them develop their novellas and writing; the critics learned vicariously about the challenges of imaginative writing, while gaining practical experience in literary criticism. Meanwhile, anyone in the community who wished to read the installments could open the *Great Expectations* folder in the BBS and download the files. Since few students had private e-mail accounts at the time, however, and we didn't wish to make criticism a public affair, the general community would serve as anonymous readers; they could browse through our collected works, but not reply to the authors via the BBS or electronic mail.

Among the greatest surprises of this project was the way in which the authors, high school seniors in their penultimate weeks, responded to their critics. Their anxiety before receiving the first critiques was nearly palpable. With each successive critique, however, they grew more comfortable with the symbiotic relationship between reader and writer. As an advisor to various school publications I've heard the complaints of student writers who encounter an indifferent audience; they often wonder if anyone reads their work. In this instance, however, there was no question. Someone was definitely reading, and responding, to their novellas. The impact of this "guaranteed" audience, and the immediacy of their responses, reinforced my belief that telecollaborative projects thrive upon authentic writing experiences and reciprocal relationships. The publication of these electronic novellas enabled students to engage in more authentic reader-writer relationships. While meaningful for both readers and writers, this was especially significant for the authors, since most student writing for an IB course is destined for an examiner's eyes only. As a result, students often feel like their writing is tossed into a void. In-class writing workshops allow for peer response and help fill that void, but over a two-year period they lose impact and efficacy. The publication of their writing in electronic form, however, stimulated these students because it transcended the usual classroom contrivances.

Many students commented on the excitement of hearing responses from relative strangers, people who—unlike classmates—came to know the writer primarily through their writing. While dreading harsh criticism, the authors also learned that the adulation of an admiring fan could flatter and worry creators, simultaneously empowering and humbling them. Because of this reciprocal relationship, authors grew more attached to their creations, giving them serious and sustained attention. Despite myriad distractions within school and their personal lives, they focused on their work and defended it against the abuses of weak readers. They experienced the bewilderment of the writer wondering if a reader's misunderstanding stemmed from poor writing or incompetent reading. Finally, the intimacy of this endeavor led to a genuine desire to communicate; the authors' vehicle was serialized fiction while the critics' was handwritten epistles, but the mutual aim was understanding "the other."

Great Expectations—Electronic Novellas in the Making reinforced my belief that reciprocity is essential to educational telecollaboration. We could very well have "published" the novellas online without seeking responses, but the project would not have been as meaningful for either the writers or their critics. The writers received a prompt response that encouraged them to continue; the critics, meanwhile, were thrilled to see the writers respond to their words by making adjustments in subsequent installments. Overall, the project demonstrated what students and teachers can achieve when their collective "voices" are allowed to find expression within the "text" of a course. This is what I find demoralizing about the carnivalesque atmosphere of many schools: it demeans the "sacred text" of our classrooms. In essence, extracurricular activities that pull students from the classroom dialogue tear the fabric of a "text," an intricate tapestry of language and thought that demands the collaborative effort of students and teachers. One cannot weave *in absentia,* nor hide the flaws of an ill-woven fabric.

While it is by no means a panacea for our problems, telecollaboration could help future language arts teachers mitigate them. In a very short time, this online activity helped my students learn the importance of self-discipline in writing—as well as how demanding, fickle, and frustrating readers can be. This, in turn, fostered questions of meaning, intention, and reader response, which compelled the authors to ask questions, take greater pains with the voice of their narratives, and strive for consistency in style and tone. Ultimately, they learned what it means to weave their words and dreams, their visions and intentions, while listening to the queries of a critical reader and the demands of a narrative seeking a life of its own.

The problems? The ease of electronic publishing, initially a blessing, can quickly become a curse. How, for example, can anyone read and respond to all the words scrolling up the screen? How can we make sure young writers pause to reflect, gaining the critical detachment necessary for thoughtful revision, rather than becoming preoccupied with superficial concerns like font styles? How do we make sure the efficiency of e-mail transactions doesn't destroy the humanity of the relationships they nurture? In many ways, it was fortunate that we didn't enable readers to send e-mail responses to the *Great Expectations* folder. As it evolves, ISKL's computer network may provide e-mail accounts for every student. Until that time, however, the use of shared accounts and a community bulletin board makes e-mail critiques problematic. This, as Lowell would quickly point out, is not a technical matter, but a social one. How so? Public responses would have made these writers more vulnerable to uncharitable criticism or *ad hominem* attacks. Imagine the chagrin of students who suffered such responses. Might it not stifle creativity and defeat a work-in-progress rather than inspiring young authors to carry on?

The creation of private e-mail accounts could solve such problems, but it might also breed hydra-headed conundrums. For instance, individual e-mail accounts could prompt an exponential growth in writing. This places remark-able strains upon teachers, compelling the adoption of new methods for in-struction, response, and assessment, along with consideration of moral and ethical questions. For instance, how much of the students' e-mail correspon-dence should a teacher peruse? After the first few installments I felt like Big Brother eavesdropping on intimate conversations, so I stopped reading the handwritten letters and simply checked to make sure the critics had done their work. How does one grade a "letter to an author" anyway? And given the collab-orative nature of this endeavor, would it be fair to fault one party for the other's failure to reciprocate? What if the reader had a mediocre author? What if the author had a negligent reader?

Telecollaboration is not about computers. It is about people learning how to read each other. It's about learning to understand the nuances of another's lan-guage, thought, and tone. However, while it accelerates the pace at which we ex-change information, it does not necessarily improve communication. The dan-ger, in fact, is that it will simply help us miscommunicate more rapidly. We of an older generation learned this from another medium: the LP. Playing a 33⅓ album at 78 rpm seldom helped one understand the song's lyrics or appreciate its tone. The same applies to e-mail. Just because I've "processed" more words, more quickly, than ever before, doesn't mean I'm making more sense. Nor does it mean a reader will apprehend an author's meaning or tone. The only way to determine whether or not we have communicated is through genuine dialogue, which demands a strong commitment from participants who alternate between the role of reader and writer in a telecollaborative project. This, I would argue, is the crux of the telecollaborative process, the holy grail that inspires us to keep trying, yet remains terribly elusive and fragile.

Utopian Visions '95 (April–May 1995)

Is it possible for a classroom teacher to run two telecollaborative projects si-multaneously? That was an important question as I entered the second half of the 1994 – 95 school year. I knew the *Great Expectations* project would require considerable time and energy, but since it was limited to ISKL's expatriate com-munity it didn't satisfy my desire for contact with the rest of the world. Lowell and I had discussed possibilities throughout the year, but the success of the *South African Elections '94 Internet Project* proved both a blessing and a curse. I've already described some of the blessings, but consider the curse: how does one construct a project that compares favorably with that one? How would we manage to keep ourselves interested, avoiding the inevitable anticlimax? The answer, it seemed, was to return to our starting point, thinking once more about what we wanted to accomplish—and why.

If there were a common thread running through our work it was "the pursuit of a better society." Although we weren't likely to find something as dramatic as the South African elections to study every year, Lowell believed the theme of utopia was an inspired one, inviting exploration of both the topic and a new medium with multinational students. There was no denying the significance of connecting students with an historic moment, particularly as it evolved. Our previous success was due largely to the dynamics of a singular moment in history, one that inspired students to ask open-ended questions, listen to multiple viewpoints, and ponder an uncertain future. If we could design a project that conceived of our time as an historic moment then we wouldn't need another "big event" to inspire discussions.

Beyond this, I wanted to experiment more with telecollaborative designs, striving for that elusive balance of academic reports and informal e-mail. Among my IB students there was a small group who chose not to take the external exams. I wanted to arrange a meaningful independent study for them, not a tedious research project that put them through obligatory paces in the library, culminating in a lifeless essay teetering upon the edge of plagiarism. So I consulted several almanacs, noting topics for which they supplied data on countries, then drafted a project design that would require both research and analysis. Lowell and I argued the details, from the number of categories to the length of respective reports, until we were suffering the paralysis of analysis. There comes a point, finally, when the rhetorician must let go of the debate. So, too, project coordinators must eventually stop tinkering, take a deep breath, and push their contraption off a cliff to see if it flies. That's when we broadcast *Utopian Visions '95*, posting a "Call for Collaboration" on educational mailing lists that had sprung up around the world.

This was the first time we "advertised" a project on the Internet, prompting a rather strange, vulnerable sensation. We felt like two people inviting everyone in town to a party. On the one hand, we worried that no one would show up, but on the other, what if everyone who received the message joined the project mailing list before they understood our intentions? Clearly, we needed to exercise discretion, so we circulated a cryptic message that we hoped would pique curiosity and attract kindred spirits, yet refrain from broadcasting logistical information too freely:

Internet Project Seeks Participants
Utopian Visions '95—An Integrated Study of the Past, Present, & Future

Ever wondered what it was like to live a century ago? Ever pondered what life will be like a century from now? This project, generated by e-mail discussions between Buddy Burniske in Kuala Lumpur and Lowell Monke in Des Moines, is designed to help students simultaneously reflect and speculate, considering their place in a fascinating continuum of history. If you're interested, please contact us at the e-mail addresses listed below. A full project description will be returned via e-mail, along with instructions on how to "subscribe" to the project listserver. Hope you and your students will join this group of "visionaries" for what promises to be an exciting discussion!

To facilitate the discussions, establishing a common frame of reference, we established ten research categories, one of which was the school's free choice. Designed as a six-week project, *Utopian Visions '95* asked participants to research the conditions of their country in 1895, compare that with their development by 1995, and, finally, describe what they envisioned for 2095. Students were asked to commit themselves to one category group, in hopes of acquiring greater depth in their study of a particular topic; meanwhile, class discussions would encourage an interdisciplinary study and more holistic understanding of historic developments. Ultimately, each category group would submit biweekly "category reports" on the respective time periods, then engage in e-mail discussions with their distant peers, providing opportunities for follow-up questions.

As a pilot project, *Utopian Visions '95* was reasonably successful, but it fell short of our expectations. Perhaps we overestimated our students, but their lack of historical perspective and global awareness limited their understanding of the people and places they encountered. What's more, participants devoted far more time to reports than dialogues with their peers. As a result, data collection became an end in itself; dialectics suffered. We were disappointed to find students embracing cliches or indulging in "infotainment" rather than thinking critically. Was this simply a poor project design? Was it a matter of student access? Or had we reached the point of diminishing returns, exposing the limitations of this medium? I left this open to conjecture, but wondered most about my students' complaints, in project evaluations, that the strict time constraints undermined correspondence. This was surprising, coming as it did from a group that enjoyed a longer interval between reports than previous groups (two weeks instead of one) as well as Internet access through a shared e-mail account.

Taken as a whole, *Utopian Visions '95* felt more like a game, a grand fiction similar to *Project Utopia,* rather than the intellectual exercise we desired. Nonetheless, this experience strengthened our resolve on two points: first, we needed to start the student dialogues sooner so that personal exchanges prior to the academic reports enabled students to introduce themselves and establish a greater sense of community; second, we had to take a more proactive stance in discussions, prompting the seriousness of purpose that infused the South African elections project. I will offer a more detailed analysis of the *Utopian Visions* project in chapter 5, but this thumbnail sketch should, if nothing else, reinforce the evolutionary nature of an educator's telecollaborative work. Had this project followed the *Great Expectations* experiment with electronic novellas, rather than evolving simultaneously, we might have spared ourselves some frustrations, facilitating dialectical discourse rather than superficial reports.

Ironically, these trials took place while mainstream media and would-be visionaries celebrated a "paradigm shift" in education. What that meant to me at this point in time, however, was the forfeiture of autonomy within a local classroom for the construction of a mercurial work-in-progress called the "global classroom." I remained hopeful that we'd get it right the next time and that we'd discover patterns that would help us anticipate problems and stimulate thoughtful discussions. For the first time, however, I had to admit serious doubts. Would online discourse ever reach the standards we set for healthy, in-class discussions? Were we wrong to compare the two? Did we need new methods to evaluate student discourse?

The Nadine Gordimer Internet Project '95 (September–November 1995)

From a personal standpoint, I might have enjoyed the *Utopian Visions '95* project more if a South African school had participated. I believed students there would offer a unique perspective while "looking backward" at their history as well as some provocative concerns when "looking forward." Unfortunately, it never happened, despite efforts to recruit people who had joined our discussions the year before. I remained in touch with South Africans, nevertheless, lurking on the "Schoolza" list and occasionally corresponding with people I had met online during the elections. This correspondence made me wish for something more than virtual acquaintance. Indeed, it compelled a trip I had long postponed.

With the aid and encouragement of online correspondents I planned a five-week trip through southern Africa, beginning with the Grahamstown Arts Festival in July 1995, and culminating in workshops and presentations at over thirty educational institutions, from Port Alfred to Cape Town, Bloemfontein to Gaborone, Pretoria to Mbabane. Thanks to the generosity and resourcefulness of South Africans we had met online, my wife, two sons, and I visited black townships, mixed-race schools, private white schools, and universities, sharing experiences with educators while discussing the impact of computer technology and the challenges of educational reform.

Upon returning to Malaysia in August, I set to work on a revised version of the Nadine Gordimer project. While retaining the focus upon story elements and analytical questions, I wanted to encourage better correspondence. Toward that end, I asked students to include a brief letter to South Africans in their reports, asking about the concerns a particular story raised ("Is this issue still relevant in post-apartheid RSA?"). By concentrating upon South African schools I hoped to build upon relationships that our visit had cultivated. Given diverse curricula and academic schedules, however, it seemed best to think of the

South African students as eyewitness experts who could supplement our study of Gordimer's fiction rather than literary critics engaged in simultaneous reading and criticism of those works. In this way, we could fulfill our curricular objectives, forge an online community, and correspond without creating logistical nightmares on both ends.

I gave schools notice in early August (the start of South Africa's second semester), widened the parameters of the project so that students would have two weeks between exchanges rather than one, and moved my classes into the newly created writing lab adjacent to my classroom. We had five new PowerMac computers to work with, meaning clusters of four to five students would gather at the respective terminals to work on their group reports. At times this was stressful, particularly since students in this tenth grade class had to become acquainted quickly, adjust to my expectations as readers and writers, immerse themselves in South African history, and push themselves beyond superficial readings to comprehend an extraordinary writer's complex fiction.

What followed was almost as remarkable as our discussion of the South African elections. Perhaps most startling was the diversity of participants, something that our previous telecollaborations had not enjoyed. Throughout the first semester, indeed well past the initial timeline I had set, we corresponded with black students from a Port Alfred township, white students from Grahamstown and Queenstown, and mixed race students from Durban. Consider what I'm describing: a North American schoolteacher in Kuala Lumpur initiates a project that facilitates conversation among black, white, and mixed-race people in South Africa, people who were constitutionally segregated just five years before, but could now be electronically connected through a listserver in Malaysia. Certainly, my visit—and the human relationships it established—helped make some of this possible, but so did our mutual access to networked technology. We employed the lowest common denominator for telecollaboration—an electronic mailing list—but each of my classes had its own shared account so that students could check e-mail during free periods or from home. Two other changes proved significant: the acquisition of an LCD panel, which allowed us to discuss selected messages and reports collectively, and direct access to the school's BBS through a telephone line in the writing lab.

Once again, the incremental changes in technology enabled significant innovations within the class, including use of the LCD panel as an electronic chalkboard upon which we could read and compose messages collectively, demystifying the reading and writing process. However, the delicacy of this endeavor was highlighted when students in one group engaged in a lewd exchange. I quickly alerted my cohorts in South Africa and admonished my classes, warning that a recurrence would shut down the project and their shared accounts. The incident helped teach the importance of responsible behavior with a new communication tool. It also served as a reminder that while students may gain technical competence quickly, and demonstrate rudimentary skills, they are still adolescents in need of guidance. Rather than make the Internet a forbidden fruit because of this episode, however, it seemed wise to address the problem, set firm guidelines, and applaud exemplary efforts that reflected positively upon the group.

There were a number of moments that did just that, including an exchange of photographs and personal effects with students in the Port Alfred township. The *coup de grace,* however, was an unexpected letter from Nadine Gordimer. Apprised of our work by colleagues in the Nelson Mandela Township of Port Alfred, she sent a message to my students via facsimile, offering insights that speak to the power of the Internet—and the writers we meet there—as well as the importance of creative literature:

There are many ways of finding out about a country, and most people think that this is done completely by listening to the news on the radio, watching television and reading newspapers. But the media does not and cannot give you a full understanding of how the people of a country live, and how they feel, inside themselves, about their lives. This you can hope to learn only from a country's writers. (Gordimer 1995)

The Media Matter (September–November 1995)

Gordimer's words spoke volumes to another group of students I was teaching that semester. They were part of a telecollaborative project that examined print and electronic media for an English elective called "Literature, Language, and Society." I asked students to analyze news stories—as rendered through newspapers, magazines, radio, television, and the Internet—then prepare media reports for e-mail exchange with other schools conducting similar research. Lowell had expressed interest in something like this a year before, in response to Neil Postman's call for schools to "engage in the task of de-mythologizing media" (Postman 1985). Unfortunately, neither of us could articulate a project design, at least not in a manner that would accommodate a high school curriculum. Working within the liberal confines of an elective course, however, I conceived of this as a study of "literature, language, and society" as expressed through disparate media. Lowell offered few complaints, a sign that he was either satisfied with the project design or too busy to quibble. He could not promise, however, that his students in a computer applications course would respond as favorably.

The Media Matter: A Communications Study, raised significant questions about censorship and media monopoly, issues my students could not have broached in a global manner just a few years before. It's worth noting that in September 1995, when the project began, Malaysia still prohibited ownership of satellite dishes and permitted the broadcast of only three television channels, all state-controlled. While arguing the merits of government control versus corporate influence, students had the opportunity to analyze media, and all who would manipulate it, from diverse viewpoints. I do not believe my students would have learned as much about the media without comparing local versions of it with their counterparts' versions in other parts of the world. This was the first time most of them had ever considered how the form of a news story influenced its content. They had never been asked to "read" a news medium before; initially, they could not distinguish between the story and the medium through which it passed. This signaled a departure from their role as passive audience to active critics, introducing them to a medium's subliminal effects, as well as McLuhan's claim that "the price of eternal vigilance is indifference" for a society enthralled with electronic media (1964, p. 43).

I wish I could report that *The Media Matter* was an unequivocal success, but Lowell would never let me get away with that. For all its potential, *The Media Matter* did not flourish the way we had hoped it would. We did receive contributions from students in Hawaii and Botswana, but after filing initial reports they failed to engage in meaningful dialogue, disappearing from the listserver without much warning or explanation. Was it a question of timing? Perhaps, though the Gordimer project, conducted at the same time, was thriving. Could it be the fate of pilot projects in general? Yes, perhaps, but that didn't hinder the South African elections project. No, there was something much deeper here, something which I've only come to see with time and distance.

I'll offer a more detailed analysis of *The Media Matter* in chapter 7, but for now let me suggest that this project was simply too far outside "the box" of secondary school curricula. It didn't fit within the confines of an IB/AP program or the conventional definitions of English, History, Math, Science, Art, etc. However, this hardly warrants its dismissal. In fact, it argues for the revision of school curricula and a broadening of the minds that shape them. Unfortunately, a reductive dichotomy prevails, reinforcing the traditional split between the humanities and sciences, a pernicious division of labor in which scholars in the humanities and many of the social sciences believe that "technology is not our job," whereas scholars in other, more technical domains believe that "technology is our *only* job" (Haas 1996, 22).

It's time to embrace the "new synthesis" that Lowell mentioned earlier, which would actually be a return to the holistic approach of the Renaissance, encouraging truly interdisciplinary courses that allow teachers to integrate language arts, computer science, history and more to awaken and stimulate "the full resources of self." A project such as *The Media Matter* argues for a "Media Studies" course situated within a social studies, journalism, or computer studies program. Frankly, I'm less concerned with its curricular placement than its educational merit, for it would offer students an opportunity to "read" various media and think critically about their impact. By liberating our curricula from rigid structures we can meet the evolving needs of our students and society. My principal aim, regardless of the technology involved, is to create the dialectical tension necessary to prompt student inquiry and learning. Without that, academic endeavors—including telecollaborative projects—deliver sterile information or political propaganda, allowing students to rest upon unexamined assumptions and suffer the delusion that they think for themselves when they are merely reciting inherited opinions or mainstream slogans.

Utopian Visions '96 (February–May 1996)

Telecollaborative projects transform not only what teachers do and how they do it, but the way in which they conceptualize a curriculum and the pedagogy supporting it. My own evolution finds me now "thinking through" the apparatus of the Internet—from e-mail to newsgroups and Web browsers—as I design a syllabus. In my final months in Kuala Lumpur I coordinated *Utopian Visions '96*, the revised version of the pilot project we'd conducted a year before. Drawing from the lessons of the pilot project, Lowell and I decided to make several changes, which I'll examine more fully in chapter 5.

To date, this remains the most "complete" project from my vantage point as a classroom teacher. This is not to say that all participants shared my experience or came away with equally favorable reports. From my perspective, though, I finally felt comfortable with the myriad demands of a position never stipulated in my job description. I was a full-time teacher with nearly 100 students, juggling the attendant duties for five classes, three of which were involved in this project (with a total of forty-six students) and situated in a writing lab with only five computers connected to the school's BBS (affording e-mail connection, but no Web browsing). I was also the coordinator of a telecollaborative project, corresponding with faculty at eight schools on three different continents, moderating online discussions while coordinating the submission of academic reports, electronic mail, and digital photos.

Utopian Visions '96—composed of participants from the Czech Republic, Germany, Hungary, Malaysia, Romania, and the United States—witnessed yet another milestone in the evolution of our work: the creation of a project Web site. This placed new demands upon us; while I moderated the mailing list Lowell had to supervise students in his computer classes responsible for the design and maintenance of the Web site. We now had reports from eight schools passing through a listserver in Kuala Lumpur and archived on a Web server in Des Moines, Iowa. As a result, we established a digital time capsule in which we could preserve reports, post student photos, and enable latecomers to catch up on earlier discussions (something a listserver had never allowed). Once again, students participated in authentic writing, composing their thoughts for a global audience, not just their classroom teacher, while engaging in the dialectics prompted by "utopian visions, dystopian realities."

However, the depth of these discussions, as measured by the duration of dialogue threads as well as the quality and persistence of student inquiry, was often disappointing. At this point, I had to wonder if I suffered unrealistic expectations, a flawed approach to telecollaboration, or deceptive rhetoric from the champions of the "Internet revolution." Did anyone else have difficulty sustaining student dialogues online? Or was this not necessary for telecollaborative learning? We will return to these questions frequently, for the issue of reciprocity remains critical to our discussion of telecollaboration in the classroom.

Utopian Visions '97–'99

Ultimately, participants in the *Utopian Visions* project considered themselves part of another "historic moment"—the end of a decade, century, and millennium—and came to see their contributions as historical documents stored in a digital time capsule (http://uv.cwrl.utexas.edu). As mentioned earlier, chapter 5 offers a more detailed account of this project's evolution, from its genesis to its adaptation for the World Wide Web and evolution over a five-year period. For now, I'll say that we've surprised ourselves by sustaining *Utopian Visions* with the help of volunteers around the world. We persevered through the year 2000, collecting disparate visions of the past, present, and future to preserve student impressions as we have found them, not as we might have wished them, thereby celebrating diversity rather than merely tolerating it.

Once again, though, we have reinvented our telecollaborative wheel. What began as a utopian vision in 1995, a project employing a listserver to distribute reports and follow-up e-mail, evolved into something far more complex. In effect, we attempted to construct an online "community of inquiry," embracing the ideals of Matthew Lipman's philosophy for children program,

in which students listen to one another with respect, build on one another's ideas, challenge one another to supply reasons for otherwise unsupported opinions, assist each other in drawing inferences from what has been said, and seek to identify one another's assumptions. A community of inquiry attempts to follow the inquiry where it leads rather than being penned in by the boundary lines of existing disciplines. (Lipman 1991, 15)

To facilitate discussions, we employed two listservers (one for student reports and e-mail, another for faculty discussions), three message forums (two for topical discussions and one for logistical concerns), and a Web site (which archived the descriptions of participants, category reports, digital photos, and e-mail discussions). The project became both a forum for contemporary debate and an archive of historical documents. Participants could contribute in more ways than ever before, joining the e-mail discussions, posting messages in the online forums, submitting book reviews in the "Utopian Library," or posting "Letters to the People of 2099" in our digitial time capsule. Nonetheless, while the technology continued to evolve, and the project's complexity grew with it, our aim remained fixed upon the marriage of healthy, dialectical discourse with thoughtful, pedagogical praxis.

From Iban to Infobahn: Integration or Annihilation?

I enjoy exploring the pedagogical possibilities of emerging media. However, such explorations, and the new opportunities they present, also invite new responsibilities. Chief among the classroom practitioners' responsibilities while creating global, telecollaborative projects is the establishment of a forum for student expression, a forum that nurtures exploratory discourse rather than the recitation of homogenized thought. Failing that, critical thinking yields to bumper stickers, encouraging the thoughtless embrace of simplistic notions. Consider, for example, the idea of a "global village," a romantic image perpetuated by mainstream media. Behind the appeal of its warm connotations lies a pernicious bit of reductionism. Is it not, after all, naive to think students separated by geography, language, and culture are "communicating" or "interacting" simply because their computers are connected via modem and satellite link? Are we not susceptible to impoverished definitions if we think that "posting" messages in an online forum is the same thing as "communicating" with people?

In every one of these projects I have seen students misunderstand e-mail messages, overreacting to what they considered "insensitive" comments; most often, however, these perceived slights proved to be honest mistakes bred by weak language skills. This can, and does, lead to painful and embarrassing moments. In each instance I've reminded students that while English may be the most common language spoken on the Internet, we remain a people divided by this common language. Many of my students in Malaysia came to English as a second or third language while their counterparts around the globe may have spoken Afrikaans, German, Lithuanian, or Spanish in all phases of their daily life except the class participating in our telecollaborative project. We must not, therefore, confuse correspondence with communication. Nor should we suffer the delusion of an integrated, harmonious village if we've annihilated unpopular views to endorse one brand of Truth.

That thought transports me to Kuala Lumpur, where the media landscape changed almost as much as the city's physical landscape during my four-year stay. The Internet was not solely responsible for this, but it had considerable impact, transforming ideas of time, space, and censorship for those previously limited to a local or regional environment. In just a matter of seconds one could "travel" from the server at the Universiti Kebangsen Malaysia, a Muslim institution thirty kilometers south of Kuala Lumpur, to the "Hollywood On-Line" Web site (Cyberspace, "Pandora"). In just a few hours' time, meanwhile, one could travel physically from Kuala Lumpur, where government officials initially restricted exploration of the cyberforest, to the oldest rainforest in the world, estimated at 130 million years of age.

I have made both journeys, the former while assisting the *24 Hours in Cyberspace* project (Cyberspace, "Bridges"), the latter with an expedition to *Taman Negara* in January 1995. Two months after my journey to the rainforests of peninsular Malaysia, I visited Borneo's state of Sarawak, taking my family for a week's visit to an Iban longhouse. One afternoon we enjoyed a picnic lunch on a riverbank, watching a man cut bamboo poles into three-foot lengths, fill them with water, and stuff rice wrapped in banana leaves inside, before bringing it all to a boil over a spit where a woman cooked a mixture of fiddlehead ferns and bamboo shoots. Two days later we returned to Kuala Lumpur. As I turned on my laptop computer to read my electronic mail the "distance" I had just traveled, from Iban to Infobahn, rainforest to cyberforest, was not lost upon me. Nor could I escape a troublesome question: Can we integrate these disparate worlds, these seemingly exclusive utopian visions, without annihilating one, the other, or both?

Something tells me the answer to that question is a sad one, but I prefer the difficult search for satisfying answers to the lethargic embrace of superficial ones. Intellectual odysseys inspired the evolution of the telecollaborative projects described in this chapter, encouraging both students and teachers to conduct their own investigations, exploring media in a responsible, inquisitive fashion rather than waiting for government officials or school administrators to blaze an "official" trail through the cyberforests of their mind. Though we may fear difficult questions, it is incumbent upon educators to engage in the dialectics they prompt. To abdicate our place in such discussions not only compromises our integrity, but allows the impassioned voices of policymakers and technophiles to speak for us. Worse still, students will forfeit the opportunity to argue one of their generation's defining issues.

Surely, few educators would boast of being *in absentia* during critical discussions concerning the role of technology in education. Fewer still would admit to the practice of self-censorship at a time when new opportunities for self-expression presented themselves. Ultimately, an open-minded discourse, from Kuala Lumpur to Kosovo, Jerusalem to Johannesburg, is essential for humanity to move forward with equal parts compassion and courage while experimenting with global, educational telecomputing. Otherwise, the evolution of technology and its *integration* will repress alternative voices, *annihilating* human diversity and expression. And who would want to live in a village like that?

4

Utopian Visions, Dystopian Worries

Lowell Monke

All technical progress has three kinds of effects: the desired, the foreseen, and the unforeseen.   Jacques Ellul (1990, 61)

From Southeast Asia to the middle of North America—as we begin to look at each project more closely we shift the point of view along with the emphasis. Here we discuss our first two efforts, Project Utopia *and* The South African Elections '94 Internet Project, *as seen from my position teaching at Central Campus in Des Moines, Iowa. Though the latter succeeded where the former fell short, we hope to convey the value of the early struggle as well as the warnings of the later success. In both cases, as our work with this new technology progressed, the most significant and instructive educational effects were the ones unforeseen.*

I agree with Buddy that the impact of technical globalization is one of the defining issues facing our youths' generation (and, no doubt, ours as well). But in the context of this discussion I think it is premature to offer a verdict on the survival of the Iban longhouse. We will return to Sarawak and a more extensive analysis of the "Global Village" in chapter 6, after we have explored in greater depth our actual experiences in cyberspace. Before I begin that journey, it is important to balance the perspective a bit. For most readers, Buddy's situation in Malaysia is a foreign one, as I reminded him on many occasions while he was there. The lens through which I viewed telecomputing, though certainly tinted from my previous experiences overseas, was quite different. Whereas Buddy was starved for information, I felt bloated by the nonstop consumption of it. Whereas Buddy felt isolated, I was so plugged-in I could almost feel the electricity buzzing along my fraying nerves. Buddy needed to break out and expose his students to the world, while my students were the incarnation of Little Eva, a hypothetical high-tech everychild, whose relationship to information here in the United States Neil Postman describes this way:

She lives in a culture which has 260,000 billboards, 17,000 newspapers, 12,000 periodicals, 27,000 video outlets for renting tapes, 400 million television sets, and well over 500 million radios, not including those in automobiles. There are 40,000 new book titles published every year, and each day 41 million photographs are taken. And, thanks to the computer, over 60 billion pieces of advertising junk mail arrive in our mailboxes every year. Everything from telegraphy and photography in the nineteenth century to the silicon chip in the twentieth has amplified the din of information intruding into Little Eva's consciousness. (1995, 43)

Having just recently returned from a three-year teaching stint in Ecuador, I was particularly sensitive to that din. My students, on the other hand, seemed oblivious to it, though hardly immune. They reminded me of the frogs that continue to swim in a pot of gradually heated water, unable to recognize until too late that they are on their way to being boiled. I felt a strong urge to pull my students out of that bubbling pot, providing them a respite from the constant, persistent flow of images and sounds that washed over and through them all day and night, making it difficult for them to quietly *think*.

By the time I started the Advanced Computer Technology program at Des Moines Public Schools' Central Campus in 1992, I was already a veteran user of online services such as CompuServe and America Online. From the beginning, my students had access to an academic telecomputing service called NovaNet, and in the first year we set up our own electronic Bulletin Board System. The issues I had to wrestle with were not isolation nor technical capabilities. My concerns had to do with an abundance of choices. Before wading into our two earliest projects, *Project Utopia* and *The South African Elections '94*, I want to explain why, with all the options available to me, and with a sense that my students were already suffering from a surplus of information, I came to the same conclusion as my isolated colleague, and decided to pursue the difficult task of developing telecollaborative projects with someone on the opposite side of the world.

Teaching in the Gaps

The Advanced Computer Technology (ACT) class began at Central Campus when I started teaching it—a pilot program inaugurated with a rather imprecise mission to give vocational students interested in computer careers a chance to work with a wide variety of business-oriented computer applications. Since no one, including my curriculum supervisor and my principal, knew how that translated into actual classroom activities, I was given wide latitude to develop the program as I saw fit.

It was an opportunity to do something teachers rarely get to do anymore—design a curriculum specifically for my students out of my own experiences and the local context I shared with them. As I explored the telecomputing projects offered by organizations such as Scholastic, AT&T, and National Geographic I gradually realized that these programs had to be designed not for particular students but for the "mass" student, that same extremely generalized "average" genderless, cultureless young person for whom textbooks and standardized tests had long been developed and for whom more recently a wealth of software had appeared under the classification Computer Aided Instruction (Noble 1991). It seemed contradictory to me to try to tailor my curriculum to my students by involving them in plug-and-play programs designed for a mass audience.

As Buddy and I began serious negotiations concerning how we might coordinate our own project, we realized that there were other concerns that made commercial telecomputing projects unattractive to us: if we were going to get consistently serious, thoughtful communications between classes, it would require a tremendous flexibility to adjust to the inconsistencies and uncertainties of school and class schedules—a flexibility only achievable through "local ownership." And if we were going to engage our students in complex issues that challenged them to think in new and deeper ways, then we as supervisors needed to have a depth of comprehension and control that could only be achieved if we were fully involved in the design effort.

Moreover, we both understood the frustration caused by the constant erosion of our roles in determining the content, mode, and standard of learning in our classrooms. Curriculum supervisors, district-wide textbook adoptions, and standardized testing all worked to crowd us out of the responsibility for determining what our students needed to learn and how. I had escaped it; Buddy was trying to overcome it. We were not inclined to step aside and let (much less pay) yet another "provider," who knew our students only as abstractions, design our telecomputing projects for us.

I think this is a bigger issue than just two bull-headed teachers insisting on going their own way. Ever since the drive for efficiency gravitated from the new assembly-line factories into the schools at the beginning of the twentieth century (Callahan 1962, Tyack 1974), the power of classroom teachers to shape the structure of their students' education has gradually diminished almost to nil. Michael Apple, among others, has pointed out that this trend continues with reliance on prepackaged computer software programs, which "can cause a decided loss of important skills and dispositions on the part of teachers. When the skills of local curriculum planning, individual evaluation, and so on are not used, they atrophy" (1984, 133). He argues that the use of predesigned computer programs contributes to this long-running trend of deskilling and depowering teachers. Certainly, this same criticism can be leveled at prepackaged telecomputing projects.

I find considerable personal irony in this critique. One of the factors that attracted me to computers in the early 1980s was the inability of anyone to tell me what to do with them. No one was able to fit them into the curricular strait jacket. Even during the period when schools were setting up separate computer literacy labs no one was successfully prescribing the instruction that went with them. Those of us who jumped into teaching with and about computers early on were able to pretty much call our own shots. We ran our programs in the gaps between the well-defined planks of the curriculum. Many of us were ceded a large degree of autonomy by administrators who had no idea what these machines might be good for (which is not to say that we did). Perhaps this is why there is such a revolutionary atmosphere at educational computing conferences. Many computer teachers have had the same experience I have had, and their eyes have been opened to the need for real change in the way we educate our children. Teaching in the gaps demanded that I rethink almost everything I knew about education. This was confusing but also liberating, for I began to understand how restricted the role of the teacher had become in the traditional classroom setting. I began to recognize the very thing Apple bemoans: that most teachers have little authority to really shape learning according to the individual and group needs of their students and themselves.[1]

Unfortunately, it seems that many computer teachers have concluded that just because the computer allowed them to slip into their own gaps in the curriculum, spreading the use of them all over the schools will somehow result in fostering the needed revolution. They don't recognize that what liberated them was not really the computer itself but its newness to education, a feature that always causes problems for rigid bureaucracies—for awhile. As I watch the way computers are being deployed in schools today I see that the bureaucrats are beginning to catch up to the computer. Apple's (Michael's, not Mac's) scenario is beginning to be played out. The trend toward networking classrooms and buying server-resident software so that each class has access to the same district-selected material is another means of standardizing instruction and further de-powering the classroom teacher (though often the teacher, in getting retrained as a technician, does experience some rejuvenating sense of power, albeit over a machine, not the curriculum).

Buddy and I both find this trend offensive, and have tried to avoid its subtle, insidious grasp. Yet it constantly tugs at us, through our own use of the technology, through the continual bureaucratic "necessities" imposed on us by school structures, and even through the language we find ourselves using. Buddy has described the subtle differences among the terms "telecomputing," "telecommunication," and "telecollaboration." What he didn't mention is that for several years we sloppily interchanged the words "telecommunication" and "telecomputing" when referring to our work. Fortunately, he insisted that we become more disciplined in the way we talked about what we were doing. While "telecommunication" was too ambiguous a term to describe it, "telecomputing" put the emphasis in the wrong place. It stressed the machinery, both the computer itself and the mechanical, technical aspects of human activity. Nothing could be further from the way we wanted to think—and have others think—about our projects. We settled on "telecollaboration" because collaborating is what human beings need to learn to do well (and it is what computers do not do, despite all the semantic gymnastics performed by the Artificial Intelligence crowd).

Throughout this chapter I have used the term "telecomputing" to describe the general activities of cyberspace. It is, obviously, the medium through which we work. But given the inflated credit computers have been given in liberating teachers from the confines of standardized curriculum, and their actual contribution to the further depowering of teachers, I agree with Buddy that it is crucial to distinguish this mechanical process from the pedagogical process of telecollaboration. I think Parker J. Palmer makes this distinction implicitly when he observes that "Good teaching cannot be reduced to technique; good teaching comes from the identity and integrity of the teacher" (1998, 10). Telecomputing is about technology and lends itself to thinking in terms of technique; telecollaboration is about human interaction and depends on the identity and integrity of the individual participants. Though it took some time to work out the language to describe it, the potential for collaboration was the real attraction for two educators yearning to break free from the stranglehold of mass education.

Ironically, I discovered that this view sometimes limited my direct involvement as a teacher in our projects. After all, the purpose of my Advanced Computer Technology program *is* to learn about the technology itself. So in the beginning, working with Buddy meant finding ways to work with core curricular teachers. It meant crawling back out of the gaps between the curricula and trying to build bridges across them—a task that has, at times, felt a lot like trying to span the Grand Canyon.

Project Utopia

Once I agreed to undertake the bridge building, Buddy and I cast about looking for material with which to build. As he indicated in the previous chapter, a project developed around the theme of utopia not only fit his literature class syllabus but it provided a means for investigations beyond both the classroom and his English department.

After a short search I was able to find a willing language arts teacher at Central Campus. Pat Ramsey is a fine veteran teacher who is not only adventurous but technology savvy. She enthusiastically signed on. I'm sure she had no idea what she was getting into.

It should be clear from the structure Buddy proposed that what we hoped to accomplish was a comparison of cultural values between midwest U.S. students and the mostly Asian students in his class. The theme of building a conceptual utopia was less a goal in itself than a vehicle for motoring across the cultural expanses of these students' beliefs. We weren't quite sure what to expect and when the project ended after four exchanges we still weren't sure what we had gotten. At first, the evidence seemed contradictory. Student evaluations were mixed, our impressions were ambivalent and on some matters at odds with each other. It took some time to sort it all out.

One thing we were sure of immediately was that we had learned some hard lessons about telecollaboration. That learning had taken place at two different levels: technical issues and human communication. These two levels actually were closely linked at several points. It was clear from the very first exchange that the medium very seriously affected the message.

Technical Issues

Buddy and I agreed to undertake this project long before we had worked out the technical details. From my end everything looked good. I had an account with AOL and was in the process of getting an Internet account through the local university. Buddy's end was where we had all kinds of unresolved problems. But with Dan LoCascio burning candles at both ends to find a way for them to get connected, I felt uncharacteristically optimistic about our prospects. We resolved to forge ahead with planning the content of the collaboration while Dan and I worked out the technical details.

Those details came very close to derailing the entire project. No matter what Dan tried at the beginning—CompuServe, Applelink, a packet switching service in Malaysia—none of it worked. How about a direct telephone link? Here is where I learned my first lesson in the bureaucratic idiosyncrasies of telecomputing. No one batted an eye at the many faxes I sent to Kuala Lumpur in preparation for the exchanges—after all, sending faxes was routine work by then. Yet when I explored the option of replacing the fax with a computer for the exchange, I found that there was no money in any budget for those kinds of phone costs. And, of course, there was no money in a budget for it because no one had done it before. I felt caught in a bureaucratic Catch-22 (I had estimated that the long-distance telephone charges might run as high as $100—I always wondered what answer I would have received if instead I had asked for $200 to plug into one of GTE's telecomputing projects).

My students had gotten our BBS online in January, about the time Buddy and I had started working on the project. Even though it meant international calls for ISKL for every exchange, we fell back on that, Buddy having been more successful at fund raising than I. We scheduled our first exchange for February 15 (even scheduling started out as a fiasco, as Monday evening for me was Tuesday morning for them; we had a lot of trouble at first keeping straight what day(s!) we were sending things to each other). On that day I received a fax from Dan saying he had tried to get through to our BBS but his computer had crashed.

I called our local telephone company who came in to check that the line was clean and static free which is what I suspected. They said they cleaned it up. Then when I went to try again, our net modem would no longer be recognized over the network. It needs to go in for repair.

He had a backup modem and said he would try again as soon as possible. Two days later I got another fax from Buddy addressed to Pat Ramsey apologizing, "due to technical concerns we must postpone the exchange until Friday, February 19 at 9:00 am our time (Thursday, 8:00 PM your time?)." At the bottom of the fax Dan attached a short note to me: "New development. Our modem was ripped off this week. I will bring in my own."

Finally, on February 19 Dan was able to get through—just long enough to send Buddy's students' vision of utopia and download Pat's students' vision. We had to celebrate with faxes to each other the next day as Dan was unable to re-connect to the BBS.

That is essentially how the technical part of the project then proceeded. Each time we had an exchange ready Dan would somehow find a window of opportunity and get the files transferred. But in between and after the last exchange he was unable to maintain a connection long enough even to send a quick e-mail. Twice he and Buddy tried to demonstrate using the BBS to others at ISKL. Both times the connection failed.

This experience may seem primitive and even irrelevant given the easy world-wide communication we have today via the 'Net. If its only significance was to show what a struggle it was to do two way global telecollaborating just a few short years ago I wouldn't have bothered to relate the story. But I think there are at least a couple of issues that emerged from that struggle, both as it took place and in hindsight, that relate to our use of the 'Net today and, thus, they merit discussion.

The first is the enormous distance that could be sensed between Kuala Lumpur and Des Moines, Iowa, when we were struggling to make good connections. It often brought to mind the difficulty I had calling my parents when I lived in Ecuador. Having to shout into the phone in order to be heard helped me keep in mind how far away I really was from home—maybe not so well as a crushed and tattered box of cookies sent fresh and whole by my mother a month earlier—but at least there was still some sense of distance suggested by the difficulty in communicating. Today, speaking with someone overseas often generates the remark, "You sound like you are right next door." And, indeed, this lack of qualitative difference between communication around the world and around the block is a hallmark of the 'Net.

I'm not so sure this is a good thing for young people, especially young people who have not had the travel experience necessary to appreciate the great physical expanse of the world. As we will see, our later projects exhibited some elements of indifference to the incredibly quick and accurate technical capabilities of the Internet, an indifference that I took to be a lack of appreciation for the enormous distances involved. Just how small do we want our children to believe the world to be? How much of the illusion of next-doorness do we want to give a student who hasn't traveled much beyond the borders of his or her state, or city for that matter? What kinds of misunderstandings about the world does this kind of undifferentiated communication give a young person? And what responsibility as educators do we have to compensate for those misunderstandings?

A second issue that arose from this experience that continues to nag at me today is the cost—not how expensive our project turned out to be, but the way in which our attitude toward paying that cost has changed over just a few years time. I'm not sure I could get $100 from my school's general fund even today to operate a similar project. Yet I can do all the projects I want now using my "free" access to the Internet through the school. In fact, I think my supervisors would be disappointed now if I didn't do some kind of telecomputing work with my students. Yet, just how free is my access to the Internet?

Des Moines Public Schools is billed nearly $500 per month to connect to the Internet backbone (the fee would be much higher except that Iowa taxpayers fund a state agency that the school connects through). We employ a part-time Webmaster and a full-time Internet consultant. I now have over $8,000 worth of equipment in my classroom that my students manage just dedicated to serving Internet traffic. The district is committed to wiring every classroom in the district (in sixty buildings) to provide all teachers, and eventually all students, with Internet access. More and more of the technology maintenance costs are network and Internet related. We are buying servers, routers, hubs and massive hard drives every month, part of which is in response to demand for Internet access. In the same three-year time period during which the district has found it necessary to reduce instructional staff by over 200 persons and administrative staff by 40%, the technology budget has more than doubled. Salaries come out of the general budget, while most of the money for new computers has come from special state funds. So while personnel have been going out one door computers have been coming in another. Yet those of us who are left don't experience this as a direct shift of finances. Rather our personal experience is that of being handed new computers and new opportunities—new resources whose substantial financial and social and professional costs lie mostly outside our professional responsibility.

With so much of the expense buried in infrastructure, there is, I suspect, no way of knowing exactly how much it costs my school district to provide Internet access to its teachers. Industry studies (Cappuccio et al. 1996) obtained by our director of technology place the total estimated cost of owning a networked computer at over $8,000 per year,[2] so it is certain that Internet access runs to much more than $100 per year per teacher served. Why is this cost so easily accepted when allocating $100 to one teacher one time in a year was too much? Have we discovered that much educational value in the 'Net and consciously determined that we will reallocate the funds to provide it? Or might it be that we have fallen into it because the costs have been hidden in up front capital and central administrative expenditures outside the shrinking budgets of individual schools? Could it be that because there is no cost attached to the individual message or even the individual accounts, we kid ourselves that the costs are not really very great? Or has the enabling technology receded so far into the background that we really have come to accept fully the illusion that the Internet is free?

These and the other questions I have offered here are not rhetorical ones. The answers are not completely clear to me. What I find more troublesome than not having the answers, though, is that so few educators are engaged in considering the questions.

Human Communications: Yamagata and Fredonia

Project Utopia began with a sense of intrigue among the students and an eagerness to correspond with peers on the other side of the world (which, as I have indicated, were still a long ways away). Students and teachers alike harbored high hopes that this connection between antipodes would yield a unique and powerful learning experience. To some extent, this goal was achieved. The development of the original utopias required considerable collaboration, negotiation, and articulation. Each group labored to produce a hypothetical society that addressed in detail the four fundamental topics Buddy's students chose as most important: government, economy, environment and education/social customs. Des Moines's utopia, "Fredonia," emerged as a smorgasbord of typically contradictory U.S. values, combining a faith in liberty, equality, and democracy with a heavy dose of socialistic programs. ISKL's utopia, "Yamagata," achieved much the same end, but arrived there via the pursuit of beauty. In subsequent exchanges the rationales were challenged, the details clarified, and a few features adjusted. The third exchange included invitations to visit the respective utopias, and acceptances and biographical sketches of the participants were offered in the fourth. All of these activities called forth analytic and writing skills as well as continuing thought about what constitutes a perfect society.

Yet with all of that accomplished, neither Buddy, Pat Ramsey, nor I felt we had achieved the success we had hoped for. When we read the student evaluations of the project it confirmed our suspicions that there was also a good deal of ambivalence among the students. To give a flavor for how these critiques were actually framed by the students I will share a few excerpts from individual comments (each statement comes from a different student):

This whole exchange thing was a really good experience to see how others want to live.

Kuala Lumpur student

When the proposition of an exchange with the students of Malaysia was brought up, I was excited about it. . . . Initially, it was fun. But as the number of exchanges grew, the novelty wore off. The topic was intangible.   Des Moines student

I enjoyed hearing the thoughts and ideas of people across the world, even though I felt some were primitive and unacceptable. . . . But overall, I felt the whole thing was too hurried and a waste of time.   Des Moines student

The fact that we're corresponding with total strangers in Iowa, who have to evaluate our accomplishments, did not really motivate me into making more effort. However, in the first response to them I liked being able to ridicule their ideas.   Kuala Lumpur student

It was interesting to compare the different values and views of what a Utopian society should consist of. This project showed me how much I have left to learn, and how one-tracked my mind can get.   Des Moines student

Like any educational endeavor that involves communicating with others, the maturity level of the students has a good deal to do with its success. That issue must always be factored into telecollaboration projects that allow for critical exchanges between students. We also found that many of the aspects of the projects criticized by some students were the same ones that were praised by others. But two observations were made repeatedly that seemed to us to have special importance for our future efforts: First, the topic was not concrete enough; either students couldn't relate to it from their own day-to-day experience, or it didn't involve a compelling real-world issue (Bosnia was mentioned) for which they had an interest.

Second, the students felt that the lack of physical presence permitted communication that was impersonal and insensitive. As one of Buddy's students commented, "This (telecommunication), I felt, made it easier to say something straight because you don't have to worry about consequences that a statement can make if you know the person." This willingness to forgo tactfulness was clearly noticeable in both camps and was constantly addressed during editing sessions. What was less easily overcome was the lack of context out of which responses were written. A well-known problem with electronic communication is the aridity of background information that accompanies it. Many discussions that degenerate into flame wars are the result of misunderstandings stemming from this lack of context. In this case, lack of knowledge of the discussions and assumptions from which the messages emerged occasionally led to hard feelings. By the end of the third exchange there was a noticeable tension between students in some of the areas. It was to combat this antagonism that we decided to include biographies of the students with the last exchange. Clearly, there needed to be some personal connections made to cushion the critical discussion of ideas.

All of these concerns were issues we felt we could address in future projects. We thought about, argued over, and planned for almost a full year before seizing our next opportunity. It proved to be well worth the wait.

South African Elections Internet Project '94

Buddy has hinted that I have the very good fortune to be married to a successful businesswoman who lets me tag along on some of her more exotic trips. In February 1994 she took me to Hong Kong with her. Kuala Lumpur looked relatively close on our world atlas so we extended the trip to visit Buddy and his family. The flight took us four hours in a jumbo jet. We stayed for four days, with most of the time taken up by sightseeing, eating the fabulous Malay food, and catching up on personal matters. Yet by the time Buddy and I finally sat down and formally went to work on the details of our next project there were surprisingly few issues left to work out. The informal conversations that had taken place during excursions to places like Kuala Selangor and La Gong, over sumptuous buttered chicken at outdoor restaurants, and during late night storytelling, had already sculpted the project structure into its basic form. Dotting the i's and crossing the t's only took a couple more hours of negotiation, further punctuated by much good-natured cursing and laughter. All of this would have taken us weeks of isolated toil to do by e-mail.

The significance of both the time differential and the quality of the experience was not lost on either of us; nor was the effect of my having actually visited ISKL, met Dan LoCasio, and gotten a feel for Buddy's situation that only could have come through firsthand contact. Throughout all the projects to come, understanding the context in which Buddy was working was a huge asset for me; one that Buddy often mentioned he suffered from not sharing.

The ease with which the structure came together should not be taken to imply that there weren't a number of hurdles we had to overcome in designing the South African Project. One of those hurdles was my own ignorance of the magnitude of the coming event. It didn't take long, once I was there and felt Buddy's passion, for him to convince me that this was one of the great historic events of the century; that it just had not yet received its fifteen minutes (or in this case, days) of fame that the U.S. media would allot it. Buddy has already mentioned some of the other technical problems we faced. However, it was clear from the beginning that this project would allow us to address the instructional problems we had recognized in *Project Utopia:* It was a real, concrete event of global significance that students could and should find compelling; the central issues of racism and democracy were ones that students could relate to their own day-to-day experience; and because there would be worldwide media coverage, we felt we could use that as a way to focus our students' attention on the tremendous effect language has on the accurate communication of ideas and events—which we hoped would help them recognize the importance of clarity and sensitivity in their own writing. By the time I left Malaysia we felt we had a project that could facilitate a truly powerful and unique learning experience for students all over the world.

Kuala Lumpur was now linked to the Internet. Bolstered by an unshakable faith that Dan LoCasio would work his typical magic to finagle a listserver for us, we began advertising the project. Our anxiety began to grow as our solicitations were met with almost absolute silence. Had my hesitation been a more accurate appraisal of global interest than Buddy's passion? Were we sending our messages to the wrong people? Weren't teachers interested in educational Internet projects after all? Was using the 'Net for this kind of serious work at the secondary level still premature? Or was our project just poorly designed? Maybe we just weren't explaining it well enough? These were the kinds of questions that crossed our minds, and our e-mail exchanges, in the weeks following our call for participation. We now understand that these are the kinds of questions you live with when you do this kind of work: Just when you want the effusive 'Net to bubble over it turns into a black hole.

Eventually, classes from the International School of the Hague and Lakeside School in Seattle joined us, as well as a number of individuals. I was fortunate to have Mike Schaffer, situated right across the hall from my room, representing Central Campus. Mike is a social studies teacher who has taught in Africa and Europe. He had a good sense of what we were undertaking and an interest in the elections that extended beyond just another world event for study. He also possesses a calm, flexible demeanor that would help a lot as we went along. And, like Pat Ramsey, he is just an all-around outstanding teacher. It was typical of him that even though it didn't really fit the prescribed curriculum he enrolled his Advanced Placement Economics class in the project.

Buddy has summarized what ensued from that point leading up to and including the week of the South African elections. To merely recount in more detail those events cannot hope to give a full sense of the experience, both for two coordinators groping around in the darkness of a new medium and for students embarking on an exploration of a kind they had not anticipated. To get a taste of the effect of this project on its participants, as well as a more intimate look at how we struggled to harness this new technology to our educational plow, I think it is perhaps best to listen in on excerpts from the conversation carried on at the time. To keep it relatively brief, only Buddy's and my voices will be heard in the early stages of development, joined eventually by a number of other significant participants. Keep in mind that the voting took place April 27–29.

February 7, 1994
From: Buddy
Re: South Africa Project

Lowell: Thanks for your quick communique. We're on-line, pal . . .

B.

Friday, March 4, 1994
From: Buddy
Lowell—Here's a revised draft of the project description . . .

As you can see I'm trying to make this thing idiot-proof. Tell me if you think I've overdone it, insulting the intelligence of participants. What I'm striving for is a document which outlines the logistics, project aims, and exchanges while establishing some clear guidelines. . . . What I find maddening is trying to strike a balance between clarity (which demands "focus" and discipline) and flexibility (which cries out for anything but discipline). Story of my life . . .

Cheers, B.

Wednesday, March 9, 1994
From: Lowell
Subject: project revision—suggestion

Buddy,

I just had a lengthy talk with Mike Schaffer who just spent some time with a South African who was passing through town. From their conversation Mike said we might want to add one category: religion. This South African says that not enough attention has been paid to the effects that the various religions are having on the situation there. The Dutch Reform Church, the Moslems, the conservative Moslems, the Hindus, etc. are all exerting pressures and influences that are being felt in all of the camps, according to him. Given your assessment of the various religious influences in Malaysia, this might indeed be an interesting topic (though certainly a hot one in some quarters).

It may be too late to add it to the mix, but I thought I would mention it. Mike is getting his troops revved up. I sent the proposal to Hong Kong and the Computer Coordinator said he would pass it along. Haven't heard anything in about a week. I'll follow up at the end of this week.

How is your exploring going? Any takers yet?

Lowell

Thursday, March 10, 1994
From: Buddy
Subject: spiritual matters

Lowell: I'm glad to hear Mike's talking about it with students. Religion is most definitely a hot item, but because of "sensitivities" I'd prefer not to isolate it, for fear that it could scuttle things. Remember where I live, after all. All it takes is one careless remark from one kid in Europe or the U.S. about Islam and we've got a Holy War via Internet . . .

Right now I'm distracted by the anxiety of slow returns. You were right. Curricular preoccupations seem to be restraining folks (am I being too polite? should we call it "apathy"?). Keep after Hong Kong. I'll resort to the FAX (how antiquated) to try to get more attention from the UK, Holland and India. I'm beginning to know how a spark plug feels . . .

Hang in there, pal. Keep plugging with me.

Cheers, Buddy

Thursday, March 10, 1994
From: Lowell
Subject: Testing

Buddy and Dan:

Both of your list messages came through loud and clear. We are definitely in business!! Now if only someone else will join us.

Lowell

Thursday, March 17, 1994
From: Buddy
Subject: Patience

Lowell: My patience is fading. I've sent messages to UK, Holland, India, Kenya, Ecuador and Turkey (colleague connection). No returns. Not even Ecuador is responding . . . this is sometimes known as a test of faith.

Unfortunately, I leave for an I.B. conference in Manila on the 23rd and won't return to KL until April (Spring break is the final week of March). Suggestions? I'd prefer to go with just the USA/Malaysia exchange rather than sacrifice the quality tremendously, but we need to start thinking this over. Any news from Hong Kong?

Hope the 2nd transmission of the project description is better.

Faithfully yours, B.

Monday, March 21, 1994
From: Lowell
Subject: Re: Testing faith

Buddy,

It's 11:21 pm, my brain is fried, my body already asleep, and now I read that we are having our faith tested! I think I will go to bed . . .

Nothing from Hong Kong. It's been a week and a half since I sent the followup message. I agree—it would be better to do a two school exchange than let this thing go to hell with just anybody. But the real kicker in all of this is the eyewitness reports. Please say it will happen.

The second description was no better than the first. I sent a reply—if you didn't get it we had better do some more work.

Have a great trip!!

Lowell

Monday, April 4, 1994
From: Lowell
Subject: Project

Buddy,

Welcome back. I just wanted to update you on where we are at my end of our SA project. No response from Hong Kong—I am assuming there is no interest, as I sent two messages along with both of your proposals.

The response here has been a little different than expected. Before Mike put the project to his 9th grade class he decided to offer it to his AP seniors as a voluntary project—no credit, no time, just anyone interested in working at it on their own could. He expected a couple of takers. Fifteen of the 22 students in the class asked to be included. They have split up the categories and will be submitting 5 different entries, one for each. I know a few of the kids in the class—it should be some good stuff.

I told Mike of our inability to enlist other schools and he agreed it would be better to do a two way exchange than open it to anyone.

Finally, I am going to have Mike send you a short note—sort of a hello, how-do-you-do type of thing. I remember your comment about not being able to communicate directly with Pat last year, so I want to get you two together at least once before the exchange starts. Lowell

Wednesday, April 6, 1994
From: Buddy
Subject: The 11th Hour Club

Lowell: Back from the beach with barely enough time to shake the water from my ears. You wouldn't believe all that happened to our baby while I was away. Faxes poured in from UK, Holland and Kenya, in response to my last gasp prior to departure. Kenya declined graciously due to the IB exams. A former colleague in London was excited and has a "definite" taker there . . .

Monday, April 11, 1994
From: Buddy
Subject: Butterflies

Question: are my personal messages garbled like the ones you've gotten from the Listserv? Let me know if there's a difference. Perhaps the problem lies more in the Listserver than it does in the method of transmission? Dunno. Dan LoCascio spent more time on Thursday and Friday just trying to clear the spools. He looked like a fly fisherman trying to cast three rods simultaneously into a brisk wind . . .

Yrs, B.

Tuesday, April 12, 1994
From: Buddy
Subject: Off and running

Dear Lowell and Mike:

Just moments after sending off our 1st report I found your Local Scene document in the mailbox. Who was up at 2 a.m. working on this? Talk about dedication! I look forward to seeing the rest of the reports.

B.

Wednesday, April 13, 1994
From: Buddy
Subject: FIRST IMPRESSIONS

Lowell & Mike:

Awesome.

How else to assess what just happened with my class. We hooked up the computer to a large screen and opened each of the reports, reading them line by line, discussing the tone, the political perspective, the implications, etc. What impressed the kids most was when I said, "Just think, on the other side of the planet they're dissecting your prose in the same fashion." Shoulda seen them squirm!

I came in to 20 Internet messages today! The bulk of them, of course, were yours, but then there were notices from Canada, USA(Seattle), Holland and Indonesia that they're still preparing and hoping to participate. Just getting into a routine for this first session was hard enough with only one school's reports to distribute. Imagine what it would've been like with eight schools!

Friday, April 15, 1994
From: Lowell
Subject: Re: Local scene-media watch

Buddy,

We got the message from The Hague. You should have seen Mike light up when I gave him the printout. His students are working on their responses and will send them Tuesday. Mike mentioned, too, that the questions seem to be the weak area of this endeavor. I think it says something about our educational system that we don't teach kids how to learn by asking good questions. But that is beside the point right now.

I think it is now time to clarify what is going to happen between the second exchange and the election . . . This thing is all over the papers now, and it is going to heat up a lot more in the next two weeks. Should we encourage the kids to submit their speculations early and have a sort of running discussion of their predictions leading into the elections? If it is feasible to get the students the messages everyday I think it would be interesting to get a freewheeling conference going for about a week. We could limit messages to 25 lines or something like that to keep the comments concise and the discussion moving. Just another thought to make your life a little more frenzied.

Lowell

Saturday, April 16, 1994
From: Buddy
Subject: Passion v. Reason

Lowell: I thought I was supposed to be the emotional one and you were supposed to be the calm, rational force in this dialectic! I refer to the fact that just a week ago you were saying "Hey, let's not depart from the script too soon or we'll have chaos" and by week's end you were ready to play nothing but jazz! God, I love it.

As mentioned last week I, too, would like to open things up a bit. Shoot, you and I are doing that, why not let the kids? The difference? Our correspondence doesn't involve a listserv. What happens if we have a few more schools join us this week?. . .

yr humble servant, B.

Wednesday, April 20, 1994
From: Buddy
Subject: Sleep?

Lowell: I may never sleep again. Did you get the stuff from Holland and Seattle in addition to ours? Hope so. Bob Mazelow assured me via private message that his kids will join the fray in the more standard format next week. For now, let Mike's students look through their stuff and see if it sparks anything. Sorry if Mike's kids feel slighted (or angered by reading "American response' from Seattle!). The kids in The Hague seem to be catching on, but they've had technical difficulties . . . even so, every bit helps. I feel like I'm just part of an enormous ant colony now.

Now for the bigger news: the UK will join us next week. They just returned from Spring break. They have a dozen kids preparing for a travel/study program in South Africa this June. Vested interest. Hope they come through.

Bigger still: Dan and I surfed the 'Net two nights ago and got into the computer at the universities of Jo'Burg, Pretoria and Durban. Downloaded a few items of general interest (peace accords, etc.) but then found a live Internet contact: Simon Tyrrell. I wrote to him immediately, requesting help. He wrote back just as immediately, offering two listservs (with folks discussing PanAfrican issues in general, S.A. in particular) and asking if I'd like some pals of his in S.A. to write to my kids. Would I? Gulp . . . just wrote back. I'll keep you posted. Stay calm now (swallow that heart, Daffy), keep fingers crossed . . .

xxxooo, bb

Wednesday, April 20, 1994
From: Lowell
Subject: Re: Sleep?

Buddy,

And to think that two weeks ago we were bemoaning our fate as lonely torch carriers . . . I am having a little trouble figuring out where some of these messages are coming from and which set they belong to . . . But I just keep downloading the messages and handing them to Mike and he seems to handle it fine.

The news about the SA contact is terrific! I have been trying off and on for weeks trying to get onto one of the Internet Gophers in South Africa—with no success (I get on one once in awhile but always get stalled and cut off). It is really interesting to me that you have more success technically than I do. It is becoming apparent that the Internet in the U.S. is beginning to suffer overload problems already.

Everyone participating here is excited as hell. Mike originally told his kids that no class time could be taken up working on this. Now they are taking time every day to go over the messages and spending a whole class period each week in the lab typing up their reports. So much for the AP curriculum.

Lowell

Friday, April 22, 1994
From: Lowell
Subject: Quick reaction

Buddy,

Just a quick question that has crossed my mind . . . How can we gear what takes place in the next couple of weeks to help our students recognize the "miracle"-ness of this experience? So much of what has crossed the oceans has been almost coldly analytical (what our students understand as knowledge). Yet your last message has affected me more than anything I have read to date. And it is based not on reason but on wonder and passion. And, interestingly, it is that wonder and passion that seems to keep your vision clear in this project. Is there some way that we can enlist the help of Simon's students, who must be full of wonder and passion themselves these days, to convey the depth of human emotion that has been expended in this struggle? Certainly we want firsthand accounts of the activities in SA right now, but it doesn't feel right to me to simply search out the "truth" of the situation as objectively as possible. This is very much a victory of the human spirit, which needs also to be expressed and appreciated.

Think it over for 30 seconds and give me a wise answer.

Hang in there. We're nearing the top of the hill!

Lowell

Saturday, April 23, 1994
From: Buddy
Subject: can you read this?

Lowell: Strange, isn't it, how so much of life returns to the dialectic between passion and reason? I agree that the reports have been analytical until now, but I think that was essential to lend substance to the project. Otherwise, we would have had a lot of uninformed, opinionated adolescent chatter.

But I think this project could endure a little passion and chaos this week.

If nothing else that'd reflect the state of the country we are all focused upon. Everyone must realize now that they may not have a reply to every one of their questions, given the free-for-all nature of this. But then again, perhaps it's time we break from the ego-centric idea of "Hey, what's in it for me?" and start thinking of this as a brilliant mosaic that we are all creating, a mosaic that is vibrant and chaotic, full of curiosities, enigmas, contradictions and questions. It will not be tidy, nor always sensible, but my god it's going to be lively. It's time we step back and let the artisans have at it, Lowell. I feel at once empowered and humbled in the face of South Africa's coming week, the Internet, and even this project.

yr humbled servant, b.

P.S.—Tell me . . . if you can even recall those lonely days of March, those wretched moments which tested faith in schools, curricula, technology and humanity? And tell me if any of the politics within one's own school or department matter when you open the I-Net mailbox, as I did just moments ago, to read the following:

"I am a South African Student. My mother is an election monitor. Ask questions, and I will see what I can do! Antony R."

Yes, o worthy pioneer, I do believe in miracles. . . . . . and yes, Antony, we have a few questions for you . . . :-) ;-)

Saturday, April 23, 1994
From: Lowell
Subject: Re: Dazed reaction

Buddy,

I can't tell you the impact that that one short, simple message from Antony had on me. I don't think there will be any ego problems in approaching these students. How can anyone who is studying this not approach them with respect and deference. This whole experience is going to take a dramatic turn, I think. I'm going to mow the lawn, fix the kitchen lights, and play with the kids. I don't figure I will be getting to any of them next week. It's a little like getting ready for the flood last year. You know it's coming but just what will be the final outcome remains to be revealed (both the election itself and our project).

Lowell

Tuesday, April 26, 1994
From: Quentin H.
To: Listserv

Subject: SA Elections

Hi. I read about your project on za.politics and would be happy to participate.

I write from my desk at the University of Natal in Durban. We are on the south-east coast of SA. We are about five hours south of Johannesburg by road and about 18 hours east of Cape Town.

This election has thrown up a series of mood swings in me. Last week when Inkatha rejoined the election race, I think we all were overjoyed. But these bomb blasts of the recent days have brought back all the old fears of civil war and racism.

My girlfriend works for the Independent Electoral Commission (IEC) in Durban— the organisation that is organising and monitoring the election. Last night she got home after 11 pm. About 600 people who felt that they had been unfairly treated by the IEC occupied the Durban offices while a solution was being worked out. The staff were trapped inside. Mercifully, no-one was injured. We will have to learn to deal with this unreasonableness.

What many hoped would be the country's finest hour will probably also be one of the saddest. But we will make it and we must make it work.

I will keep you posted as the election develops.

Hamba kahle : go well/keep safe/bye-bye

Quentin H.

Tuesday, April 26, 1994
From: Buddy
To: Lowell

BIG DAY TOMORROW! Exhausted, but wired . . . nothing new there. LOTS of news in my mailbox, though . . .

God how I do hope for more tolerance, less violence, in the coming days . . . (I speak of Jo'burg's bombings, not an upcoming faculty meeting).

b.

Tuesday, April 26, 1994
From: Yorke R.
To: Multiple recipients of list
Subject: Personal encounter with a bomb scare

Just an few hours ago I took my son, Peter, and a friend of his to a shopping centre in Pretoria to get some rechargeable batteries. My wife said that we should not go because of the bombs around. My reaction was—no it is only Black Taxi ranks and poling stations that are targeted.

Well I parked the car, paid the parking metre and we walked to the centre. Suddenly we saw traffic police on motorbikes followed by 6 or 7 large police and army troup carriers. Had they passed through all would have been fine—but they stopped outside the shopping centre and blocked road.

We are getting out of here I told the boys. I had no trouble getting them to obey me. Better a live dog than a dead lion.

It is very sad that the people who are the target of the bombs are black people—often those who have suffered in the past. The joy has been taken out of this wonderful time for many of us.

Last night a young friend of mine, William M., phoned to ask me to pray for him. He is young, enthusiastic and full of life. He is only 24 years old and has been appointed "Presiding Officer" at a polling station in Tembesa.

The wife of Paul N. also asked me to pray for him as he is away from home for 5 days working at the counting of the votes. He is the computer boffin who has provided me with this link into the internet.

I do not think that the right-wing will have much more success. They have managed to steal some of joy but I am convinced that they will not steal the real victory that this land is going through.

God Bless you all!

Yorke

Wednesday, April 27, 1994
From: Quentin H.
To: Multiple Members of the List
Subject: SA Elections

If you received my post of yesterday, you might have noted the despondency in my tone. Well that has been overcome by a great sense of joy at the outset of these elections. Watching Nelson Mandela cast his vote this morning was a very special moment—not because I am supporter of him or his party, but because that sight was unimaginable when I joined this university not so long ago.

People stood firm in the face of bomb blasts and disorganisation to make democracy work. All South Africans will be linked by the symbolic gesture of having a say in how this country should be run. In a very short time we have gone from being a symbol of oppression to being a symbol [of] freedom. That makes me, at least, feel so good. For the first time in my life, I can truly say that I am proud to be a South African. I am proud to be associated, by virtue of my birthplace, to those people that rose in the early hours of this morning to ensure that they would participate in elections.

There must be few places in the world where the right to vote is so dear.

Bye now—I am off to vote!

Quentin

Durban, South Africa

Date: Thursday, April 28, 1994
From: Buddy
Subject: sigh . . .
To: Lowell

Lowell: I think I sent you a note yesterday, but I'm not sure. In fact, I'm not sure of much right now, but I do find myself feeling pretty good of late. Perhaps it's the news that the elections are taking place and 31 AWB thugs were just arrested. Perhaps it's the knowledge that Nelson Mandela just voted (I pause for the chill to run through my body). Perhaps, too, it's the knowledge that our little baby has mushroomed into an int'l dialogue which is at once thoughtful, intriguing, terrifying, overwhelming and wonderful.

One area to discuss: the private/public dichotomy in correspondence via this medium. As a man of letters I retain the old fashioned belief that The Word is sacred and any offering of words should be accepted as a gift (not always the gift one wants, needs or likes . . . and sorry, there are no customer service reps waiting to exchange this one at the counter over there by the express lane). So I'm still feeling a bit awkward about loading a remarkable personal communique like Quentin H's into the Listserv for all to gawk at. And yet, all I really want to do is share, have others admire it, sighing as I do because I think it is so remarkable and just the tonic we need to refresh ourselves in this dizzy, tense world of ours.

I look forward to talking about that—and a few thousand other items—with you in the future. For now, let's just stick to S.A. and enjoy this precious sigh . . .

yrs, bb.

I end the sequence of messages here, in part because these last three messages represent the emotional peak of the project. And the emotion involved is important. As indicated in the earlier exchanges between Buddy and myself, the conversation among participating schools tended to be analytical and abstract. It was necessary, as he said, to establish the context of the struggle that led up to the elections. Yet it would have remained mostly an intellectual exercise had not Yorke, Quentin, Antony, and a number of others appeared just as the voting began. When their messages started arriving from South Africa everything changed.

It hit me first as I read through Yorke's message. Tears welled up in my eyes as I considered the tremendous amount of courage these "ordinary" people had to summon in order to accomplish what we take for granted. I didn't get to witness the reaction of Mike's students when they read Yorke's message that same day though he reported to me that the room became extraordinarily quiet. The extent to which his students were affected by this and other impassioned voices from South Africa varied a great deal, I'm sure. But in the student exchanges that followed the election, the tone changed dramatically. Intellectual analysis was muted by a respectful appreciation for what the people of South Africa had accomplished and heartfelt concern for the enormous task ahead of them. The students' final reports were full of words like "hope," "amazing," and "wonderful." And the contrast between the South Africans' determination to vote and Americans' apathy was not lost on them. "Recently I was at a shopping mall trying to get people to register to vote," wrote Liz Baldwin in her final report. "Many people said, 'I'm not registered and I don't want to,' yet they're all too willing to complain about what our government does."

It's impossible to evaluate the learning that took place. Perhaps if it had remained a strictly intellectual endeavor some kind of test could have been given to determine how much knowledge had been consumed. But how does one assign a numerical value to the effect that messages from Yorke and Quentin had on a student's understanding of oppression, democracy, politics, or life? That kind of knowing can't be quantified, standardized, or perhaps even verbalized. It can only be recognized by those who, like Liz Baldwin, find meaning in it for their own lives.

With all the push toward standardization and "measurable outcomes" it was eye-opening to witness, and experience for ourselves, this type of learning, that reaches us through our hearts. Such a powerful educational experience is only diminished and degraded by efforts to measure it. As far as I know, no one received a grade based on what they had learned from this project. Soon after the election Buddy wrote to me, "I think we've had a pretty good lesson in the potential good of the human spirit these past few weeks." That's an unusual lesson to learn in school, but one we might do well to strive for more often, even if we can't grade it.

Meanwhile, Back in School—More Lessons Learned

It took some time to separate out from the emotion of the experience the pedagogical lessons learned from the South African project. Certainly, the use of the Internet had improved communications enormously. The listserver had proved crucial for multi-school participation. The students had compiled reports that constituted well over 100 pages of thoughtful, well-researched analysis that related the elections to their own situations. Their own evaluations were uniformly positive. Any way we wanted to look at this project it came out a success. Still, there were issues that emerged that troubled us, and they are worth noting here.

For the first time we had recognized a particular deficiency in student communication that would prove to be chronic: the lack of ability and/or inclination to ask questions that stimulated dialogue. For all of the electronic traffic that flowed through the project, precious little of it included inquiries of others that sought further explanations or deeper insights. Given our goal of helping students learn to collaborate in their learning, this was a troubling observation.

Then, of course, there were the curricular problems. In Buddy's description of the project he shared the message I had to send him just a week after the election informing him that Mike's students had to pull out of the continuing dialogue. Advanced Placement exams were beginning and he had to concentrate on getting his students prepared for them. Many of Buddy's students followed suit, having to prepare for the equally rigorous International Baccalaureate exams. This we had anticipated, but with the discussion still full of youthful vigor it rankled us just the same. We were beginning to sense an ominous pattern developing already in our projects: structural and bureaucratic impositions that sucked at their life blood. In the next chapter Buddy will discuss these problems in greater detail. To close this chapter, however, I would like to offer some reflections on a different problem, one that could actually grow out of the success of projects like this one.

The Big Event Syndrome

We had never envisioned the South African project as a model for future efforts. It was unique in nearly every way. Still, in the semi-euphoric afterglow there was talk by some participants of locating another big global event and studying it. Bosnia was mentioned. Having recently visited Hong Kong, I suggested that we might plan on studying its return to China in 1997. But these proposals quickly faded as we came to conclude that searching the globe for exciting events would, in the long run, do our students more harm than good.

At the time I was reading the draft of a chapter from Stephen Talbott's book, *The Future Does Not Compute* (1995). The chapter was titled "Impressing the Science Out of Kids." Though Talbott works deeper soil than I can get into here, his basic argument that motivating science students with awe-inspiring multimedia programs (the "wow" factor) is counterproductive, seemed applicable to our work as well. A concentration on the sensational distorts the level of student expectations with regard to learning. Pulling them back down to the earth of their immediate surroundings inevitably results in a feeling of boredom and disinterest. Students become big event junkies, and in order to keep them engaged classes have to be conducted with all the multimedia sensationalism of the nightly news.

With the advent of the Internet we now have ample opportunity to cruise the world, dropping in on whatever happens to be the big event of the semester. No matter how well prepared, how pedagogically well designed, the activities might be, the cumulative effect of this approach to learning is, I believe, destructive. The South African project affected students so strongly, in part, because they had never experienced anything like it in their high school careers. But I have to wonder if students raised on a steady diet of virtual trips to the Antarctic, virtual climbs to the summit of Mt. Everest, and virtual trips into orbit will be affected so strongly by a similar project? Will the courage displayed by the next William M and Paul N be so meaningful? Or will the ante of sensationalism have been raised to such heights by then that such simple acts of personal courage will seem mundane and boring? Over the years, TV has only been able to keep viewers plugged in by providing an endless escalation of sensory arousal. Do we really want to go this same route with education—replacing purposeful inner drive as the motivating force in education with external stimulation? For all the anti-drug talk that goes on in schools, this willingness to use computers to seek ever higher doses of excitement in order to get students engaged in learning displays an all too familiar approach to coping with the arid, dehumanized and purposeless environment we allow our young people to face each day.

There was always a small twinge of voyeurism that accompanied the South African project. Our students obtained a sort of vicarious gratification from the actions of others, much as we all do as spectators at a great sporting event. This sensation was one with which Buddy and I were all too familiar. Television has already created a pervasive spectators-of-life mentality among many young people (not to mention adults). In our own travels Buddy and I had encountered far too many of these snapshot tourists who carried this "been there, done that" philosophy around in their fanny packs. We did not want to promote this mentality in our work. We wanted our students to be the cast, not the crowd, and in a real, not virtual sense. We believed that the only way to really help our students make learning deeply meaningful to their own lives was to focus their attention on what was happening in their immediate surroundings, trying to bring it to life so that those local activities that seemed of little consequence when compared with what was experienced through the electronic screen would take on greater significance.

Project Utopia had sent us far out into the abstract space of idealism. South Africa had brought us down to earth, idealism intact, but far from home. It was now time to see if we could carry that idealism into our own backyards.

5

Out of the Labyrinth, Into the 'Net

R. W. Burniske

I warn you Icarus, he said, you must follow a course midway between earth and heaven, in case the sun should scorch your feathers, if you go too high, or the water make them heavy if you are too low. Fly halfway between the two.

Ovid (1985, 184)

Like many adolescents, Icarus failed to heed his father's advice. "Drawn on by his eagerness for the open sky, he left his guide and soared upwards, till he came too close to the blazing sun" (Ovid 1985, 185). His subsequent fall served a didactic purpose, however, warning against hubris, *the deadly sin that invariably prompts tragedy in the ancient Greek myths. We would do well to remember Icarus while preparing students and teachers to fly from the labyrinth of curricula into the information skyway of the Internet. The temptation, for both students and teachers, is to shed curricular restraint while placing their faith in technology. What might Daedalus, the creator of the technology that gave his son flight, say to us as we embark upon telecollaborative activities? Despite his brilliant vision and skilled craftsmanship, Daedalus approached his inventions with wariness and caution because he understood the laws of Nature as well as the limitations of humans and machines. Unfortunately, while his technical expertise made it possible for his son to fly, it couldn't compel good judgment or the responsible use of his invention.*

Despite our technological innovations, teaching adolescents to think critically and behave responsibly is no easier today than it was for the ancients. Nonetheless, the social impact of modern technology—from automobiles to firearms and computers—compels us to emphasize far more than technical skills, lest our students suffer a tragic fall of their own. The key to guiding them in telecollaborative activities, we believe, is creating the dialectical tension necessary to transform the Internet from a container of information to a medium for communication. To achieve this, however, we must encourage teachers to "follow a course midway between earth and heaven" when launching into cyberspace. Failing that, educators could mistake casual Web browsing for critical thinking. And what good will the Internet do for students if it becomes just another mind-numbing diversion similar to television "channel surfing"? What, ultimately, might happen to a society in which children dismiss the wisdom of their elders, forsaking a disciplined approach to education for the intoxication of technological toys?

The Curricular Maze

Given the wariness and concerns that Lowell and I have already expressed, we need to address a fundamental question at this point: Why should we, as educators, introduce telecollaborative learning activities to our classrooms? There are no simple answers to this question, but I would begin by arguing, as I have in faculty meetings throughout my career, that a curriculum ought to be more an expression of the individual teacher than a bureaucratic system. In the ancient Greece that bred stories like "The Death of Icarus," the *paidagogos* was a slave who escorted children to and from school. Thus, "pedagogy" described the strategies employed to accomplish this task (Oxford 1993, 2136). Sadly enough, modern educators in K–12 schools often feel like the *paidagogos*. They have good reason: state and local organizations deliver prescribed curricula to administrators who enforce them through the assignment of designated texts, regimented report cards, and standardized tests and teacher evaluations.

This is hardly a conducive environment for innovative teachers. If anything, the system's design frustrates innovators and impedes the diffusion of their innovations (Rogers 1995). Nonetheless, if something good is to come from networked computers in the classroom—and the jury should definitely continue its deliberations on this—I'm convinced it must come from teachers and students. Otherwise, telecollaboration will become yet another prescribed piece of an outcome-based curriculum that restricts individuals, yet seldom inspires them. In my first year of teaching, as a physical education instructor at an international school in Cairo, I learned a valuable lesson about schools' resistance to innovation and administrators' tendency to prostrate themselves at the altar of The Curriculum.

During the "Fall" semester (a ridiculous concept in Egypt, but an obstinate term in this American school), I introduced my students to "Carolina Flag," a variation of flag football that I had encountered as an undergraduate at the University of North Carolina. It required none of the pass blocking that accounted for most of the brutality in my co-ed classes, waiving the requirement of passing from behind a line of scrimmage. Offensive players could throw the ball from anywhere on the field, proceeding downfield until an opponent either stripped them of a flag attached to their belt, intercepted a pass, or caused an incompletion. I opted for this after a week of dreadful skirmishes left several students physically damaged or emotionally wounded. The talented minority had gleefully excluded less skilled players and protested whenever I asked them to play an alternate position. With each new day of the traditional approach the number of medical exemptions for the less talented majority increased. "Carolina flag" seemed the best solution, as it enabled every offensive player to become both a quarterback and a receiver on every play, removed the ugly job of pass blocking without padding, and dismissed rules that prompted incessant disputes. A few days after introducing this alternative, which the talented minority disliked because it allowed for more democratic play, and the less talented majority enjoyed because it was so liberating, my initiation to administrative hegemony began.

The head of the Physical Education department called me into his office shortly before classes began that day. He handed me a memorandum from the high school principal. In the formal, terse language of a career administrator addressing a department head, the memo censured the "new appointment in the physicial education department" for his "obvious deviations from the game of American Football, and inappropriate instructional methods." Copies of the letter were forwarded to the school's superintendent and my professional file. My department head, a dedicated athlete from the Netherlands who confessed he did not understand the rules of "American football" or "Carolina flag," asked what I thought of the memo. I said it lacked respect for the instructor's judgment. The principal had never spoken to me of these "obvious deviations" or my "instructional methods." I defended this innovation on the grounds that it led to more aerobic exercise, better teamwork, and more appropriate activities for this age group.

The department head took this reply to the principal. A response was waiting in my mailbox at day's end. Among other things, the principal's second memo reminded me, my department head, and the superintendent, that I was not a certified teacher of physical education and that my status as a substitute (due to an abrupt resignation one month into the school year) did not give me authority to "alter the curriculum" without prior approval of my department head, the high school principal, and the curriculum and instruction committee. My career as a subversive educator had begun.

In retrospect, the Carolina flag episode demonstrated how easily The Curriculum, a supposed tool or guideline for teachers, can be used as a weapon to frustrate innovations. It also says a great deal about the power structures within schools, particularly when an inflexible administrator enforces a status quo curriculum rather than encouraging the introduction of new ideas. Why didn't the principal speak with me about my "obvious deviations" from the norm?

R. W. Burniske   89

Why didn't he trust my assessment of the students' needs and my vision of how best to convey the necessary information to "teach" them this subject? In a word, I lacked that one, fundamental prerequisite that all educators must earn: respect. The principal did not respect me or my methods because I lacked "certification" and formal experience. My department head could do little to protest since he, though certified to teach physical education in Europe, hadn't a clue when it came to American football. I gave him credit, nonetheless, for respecting my judgment of what I thought was best for my students.

Those Who Can, Teach

I share this anecdote because it exposes a fundamental tension within our schools, one provoked by the differences between the work of administrators and classroom practitioners. My experience in Cairo made me wonder why such a pernicious dichotomy exists, giving rise to the "Us against Them" mentality. It is a power struggle, certainly, but also a dialectical tension that emanates from different views of the world, school, and individual purpose. Administrators must solve problems ("How can we keep students from looking at pornography on the Internet?"); teachers must create problems for students to interrogate ("What is pornography and how do we define it?"). Administrators are eager for answers to close-ended questions ("Which computers would be most cost-effective within the existing budget?"); teachers are thrilled to hear students ask thoughtful, open-ended questions ("Why are we using computers for this instead of doing it face-to-face?").

In essence, I'm describing a division between the Land of Answers and the Sea of Questions. Administrators step off *terra firma* when they enter a classroom in which Socratic methods lead to an infinite exploration; teachers, meanwhile, bemoan the tedium of simplistic answers they must endure upon the shore of supposed "faculty meetings" run by administrators. The integration of networked technology may exacerbate these tensions, drawing a line between those who believe this innovation heralds a brave new world and those who fear that something wicked has arrived. It also forces us to consider the rationale behind the adoption of innovations. When should a school adopt a new innovation? When should it resist? Who should determine the diffusion of that innovation?

I understand why many veteran teachers resist telecollaborative learning. Although society assigns positive connotations to the term "innovation," not every change of curricula or pedagogy is a sign of progress. From the veteran teacher's perspective, the rush to network classrooms and integrate technology into the curriculum could deprive them of even more autonomy. If the *integration* of technology *annihilates* dialectical discourse within our schools, then might it not force teachers to follow new mandates rather than trust their own intuition and judgment? This may sound hysterical, but consider the teachers' viewpoint, tempered as it is by the history of education in the United States of America. Despite all the ink spilt over the plight of education in this country, can't the mainstream American attitude toward teachers be expressed by one famous slight?

"He who can, does. He who cannot, teaches" (Shaw 1965, 183).

Let's not kid ourselves. Publicity stunts like "Technology Teacher of the Year" awards will not solve the problems; they inflate a few egos, but do little to aid the average teacher. Instead, we must address a fundamental issue, one that will make people squirm if they discuss it with their children, and admit that an unhealthy attitude has settled as deeply as their bone marrow: Most Americans don't respect schoolteachers. We're quick to say how important it is for students to "get an education," but that has become another way of saying how important it is for kids to "do well" so that they can get into the right schools which will get them the "right" jobs. But who's kidding whom? Are we talking about developing minds, encouraging imagination and intellect, or are we talking about socializing children so they'll know what "really counts"? Do we offer courses in the humanities to help initiate children to the world and themselves or to fulfill requirements for college admission? Are we, ultimately, talking about educating or manufacturing, nurturing young minds seeking wisdom or conditioning them to think of an education in terms of degrees and themselves as "products" of their institutions?

For all our platitudes about the importance of education it's apparent that many high school students and their parents still believe a schoolteacher is a schoolteacher because he or she couldn't succeed at something else. This unfortunate misunderstanding of teachers and the teaching profession, which breeds disrespect and low wages, deters the best and brightest from filling its ranks. This, in turn, encourages restrictive curricula designed as idiot-proof restraints, perpetuating a vicious cycle that technology alone will never solve. Such a misguided approach paints all educators with one broad stroke while neglecting their need for continuing education. Thus, we fail to nurture teachers as learners, forgetting that active learners are the ones who make the best teachers.

Might this not account for the "burn-out" suffered by dedicated professionals, the veteran teacher who commits endless hours to the craft of teaching, striving for the requisite understanding of both children and subject matter? Imagine what it is like for someone with an advanced degree, a decade's experience, and ideas of their own to be told not only what to teach, but how and when to teach it, as well as how to evaluate and report that evaluation? This is not a healthy environment for talented, creative individuals or even less talented ones who'd like to develop new skills. Nor does it foster a humane environment for children. Schools will never be good places for children until they are good places for the adults who teach them. And how good can any school be for an adult still treated like the *paidigagos* of the ancient world? Many teachers are sustained by the conviction that their contributions can, and do, make a difference in a child's life. Anyone belittling that conviction demoralizes the teacher, discouraging experimentation and perpetuating the status quo rather than invigorating the learning community.

While all of society is responsible for this situation, educational leaders must take a more active role in its reversal. I do not wish to ostracize school administrators. Not at all. In fact, I've served in that capacity myself, as an activities director, dean of students, and assistant principal. However, in each instance, I continued teaching while fulfilling administrative duties, which seems a much healthier balance than we find in most schools today. We have drifted much too far from the idea of a "principal teacher" or "headmaster" as, first and foremost, accomplished educators. In the evolution of the school-as-factory metaphor that has allowed the language, hierarchy, and mentality of business to put a stranglehold upon schools, the term "administrator" has supplanted this idea. Instead of the "principal teacher" we find a company manager.

If this were not so, then faculty meetings might be arranged like classes in which a community of learners engaged in genuine inquiry and discussion. What we find instead is the "press conference" format: an administrator stands at the front of the room repeating statements made in the daily bulletin before fielding questions from the audience or calling upon a coterie of assistants to offer predictable reports. In this arrangement the ego of the administrator is gratified as CEO, while teachers play the role of expendable day laborers. This does little to build a bridge between the Land of Answers and the Sea of Questions. In fact, it represses our desire to tinker with the status quo, to experiment and innovate. I'd like to change that, to help teachers become innovators so that pedagogical innovations respond to the individual student's need to question, explore, and discover. Without this, classroom teachers may forfeit what little autonomy remains, forcing them to satisfy institutional demands so that policymakers can justify outrageous expenditures on Internet connectivity.

This presents a remarkably complex challenge, particularly when we consider the average teacher's shortage of time and surplus of predicaments. I recall the colleague who shook her head following a workshop I had given in Kuala Lumpur, asking: "Why should I bother going online if it means losing more control of my classroom?" She had just itemized the list of classroom disruptions due to extracurricular activities that pulled students away for the Choir Exchange in Singapore, the Forensics tournament in Manila, and athletic tournaments all over Southeast Asia. It had been several weeks since she had seen a full class in attendance, and not once in the second semester had she seen the entire group for a full week. The school may have run on an industrial model, but the classes it bred were dysfunctional families trying to carry on conversations despite their rare communion. Why, my colleague asked, should she invite further fragmentation, jeopardizing what little autonomy and cohesiveness her classroom retained? It was a good question. I offered a one-word reply: "Empowerment."

What appears to be forfeiture of control, yet another loss of power and academic freedom, has the potential to liberate and empower both students and teachers. This is yet another paradox, one that sits at the crux of telecollaborative learning and the dialectical tensions within this book. Despite his reservations, Lowell concedes that telecollaborative projects prove intellectually stimulating, though often in spite of the technology, not because of it. Myriad challenges call attention to the computers in a classroom, often distracting students and teachers from their purpose. However, they also inspire genuine problem-solving, which fosters dialogue and collaboration, enabling students and teachers to find solutions together that they couldn't discover alone. While this may not improve test scores, it can enhance classroom dynamics, liberating students and teachers from the traditional roles that defined and limited their inquiry. Certainly, we need to go beyond technical troubleshooting to fulfill curricula, but perhaps by transferring the collaborative spirit from one form of problem-solving (technical) to another (academic inquiry) we may effect positive change. By creating an original, telecollaborative project the teacher becomes a creator, learner, and collaborator rather than an extension of the curricular bureaucracy devouring our schools. To succeed, however, the teacher must begin with student needs and a personal vision, rather than a bureaucratic decree or corporate agenda. It also helps to have a philosophy informing the design of such projects.

The Teacher as Gardener

I grew up in the farmlands of Western Massachusetts, tutored by Polish farmers, a fickle climate, and diverse crops ranging from cucumbers to tobacco. As a result, gardening has become more than just a hobby, providing a connection with my past as well as an important educational metaphor. I like to think of teaching in organic terms, acknowledging the educator's responsibility to nurture young minds and help them grow. If saturated with facts, they'll go soggy; if exposed to the brilliance of multimedia, audiovisual displays without discussion and argumentation, their critical acumen may wither and die. So they need careful attention, and a regimen that includes fertilizer (reading), irrigation (discussion), sunshine (praise), and weeding (of hackneyed, unexamined ideas). We attempt this through the repertoire of activities that constitute one's pedagogy. There's yet another ingredient to consider, though, one we may neglect because of competing demands on both teacher and student: time for reflection. Plants, as every gardener knows, often grow best at night, away from the prodding of the gardener's well-intentioned, but occasionally misguided hands.

The implications of this are profound. If nothing else, it illustrates the need for a collective pause that invites deep, sustained reflection. This the teacher cannot *do* for the pupil. However, we can provide opportunities for reflection, which begin with the recognition that overzealous attention and hyperactive classrooms may prove counterproductive. The teacher as gardener learns to create structures that guide and support the growth of students, without strangling them at the curricular stake. This same educator is sensitive to anything that encroaches upon the life of the mind, the life she hopes to stimulate through the creation of an environment conducive to learning. Is it any wonder why someone who has done so much to create that environment would defend it against the extracurricular logging companies, the administrative legislators, and special interest groups who think the best way for young plants to grow is to continually transplant them to other locations, exposing them to a variety of activities without pausing to make sure their roots aren't stunted?

Beyond the self-inflicted wounds lie a number of predators. These take many forms, but an especially troublesome one is the commercial farmer preoccupied with the short-term boon of chemical fertilizer rather than its long-term effects. I've never understood, for instance, how a language arts teacher can use a prescriptive anthology of literature imposing a chronology and selection, as well as questions (and answers!), that the humanist ought to find intrusive. The sales reps for CD-ROMs are little more than the print anthology's wolf in the disguise of multimedia sheep. I don't want either of them in my garden because they don't really care about educating or, by extending the metaphor, cultivating young minds. One person's fertilizer is another's poison, I suppose, but there's a fundamental difference between the way a teacher thinks of books or software and the way an administrator or businessperson views them. Where the teacher sees a tool, the administrators see a container.

This occurred to me several years ago, while discussing textbooks with a representative of a large New York publishing company. She was "on the circuit" through Latin America and had stopped in Ecuador to visit schools and universities in an attempt to expand her company's market. None of the anthologies she presented that day, replete with worksheets and "guiding questions," made any sense to me as an educator. To ask my students to open an anthology and read from page 1 to page 999 in sequence, stopping to read generic questions that implied certain answers that certain authorities possessed, seemed like intellectual suicide. That's the "container" approach to education, one that appeals to inexperienced, ill-trained, or simply mediocre teachers.

The master teacher, the educational gardener, knows that there must always be room to breathe, room for serendipity and a dynamic interplay of teacher, students, and texts. Books and syllabi, curricula and pedagogy, are tools that the teacher employs, not containers carrying gifts from the gods. This may explain why no two courses are ever alike for the master teacher. They each have a life of their own. The unique blend of interests and personalities inspires questions and concerns that no formulaic anthology, worksheet, or software could ever fully anticipate.

The Curriculum as Tool

This brings me to an item that arrived just before I began writing this chapter. To most people this item might signify little more than junk mail, but imagine my reaction to a brochure promising recipes for the "Internet made easy in the classroom." Coincidence? Perhaps, but it strengthens my resolve to help educators become proactive in the integration of technology in their classes. Quite simply, if we don't take that initiative, someone will take it for us, someone who may not have the best interest of students in mind. I'm astounded, for example, by how many state and federal politicians have adopted the "computer as container" metaphor, giddily expressing their support of "education" by advocating expenditures on boxes and wires without pausing to think about teachers' professional development. This disparity makes our schools susceptible to commercial enterprises promoting the sale of Internet "content" and pedagogical recipes. While pondering how to describe the creation of a telecollaborative project, one that satisfies a teacher's personal vision of what suits a particular group of students in a specific school and curriculum, promotional material with the following message appeared in my mailbox:

Dear Educator:

When it comes to bringing the amazing world of the Internet into daily K–12 instruction, up to now you've had to build it yourself. First, find good sites. Then, write smart lesson plans. Figure out cross-curricula angles. Compose useful activity sheets. Brainstorm project ideas. But what if using the Internet in your classroom was as easy as changing a light bulb? What if all you had to do was open a binder, and out poured everything you needed?

In short—what if somebody did all the work for you?

We have.

Presenting the Internet Curriculum Planning System . . . the integration tool you need to light up learning!

In one incredibly affordable binder/subscription system, we've assembled everything you need to turn the Internet into a "teacher's aide" you can power-up in any curriculum, any grade level. (Young 1997)

Note the mixture here of the two metaphors I've described: the container and tool. This company's binder presents another version of the magic genie in the lamp ("What if . . . out poured everything you needed?"). To pitch this magic lamp with its equally magical elixir at educators who ought to know a placebo when they see one, the writers of this brochure appeal to traditional marketing tools: fear and fatigue. The "Internet Curriculum Planning System" is not only a tool, we're told, but a "time factory that lets you pour hot Internet content and resources right into existing curricula" (Young 1997). Under the guise of helping the weary educator these duplicitous Samaritans offer a discounted price for materials that "do all the work for you: site searching and analysis, lesson plans, activity sheets, project ideas, you name it. All you have to do is read, use . . . and enjoy!" (Young 1997).

What ought to be apparent, but frequently escapes attention, is that the authors and promoters of such materials don't know much about education or children. Evidently, they hope educators know even less about the Internet. If their executives knew something about treating students—and teachers— with respect, as active learners rather than receptacles waiting for that magical elixir to be poured into their heads, they'd know that few competent teachers would "find good (Internet) sites. Then, write smart lesson plans. . . . Compose useful activity sheets." Returning to my earlier metaphor, this is akin to tying off plants before their sprouts have popped through the soil. Quite frankly, anyone talking about the Internet solely as a container is full of toxic fertilizer.

We need to think of the computer as a tool—for communication as well as research—rather than a container. Yes, network servers "contain" data, but what kind of educator does all the work for students instead of inspiring them to pursue their interests within broad areas of inquiry, discovering far more Web sites and resources collectively than any one individual could? Of course, the audience for this pamphlet isn't the teacher who asks such questions, for she'd fail to flinch at the sight of their trump card:

If the world's on the Internet . . . where will you be if you're not?
    What's the cost of not bringing the Internet into daily teaching?
    How much could your students lose in the long run by not mastering the Internet today? And how competitive can you be in the "education economy" if your Internet skills fall behind the curve? (Young 1997)

Indeed, the stakes are high, but this rhetoric is designed to heighten anxiety and sell products, not educate students. To accomplish that goal, serving the needs of students rather than salespeople, we must help educators fly between "the blazing sun" of cyberspace and the stagnant water of prefabricated projects and curricula.

Utopian Visions '95: Looking Backward

Before you "plug the power of the Internet right into standard curricula" it's a good idea to question your goals as an educator. In the beginning, Lowell and I overwhelmed each other with questions, relying primarily upon experience as classroom teachers and convictions about what should transpire in good classes. These two assets—experience and conviction—would guide us. The rest would require trial and error, dialectical tension, and reflection. I reiterate this because of the hype assaulting educational ears, which frequently employs manipulative rhetoric like we just heard from a promotional brochure. What's more, it would be disingenuous of me to suggest that this has been one happy ride with a few bumps along the way, resulting in a tidy, sequential list of things-to-do when we design and coordinate a telecollaborative project.

If this book were hypertext instead of print, I would offer a link right here to illustrate this point. The uniform resource locator (URL) would lead directly to the *Utopian Visions* project, which began in 1995. If you care to interrupt your reading of this printed codex and turn to the electronic medium for a moment, please take a look at the project Web site: <http://uv.cwrl.utexas.edu>.

Now then, let me ask a few questions:

- How did the *Utopian Visions'* Web site evolve?
- Is it possible to detect the process involved in its construction?
- Is there a relationship between the site's form and the project's function?
- What principles, if any, informed the site's design?
- What obstacles did its creators overcome and how did those obstacles shape the project and Web site?

These are not merely rhetorical questions. They are essential ones. We ought to apply them to every educational Web site we encounter. Too often, though, I hear students sing the praises of "cool" graphics and educators award high marks to a Web site that has "some really cool links." Once again, infatuation with the container overwhelms critical assessment of the tool. I'd be happier if those students were to say "the graphics helped me think about this" or my colleagues were to notice "the sites ending with 'com' read like propaganda." Unfortunately, though, coolness rules and surfaces frequently disguise a lack of substance. None of this helps the educator who, while pondering how to design a telecollaborative project, asks: "How do you begin?" Or, perhaps more to the point: "Why do you begin?"

The *Utopian Visions* Web site did not spring like Athena from Zeus's head. Nor would it be fair to say it sprung from two heads. When we began, in fact, neither Lowell or I mentioned creating a Web site. We had never attempted such a thing. By starting with the present Web site, though, we simulate the experience of educators trying to learn from existing projects. In effect, they must work in reverse, trying to divine the process that led to this "product." In this case, however, there's a difference: One of the principal designers of that project and Web site will serve as the guide on a journey from its conception and birth, to its infancy and adolescence. I can't promise to answer every question, but perhaps this odyssey will provide a useful glimpse of the dialogical process that enabled two classroom teachers to create and sustain a global, telecollaborative project.

That Thing You Do

Nearly a decade has passed since our first telecollaborative efforts, providing Lowell and I with a better perspective of what we did, and how we did it. However, this does not necessarily mean we know how to articulate our actions. Like the poet asked to explain her poem, a teacher often cannot articulate the rationale for why she does certain things, in certain ways, at certain times in the midst of a class session. We simply internalize the process, relying upon instinct and intuition, a holistic "feel" for the class. It isn't until we're asked to articulate matters, to externalize what we've internalized, that we become self-conscious of our thought process and the "cognitive artifacts" we employ (Hutchins 1996). I learned this lesson when asked to "teach" poetry for the first time. How does one "read" a poem? How does one teach someone else to "read" a poem? The novice draws upon a limited repertoire, vainly attempting to "tell" students what to think in response to the question, *What* does the poem mean?" The more experienced and enlightened teacher, however, draws upon diverse strategies to help "show" students how to address a more meaningful question: "*How* does the poem mean?" (Ciardi 1960).

   With the introduction of telecollaboration to the classroom we become novices again. This, too, explains why veteran teachers often resist new technology. The veteran teacher's comfort in a classroom is built upon years of experience and numerous trials. Over time, one gains confidence in certain pedagogical strategies and a particular learning environment. New ideas and methods threaten that environment and comfort. The prior experience that helped us "show" students in some external manner what we would otherwise "tell" them as abstractions may lose its relevance. How can teachers externalize telecollaborative concepts for students when they've not fully internalized them? How might they relax their hold of the classroom reins, when they're uncertain of where they are going? Think how long it takes to develop good judgment in facilitating a classroom discussion, deciding when to allow digressions, when to pull students back to the original topic, or when to bring it to a halt. Given their conditioning as *paidagogos,* and lack of professional development, how many teachers are prepared to make such judgments in cyberspace?

There are enough false prophets offering "simple" answers to such questions at professional conferences. They thrive on the hype and hysteria attending current debates, and like the Man in Aesop's fable they concentrate on anecdotes supporting their argument, as though they've possessed the answers all along. So let me be clear about something that we may not have conveyed forcefully enough before: None of this was easy. Lowell and I were making it up as we went along. We never knew if any of it would work. We suffered more obstacles than many teachers today, since this work began before e-mail addresses became ubiquitous and Web sites even existed. Our primary resources consisted of our experience, passion, and educational principles, all of which would be channeled through the secondary resource: a telecommunication link.

Argue for Your Imagination

As mentioned in chapter 3, a repressive environment motivated my telecollaborative experiments. One would not gather that, however, from a cursory glance at the *Utopian Visions* Web site. This is the problem with looking at the graphical representation of a project as opposed to its function as a pedagogical and curricular tool: The product consumes the process. It's far more instructive to learn how it all began and what decisions the coordinators made along the way. I've already described our sequence of projects, indicating how *Project Utopia* led to the *South African Elections '94 Internet Project* which, in turn, led to the *Nadine Gordimer* project and so on. This does not, however, account for the evolution of the *Utopian Visions* project, which remains our only sustained, mutual effort to date. Like all of our work, this project began in our imagination and evolved through dialectical exchanges rather than prescribed curricula or lesson plans.

I call attention to this because a preoccupation with hardware, software, and logistical matters frequently overwhelms discussion of computers in education. Yet, the most important resource remains the teacher's imagination, which the anxiety of technical concerns often stunts. What software should I use? Which search engines will help me find the best sources on the Web? How do I create a Web site? Do I save graphics in JPEG or GIF format? These go on and on, *ad nauseum*. And what becomes of the teacher's vision as a result? We'll never take those first, tentative steps if preoccupied with such details. If the telecollaborative project is a journey, then preoccupation with details is the first obstacle one must overcome. By their very nature details conjure more problems than solutions, troubling us so much that we may postpone the journey altogether.

When I was a humanities teacher equipped with little more than a book, chalk, and a slate board, such details didn't interfere with my focus upon Shakespeare's drama. The focal point had to be the play itself, and the meaning that an audience constructs from its rendering, not the media that assisted class discussions. Similarly, educators initiated to new technology must not lose the forest for the proverbial trees, nor cling to their relative ignorance like it's a crutch. "Argue for your limitations, " as the novelist Richard Bach observed, "and sure enough, they are yours" (Bach 1977, 75). Personally, I'd prefer that educators argue for their imaginations, rather than personal or technological limitations. After all, as educators we know that "so long as a (student) imagines that he cannot do this or that, so long is he determined not to do it" (Spinoza 1994, 193). If we wish to open student minds, therefore, we must keep our own minds open to new possibilities.

So with the reader's indulgence, I shall utter a few absolutes in the hope that they will help teachers set aside familiar crutches:

- There will never be enough "good" computers in your school or classroom.
- Classroom computers will never have enough random access memory (RAM).
- The disk space on hard drives and floppies will never be sufficient.
- The Internet connection will never be fast enough.
- The technological conditions will never be optimal.
- The school curriculum will never be written by individual teachers for individual teachers; they will always be written by committees and for committees.

I know, we should refrain from uttering absolutes, but sometimes a teacher must violate the rules to teach a lesson. These would-be obstacles provide a convenient excuse for resisting innovations or failing to conduct experiments of one's own. They are not insurmountable, however, for those equipped with desire and imagination, educators capable of beginning with a vision like we had back in 1994, when we imagined that:

1. Students could discuss historic events and personal views in a virtual United Nations without leaving home or missing classes.
2. Educators with vision and a tolerance for risk could telecollaborate in a project integrating technology across academic disciplines.
3. Academic institutions, and their administrative staffs, could tolerate "obvious deviations" from conventional pedagogy.

This is how *Utopian Visions* began. Before the "cool Web site" replete with message forums and automated archives, before subscription to the electronic mailing list and the minutiae of logistical concerns, there had to be a vision. Obvious though it is, this bears repeating because so much of the rhetoric describing a "paradigm shift" implies something revolutionary has arrived in our classrooms. Perhaps if we shift attention from technology to pedagogy, however, we will perceive the evolutionary character of this supposed revolution. What follows is a discussion of how Lowell and I initiated a telecollaborative project with dialectics as our guiding principle, striving for dynamic endeavors that help students develop not just computing skills, but aptitudes for critical thinking. I offer this not as a blueprint, but as a glimpse of how one telecollaborative project evolved.

"The Vision Thing"

Lowell and I began with what a former U.S. president called "the vision thing." We wanted to apply what we had learned from the South Africa project to another "historic moment": the end of our decade, century, and millennium. We knew we wanted dialectics, which would allow us to avoid "keypal" exchanges that frequently deteriorate into frivolous "chat room" discussions. Equally undesirable were scavenger hunts treating the Internet like a container, compelling students to conduct "fact-finding missions" without thinking critically about their information or its sources. So whatever we constructed would have to be flexible enough to accommodate disparate curricula and pedagogical styles, yet structured enough to inspire meaningful research, critical thinking, dialectical discourse, and communication skills.

We weren't asking for much, were we?

Of course, a vision alone is not enough to answer all the questions that arise, though it remains an essential compass. We relied upon our personal dialectic, conveyed entirely through electronic mail, to address the troublesome questions that most teachers encounter while making their initial foray into educational telecollaboration. How do you break out of the labyrinth of prescribed texts and activities to experiment with this new medium? Where do you begin? How do you "fit" it into an already crowded curriculum? My answer to these questions, like so many efforts to externalize what we've internalized, relies upon an analogy. Think for a moment of parallels between the Internet and the automobile.

At the end of the nineteenth century the automobile was introduced to Americans with much the same fanfare that accompanied the Internet's introduction at the end of the twentieth century. "It will change your life," its proponents claimed, assuming this change was all for the better. "It will allow you to go places you never could have gone before," they boasted, revealing another positive assumption. There's an instructive parallel here, for telecollaborative learning activities share certain qualities with a journey by automobile, and their design demands a similar thought process. Before making a trip by automobile we must ask:

- What's the destination?
- Who are the passengers?
- What kind of vehicle will I be driving?
- What's the best route to get everyone safely there—and back?

There are others, of course, but these four will do for now. The educator thinking about telecollaboration will be better served by these questions than any prefab, "plug-and-play" program. If one begins with an educational vision, the philosophical grounding that all educators need whether they are conscious of it or not, many of the supposed obstacles begin to dissolve. The vision informs decisions along the way, helping one decide which of many forks in the digital road to take.

In our case, the destination was dialectical discourse emanating from the study of an "historic moment"—the end of a decade, century, and millennium. Our passengers would be international, secondary school students from diverse academic disciplines. The "vehicle" would range from state-of-the-art networks to wing-and-a-prayer connections, but the lowest common denominator would be electronic mail and a mailing list. The best route would be shared learning activities and a common "curriculum" flexible enough to accommodate a range of academic disciplines and calendars, while stimulating reciprocal discussions.

Sounds easy, doesn't it?

However, nothing is certain when it comes to telecollaboration. After going to all the trouble of designing a project, how can we be sure anyone will be interested? On the other hand, how will we manage things if a large number of people should join us? Each time I call for telecollaborators via electronic mailing lists I'm reminded of Oscar Wilde's ironic observation: "In this world there are only two tragedies. One is not getting what one wants, the other is getting it" (Wilde 1973, 83). Returning to our automobile analogy, this is the equivalent of posting a "Rider Wanted" notice on a public bulletin board without setting any restrictions. Initially, the driver may hope someone—anyone—will offer to share the expense and experience. What happens, though, if that volunteer shows up with six friends for the trip from Boston to San Diego in a compact car?

Anticipating Extremes, Limiting Chaos

When we began drafting the *Utopian Visions* project I had no Web access, few resources for discussions of instructional technology, and no colleagues engaged in similar work. However, the *South African Elections '94 Internet Project* had taught me to anticipate some fundamental challenges. It was evident, for example, that we needed to simultaneously stimulate discussion and limit the length and number of submissions. If we failed to stimulate participants, the discussions would never evolve from data reports and superficial repartee to more thoughtful dialectics. If we neglected to limit the length and number of individual messages, meanwhile, we would subject participants to "information overload," prompting declamations but not necessarily dialogues.

To help us think through some issues, and simulate the experience of our students, I initiated an uncharacteristically formal dialogue with Lowell in October 1994. We conceived of this as an exercise that would impose constraints similar to the ones we placed upon students. We would take turns, allowing each other a week to respond to a message, while limiting ourselves to 250 words per message. By adopting the constraints of weekly exchanges, limited word counts, and electronic mail, we acquired the experience necessary to internalize new methods and empathize with our students. We were, as the constructivists like to say, "learning by doing." What follows is far more succinct and self-conscious than our usual correspondence, but it offers a glimpse of one project's genesis, as well as the method to our telecollaborative madness.

Date: Wed, 5 Oct 1994
From: Buddy Burniske
Subject: Project 1999
To: Lowell Monke

PROJECT 1999—Global Internet Project

The end of a millennium approaches, announcing the close of one chapter in human history and the opening of another. As always, the ending inspires reflection. We stand upon a moment in time and simultaneously look forward to the future, backward at the past, while living in the present. How did we get to this point? Where do we go from here?

Profound questions generate profound studies. Call it "Project 1999: The Third Millennium." Call it what you will. What matters most at THIS moment is exploring how we could stimulate students around the world, exciting investigation of their past and speculation of their future. This could be a remarkable fusion of academic disciplines and international perspectives.

In very general terms, this is what I envision for such a project:

1) Participating students speak from the viewpoint of the country in which they reside.

2) Looking Backward—Students report on where their country stood in the year 1899.

3) Looking Forward—Projections for their country in 100 years—the year 2099.

4) The "Present"—What will be the situation as of 1999 in that country?

5) Specialists—students cluster as "experts" in broad areas such as: Government, Economics, Environment, Education, Communication, Transportation, Arts/ Literature . . .

6) Reports sent to a worldwide "listserv," then placed into a database "Time Capsule."

So, how do we get THERE from here? How do we give this more shape and "focus" so that it doesn't become another exercise in chaos theory? How do we help students find meaning in all the information they're asked to process?

(Word count: 263)

Date: Thu, 13 Oct 1994
From: Lowell Monke
Subject: Project 1999/#2
To: Buddy Burniske

Your last question is the most crucial one. After all, helping young people find meaning in their lives should be the highest goal of education. If we can find ways to give our students a sense of connectedness—in terms of time, place, people, beliefs—then I think we will have provided one crucial element in achieving that goal. I suggest that all of our ideas for this project point toward achieving that sense of connectedness.

Let me put off answering your structural questions for another time. I need to ruffle your six general proposals a bit first:

1) Should international students connect with their residence or their homeland? Would that be an organizational nightmare for international teachers like you?

2) This is also the end of the millennium. Is 100 years enough to really give students the perspective they need? How about 1,000?

3) I'm not so foolish as to suggest looking forward 1,000 years. Ten years might be more realistic.

4) Good, but again which country?

5) I suggest these categories: Government, Economics, Technology, Arts/ Literature and Religion (tricky, I know, but I don't think we can ignore it).

6) Excellent! But let's keep a hardcopy backup.

More questions: do we create five clusters of experts within the local groups or should we have several units within each local group, each unit composed of five persons, each representing one of the categories? Do we try to make this a cooperative project for teachers in a school as well as students? How far can we stretch across the curriculum? (Word count: 260)

Date: Wed, 19 Oct 1994
From: Buddy Burniske
Subject: Project 1999/Installment #3
To: Lowell Monke

Yes, let's aim for "connectedness." I like it more than "integration." Integration suggests coercion, often homogenizing, if not annihilating, disparate views. Let's not sacrifice diversity at Unity's altar. Metaphor? Create a salad bowl, not a crucible; the former allows for differences, the latter doesn't.

Ah, metaphysics! It's essential that we begin there, isn't it? Too often technical logistics preoccupy educators on the Internet. Frankly, it bores me. Technology's the starting point, the means by which we help students explore the world and themselves, but not the answer to life's mysteries.

Now then, off the soapbox and on to pragmatics:

REPORT VIEWPOINTS—Dozens of nationalities are represented in this school's classrooms. The best way to "connect" without homogenizing is through the shared experience of living in Malaysia.

TIME FRAME—I like the symmetry of a century forward and backward. The century becomes a yardstick, allowing us to measure dramatic changes in human population, environment, technology, etc.

CURRICULAR ISSUES—Let's brainstorm some more before we commit ourselves to categories and sub-categories which become straitjackets (no one looks good in straitjackets).

QUESTIONS: With all the electronic junk mail out there, how do we (a) distinguish Project 1999; (b) attract various disciplines and (c) establish a manageable time frame? Then: how do we help people go beyond technical concerns? How do we stimulate all that's best in humanity—compassion, thoughtfulness, creativity and hope—to inspire genuine reflection and speculation? A starting point: What excites you about the future; what fascinates you about the past? (Word count: 251)

Date: Thu, 27 Oct 1994
From: Lowell Monke
Subject: Project 1999—Installment #4
To: Buddy Burniske

Salad bowl? OK. But be careful lest we leave out some ingredients because their flavors are too strong. No shying away from the pungent taste of controversy just to make the biggest salad possible. As for technology not being the answer to life's mysteries, I would say that it IS one of life's mysteries.

REPORT VIEWPOINTS—Agreed.

CURRICULAR ISSUES—Maybe we should attack this holistically, with each small group developing its own categories of society—a learning experience in itself and opens the doors to more creativity.

TIME FRAME—Symmetry, Shmymmetry. You sound like a math teacher! A century doesn't give us a long enough yardstick to see the big picture. With technology alone, nothing happening today makes sense without going back at least to the beginning of the Industrial Revolution.

DISTINGUISHING PROJECT 1999—Commercial programs are mostly K-Mart stuff—off the rack. Their motivation is to push telecomputing and they charge a fee to boot. We customize at no expense. We focus on our students, not the technology. AND WE SET VERY HIGH STANDARDS. If we make it academically demanding and technologically unobtrusive it will step out from the crowd.

BRAIN-STORMS: (a) Try to bring on-line futurists; historians (you live close to Arthur C. Clarke, don't you? ;-)) (b) What fascinates me is whether we are making progress in the quality of life on this Earth? In what ways is life better? at what (and whose) cost? How will life improve? at what (and whose) expense? Can we use that as the investigative context? (Word count: 256)

Agreeing to Disagree: The Call for Collaboration

Our lack of a clear project design should be self-evident. Even more apparent is our concern with what we didn't want to accomplish. What's most significant, though, is the way we used our differences to brainstorm ideas and further our dialectical exchange. In time, we concentrated upon details that teachers would seek before committing themselves to this endeavor. We continued arguing over the particulars in the final months of 1994, but failed to resolve a number of issues. Finally, we agreed to disagree and see what happened. As with any educational endeavor, there was only so much we could do to "prepare" for it.

The rest would depend upon the dynamics of an online community. If this were to be a truly collaborative project, then it would have to be flexible enough to support teachers with diverse curricula and schedules, holding them and their students accountable without regulating their actions. Fortunately, we did reach agreement upon one minor detail: dropping the name *Project 1999* for *Utopian Visions*.

In February 1995, two months prior to our scheduled beginning, we posted a "Call for Collaboration" on educational mailing lists in Africa, Asia, Europe, North and South America. If anything, we favored regional lists maintained outside North America, since we hoped for a geographically diverse group of participants. We wrote the "Call for Collaboration" with a dual purpose in mind: first, to attract educators interested in an ambitious project; second, to advertise the project idea without divulging logistical matters, such as the instructions for subscribing to our mailing list. In this fashion, we hoped to locate kindred spirits who wished to make a strong commitment to telecollaboration, rather than attract "lurkers" or irresponsible hackers. Once they contacted us, and expressed a genuine interest, I forwarded the full project description, which began with a statement of our intention:

I. Our Aim: The end of a millennium approaches. As always, the ending inspires reflection. We stand upon a moment in time, looking forward to the future, backward at the past, from the promontory of the present. How did we get to this point? What "utopian visions" guided us? Where do we go from here? What "visions" will lead us?

Students will examine the "quality of life" in their respective countries over a two hundred year interval. We will begin by "Looking Backward" to 1895, then consider "The Present" of 1995, before "Looking Forward" to 2095. In this manner participants will be encouraged to view history and current events as part of a continuum, pondering personal as well as collective issues. We will consider the end of this century and millennium as an "historic moment", and think of all contributions to this project as a time capsule for scholars of the future!

The rhetorical questions, appeal to intellectual curiosity, and suggestion of historical significance were designed to attract a certain type of educator, as well as indicate the seriousness of our purpose. With Oscar Wilde's observation in mind, we had to take special care not to attract people who were simply looking for electronic diversions. We wanted to collaborate with educators who would make a serious commitment to a project that would demand much of them and their students. We decided to center the project around the year in which it took place (1995), with an eye toward possible sequels. The century would be our yardstick, providing what my partner had delicately termed "symmetry, shmymmetry." Following this broad sketch of our objectives, culminating in breathless enthusiasm, it was necessary to narrow the focus, indicating our intended audience:

II. Applicable To: Secondary students (ages 14 –19), from virtually all disciplines (or extracurricular activities). Participating groups may be large or small, gathered within an organized body or brought together specifically for this project. An implicit aim is to knock down classroom walls without causing educational roofs to collapse. What matters most is inspiring students, stimulating investigation of their past and speculation of their future.

Notice the attempt to limit the chaos, by specifying student ages, while accommodating a full range of academic disciplines. In 1995, we knew most schools with e-mail access probably had gatekeepers in the computer science department. Thus, if we had narrowed the focus to, say, only the humanities teachers—who were most likely not at the forefront of telecomputing in their school—our work might have resulted in little more than a brief look by the computer coordinator, who would either print out the project description and pass it on to the respective department heads, or, worse still, delete it from his or her files. Appealing to all disciplines improved our chances for recruiting participants, while also supporting our philosophical belief in holistic learning. This was fine and good, but what about the logistics? What would we actually *do*, and when? Equipped with a vision, a relatively clear destination, it was now time to address the details that potential collaborators would demand before making a commitment.

III. The Structure: In general terms, this is what we envision:
a. Students around the world discuss *Utopian Visions* (and dystopian realities) from the perspective of the nation in which they reside.
b. Biweekly exchanges—Each school will file three sets of reports to the project listserv:

   April 14—1st Exchange = "Looking Backward"—1895.

   April 28—2nd Exchange = "The Present"—1995.

   May 12—3rd Exchange = "Looking Forward"—2095
c. On-going e-mail correspondence will allow students to ask follow-up questions, clarify reports, and discuss issues that emerge from the exchanges.

Every classroom teacher who wishes to inspire dialectics knows how important it is to establish the proper atmosphere in class. We may *say* that we value different opinions or critical thinking, but if we spend the majority of our time lecturing and administering tests, providing little opportunity for discussions, students will quickly note that our actions fail to support our rhetoric. *The*

South African Elections '94 Internet Project required weekly reports from students, which turned them into reporters without allowing sufficient time for cross-examination and dialogue. With *Utopian Visions '95*, therefore, we opted for fewer reports (three instead of five) over a longer time period (six weeks instead of five) to encourage better dialectics.

How did we choose these seemingly arbitrary report dates? Were we simply following the South African project's schedule with slight variation? Yes and no. While our schedule was not constrained by an actual, historic event, we were cognizant of the internal rhythms of classrooms and schools. Most northern hemisphere schools observe a spring break in March, which meant it would be difficult for discussions to gain momentum at that time. April seemed more conducive to active participation, though May would bring external examinations for students in the International Baccalaureate and Advanced Placement programs. So, if we could recruit participants in February, test our listserver in March, and begin the biweekly exchanges in April we'd improve our chances for accommodating a wide variety of school calendars as well as academic disciplines.

As classroom teachers ourselves we understood the significance of these matters. Contrary to what technophiles would have us think, we knew it would be difficult for teachers to juggle the constraints of a curriculum, student absences, extracurricular activities, school holidays, and external exams while weaving a global, telecollaborative project into the fabric of their daily lives. Nonetheless, without a schedule, deadlines that gave everyone a sense of where we'd be in the project at a given time, the dialectics would suffer. It would be like trying to have a class discussion with students dispersed throughout the school. The prerequisites for healthy discussion, we believed, were high participation rates and clear guidelines for discourse.

Which leads to an obvious, though critical, point: for telecollaborative activities to thrive we must make communication a priority. Think how many conventions we take for granted in "face-to-face" classroom discussions. These habits require years of training: from active listening to the raising of hands, signaling the desire to speak, and a civil taking of turns. Our ideal of dialectics, threatened by so many variables in actual classrooms, was even more fragile in the virtual meeting place. So the schedule was an attempt to say when we'd be talking about the nineteenth, twentieth, and twenty-first centuries. What, exactly, would we talk about when we convened? That brought us to the specifics of the exchanges themselves. Once again, it was time to guide the discussions, limiting the chaos that would naturally ensue if we adopted a laissez-faire approach. Here's what we conceived:

IV. The Exchanges: Each exchange will consist of ten category reports, each of which includes: (A) Data Report, (B) Narrative Analysis.

Initial Question: "Describe the following in your country as of 1895 (1995, 2095) and significant events which led to these conditions (footnote all sources)." Obviously, no listing is ever complete, or completely satisfying, but we hope the following will provide common grounds and the structure necessary for a meaningful discussion.

A. Data Report (500 words maximum)—Address each category, but allow students flexibility within them.

    * Name of Country (in 1895. . . 1995 . . . 2095)

      1. Environment—total land area; climate, average temperatures, rainfall, natural resources, percentage of cultivated / developed land.

      2. People

          a. Population—density, largest city, growth rate, total population, etc.

          b. Demographics—ethnic breakdown; immigration / emigration; country vs. city, coastal vs. inland; dwelling types, etc.

          c. Religion—major religions, approximate numbers and percentage of citizens who are followers, "freedom" of worship.

      3. Education—educational system and methods; literacy rate, number of schools, libraries, universities; number of students enrolled and grade levels attained.

      4. Government—gov't structure; seats of power: legislative, judicial, executive powers, etc.; size of police force, military, special services.

      5. Economy—

          a. describe main goods / staples and % of people working in agrarian vs. industrial jobs; imports v. exports, cost of staple goods; currency.

          b. Employment—% of unemployed; male / female work ratios; welfare.

      6. Health—common medical practices, medical facilities, epidemics, infant mortality, life expectancy, mental illness, homicide, health care, insurance and social support.

      7. Transportation—primary travel mode; approximate number of motorized vehicles and relative transience.

      8. Communications—primary means of communication; circulation of print publications; estimated number of citizens who use print and electronic media.

      9. Arts / Recreation—indicate primary artistic / recreational activities and relative significance in defining national identity / culture of that time.

     10. *Wild Card*—School's choice of additional category (MUST be standard for all three school reports).

B. Narrative Analysis (500 words maximum)

> In light of the information gathered, describe the overall "quality of life" in your country as of 1895 (... 1995 ... 2095). This is a subjective analysis. Feel free to discuss what you consider the advantages and disadvantages to life in your country as of 1895. What industrial/technological developments affected the quality of living? Were the advantages of these innovations for the majority or a privileged minority? What "utopian vision" guided your nation at this time? How influential has that vision been? Are there still vestiges of that "vision" at work today? What "intangibles" are not revealed through the Data Report? Why are these intangibles significant in determining the "quality of life" in your would-be Utopia?

How to explain all of this? To begin with, we knew from *Project Utopia* that we wanted far more than fanciful exchanges. That meant designing the project so that students felt compelled to conduct research. However, we also knew, thanks to our experience with the *South African Elections '94 Internet Project*, that the collection and distribution of data alone would not satisfy our goals. So we hoped for a balance, which is why we allotted 500 words for both the Data Reports and Narrative Analyses. The creation of categories, meanwhile, would allow for a range of class sizes to participate if the teacher arranged collaborative work groups. Thus, a teacher with thirty students could have ten groups of three specialize in the respective categories, prepare a single report composed of Data and Narrative Analysis, then submit it to the project listserver. This accomplished several purposes, not the least of which was limiting traffic on our electronic mailing list. Instead of getting thirty submissions from a school with thirty participants we would receive only ten; word limits would mitigate the information overload and encourage judicious editing. It was worth repeating this while mentioning special concerns in the next section of our project description:

IV. The Exchanges—Special notes

* REPORTS must not exceed the word counts (500 for Data; 500 for Narrative). Teachers are kindly requested to observe these restrictions, which will encourage revision/editing, prevent information overload, and generally sharpen the focus.

* SUBMISSION of reports must be to the listserver—see Logistics—and identified as follows: "School/Date/Exchange Title" atop the document.

Example: ISKL/APRIL 14/LOOKING BACKWARD

* CONTRIBUTORS' Names should be listed at the bottom of respective report sections along with age and nationality. This will help personalize the e-mail correspondence.

Every teacher knows how difficult it is to give clear, concise directions. It's even harder to get students to follow them. In this instance, electronic mail's "narrow bandwidth"—which didn't, at that time, allow for graphic representation, facial expressions, body language and the other "tools" an educator employs to convey important information—exacerbated matters. By reiterating the word limits for reports we hoped students and teachers would take them seriously. However, the directions for identification were equally significant because submissions identified only as "Reports" from anonymous authors who failed to contextualize their remarks would subvert dialogues. Now came the matter of subscribing participants to the project's mailing list, and teaching them the difference between public and private e-mail.

V. Logistics

   a. Coordinator's e-mail address: buddyb@iskl.po.my

   b. Listserver Subscription—Send this message, "Subscribe isklproj YOUR NAME" to the following address: listserver@jaring.my (Be sure to include your name and e-mail address).

   c. Once you've subscribed to the listserver you will be included in all communiques. However, be sure to send your mail to: isklproj@jaring.my

All items sent to this address will be "public" to all subscribers. Private mail should be sent to individual addresses. PLEASE give this rehearsal before the first exchange of reports: April 14, 1995.

By the time this book goes to press these concerns may seem irrelevant. New software could simplify matters, enabling subscription to a mailing list through the click of a digital icon. However, we should never presume too much when it comes to logistical matters. The "digital divide" makes it increasingly difficult for educators around the world to enjoy the same technological advantages. By April 1995, Lowell and his computer class in Des Moines had access to the World Wide Web through modems running at 19,200 bits per second. They also had relatively secure connections and reliable electricity. I, meanwhile, relied upon a 4,800 bps modem with a tenuous SLIP connection that rarely lasted more than five minutes. When I "surfed" the Web, if I surfed at all, I would automatically set the browser to deliver text only, switching off the images that would otherwise take several minutes to load.

I point this out because many educators suffer the delusion, even as they design "global" telecollaborative projects, that their local conditions are somehow universal. We do not enjoy the same hardware and software availability, technological expertise, telecommunications experience, language abilities, or curricular control. We know this and yet we still grow impatient when two days go by without a reply to e-mail sent from one continent to another. So when confronting logistical concerns it is best to adopt a philosophical stance: "Whenever you feel like criticizing any one . . . just remember that all the people in this world haven't had the advantages that you've had" (Fitzgerald 1979, 7). With this in mind, we concluded our project description with ideas that might help teachers overcome inertia. This allowed us to share ideas and reiterate our concern for individual autonomy, while demonstrating the potential application of this project to a variety of disciplines.

VI. Teaching Strategies/Starting Points—While we hope this structure is helpful, minimizing the chaos of listserv communication, we do NOT want it to dictate what happens in classrooms. Teachers are encouraged to work this into an already existing curriculum, rather than trying to attempt it "in addition to" other demands. We offer the following ONLY as suggestions/strategies for those wondering where they might begin, how they might incorporate this project into a crowded curriculum. By all means, share YOUR suggested readings/ideas with us!

- Language Arts Teachers—study a novel which offers a utopian/dystopian vision: *Looking Backward, Fahrenheit 451, The Handmaid's Tale, Animal Farm, Brave New World* . . . Discuss how/why "utopian visions" can become "dystopian realities."

- History Teachers—study constitutions, laws, treaties, etc. which shaped your nation. Research actual utopian societies/communes and discuss what "vision" led to their creation. Where might one find evidence of their ideas in mainstream society today?

- Economics Teachers—read a futurist's view of economics: *Megatrends, Powershift.* Discuss "alternative" approaches to economic development and utopian economic ideals.

- Theory of Knowledge/Philosophy Teachers—what is progress? What would be the "perfect society"? Please define. Reading: Toffler's, *The Third Wave.* Le Guin's "The Ones Who Walk Away from Omelas." Vonnegut's "Harrison Bergeron."

- Science/Environment Teachers—read Quinn's *Ishmael* or Suzuki's *Inventing the Future* and discuss how the "history" of human attitudes toward the environment shapes our future.

- Computer Teachers—what were (are/will be) the benefits brought to society by technology? What were (are/will be) the negative effects? Will the positives outweigh the negatives? Read a text that challenges the role of technology in society: *Technopoly, The Machine Stops, In The Absence of the Sacred,* etc.

- Journalism Teachers—have students survey residents, older shopkeepers and younger enterpreneurs, local officials, environmentalists, business people, etc. about the past, present and future in their country. Quote interviews in your narrative analysis.

Utopian Visions '96: Reinventing the Wheel

Obviously, we were rather ambitious with the *Utopian Visions* pilot project. The truth of the matter, though, is that we didn't think of it as a pilot project. We were gaining momentum, finding our way by trial and error, yet drawing upon previous experience to refine a telecollaborative project. In this, too, telecollaboration challenges the status quo, for it allows teachers to transcend the boundaries of a "unit" of study or academic time period. Telecollaboration diminishes the significance of artificial boundaries like academic disciplines, and grade levels, while conflating time and distance. A project doesn't necessarily end with a particular group or school year, the way conventional studies often do; instead, it has the potential to evolve with future groups, establishing an archive from which they can learn and to which they may contribute.

Utopian Visions '95 enjoyed several accomplishments, including the participation of schools in six countries: Canada, Finland, Indonesia, Malaysia, the United States, and Venezuela. However, the narrative analyses and dialogues were weak. Students spent far more time on the presentation of data in their reports than on the analysis of it. We pondered reasons for this, blaming ourselves for poor design and educational systems for conditioning students to believe "facts" were all that mattered, instead of critical thinking. The dialogues failed to move beyond superficial responses, though many students asked thoughtful questions to prompt further reflection. What's more, we heard very little from coordinators at other schools. This was both puzzling and disturbing. Did coordinators not see the value of collaborating or were they simply not prepared to make that step? Perhaps they believed their job was to have students produce reports, submit them to the mailing list, then move on to the next report? Or perhaps they simply lacked time to correspond? Regardless, we were determined to do better with the second edition of the project, *Utopian Visions '96*, drawing upon the project evaluations of participants to make alterations.

The results of this effort are displayed at the original *Utopian Visions* Web site (http://www.cwrl.utexas.edu/~burniske/uv96/uv.html), but the rationale for changes to the project's design and coordination may be of as much interest as their consequences. Again, our goal was dialectical discourse for a global community of inquiry. Of the eight schools participating (from six different countries) in *Utopian Visions '96*, only a few had reliable access to the Web, which meant employing the lowest common denominator, electronic mailing lists, to facilitate our discussions. While the alterations addressed a number of concerns, our central aim was the improvement of discussions, which we hoped to achieve by the following means:

- Lengthen the project time frame (January–May)—to give relationships more time to develop, allowing participants to gain confidence with the technology and greater familiarity with their counterparts.

- Narrow the focus from *country* of residence to *municipality*—to limit generalizations, focusing upon "local" concerns as well as the global picture, and accommodate more than one school from a single country.

- Emphasize the importance of dialogues early and often—to place dialectical discourse in the foreground and information collection in the background.

- Begin with personal, informal exchanges to introduce participants—to allow students to discuss what mattered to them before they began more formal academic work. Increased ownership and "keypal" connections might encourage better engagement and dialogue.

- Merge the data and narrative analysis into one 350-word report—to limit the information overload and encourage more analysis; compel concise prose, and shift the emphasis from reports to follow-up dialogues.

- Drop the "Wild Card" category; split Art and Recreation; add Religion and Crime to bring the total number of categories to twelve—controversial topics like Religion and Crime would encourage dialectical exchange; Art and Recreation deserved separate attention; the Wild Card category had caused only confusion or neglect.

- Require a "Cumulative Report" assessing the municipality overall—to encourage full-group discussions and holistic analysis, drawing attention to the dialectical tensions caused by conflicting interests (Environment vs. Transportation, etc.).

- Construct a project Web site—to enable publication of student work and archive information so that it could be retrieved and discussed more easily.

Many of these changes helped improve the project, most notably the longer time frame, focus upon municipalities, and initiation of discussions through personal visions. However, the goal of dialectical discourse remained elusive. Only three of the school coordinators had been involved in the pilot project, so for the majority this was still a new experience. Several of the coordinators faced severe limitations, including access to e-mail through one dedicated computer terminal. Others had too many filters between the students and online dialogues, as in Lowell's case, where students wrote their reports and replies by hand, submitted them to another class to be typed, before they were collated and submitted in one batch through a shared e-mail account. My students, meanwhile, had a shared account for each of three classes and, as a result, found it much easier to contribute to the discussion. They liked the "idea" of telecollaboration and brought remarkable energy and enthusiasm to the enterprise. However, they felt betrayed by unrequited messages, which they often interpreted as a sign of indifference rather than limited access. The distinction didn't matter to them; the effect was the same. Their disappointment prompted emotional discussions in class, and blunt commentaries like the following, which appeared in a project evaluation:

The use of the Internet for this project increased our understanding of how the use of technology can not only affect the way we write, but also the way we communicate. It was really amazing to be able to share thoughts and ideas with people in different countries! However, at times the thought that we were in this alone was not very rewarding. The feeling of writing a report and not getting any responses was a very frustrating one. At many times I was discouraged to keep going and I don't think that is something anyone should feel. This is a project where people should really express their thoughts and ideas. One thing I would change about the project if I could would be to make sure that everyone gets involved. (Rocio T. ISKL)

Reciprocity remains a critical issue, and one that requires careful vigilance. Overall, the dialogues showed subtle, qualitative improvement, though they lacked the urgency and authenticity of what transpired during the *South African Elections '94 Internet Project*. Improved correspondence had as much to do with our presentation of the project, emphasis of its respective components, and evolving interaction as it did with hardware and software. It could be argued, of course, that the less awkward we felt with the latter, and the less visible they were, the more comfortable we became with the former. Nonetheless, we needed to give more thought to the project's design and facilitation, while helping participants understand the importance of the dialogues, shifting their attention from research and reports to subsequent discussions of them. This would prove far more difficult than gaining access to the Internet or creating a telecollaborative project design.

Beyond Design: Communicate!

As I've said before, telecollaboration is not about computers. It's about people learning to communicate through new media. Unfortunately, this escapes many of the people who enable telecollaboration in the classroom, from the technicians who manufacture the "boxes and wires" to the programmers who write the software and even the educators who use these instruments for instructional purposes. In retrospect, I see the work that Lowell and I have conducted as a response to this oversight. What began as a telecommunications experiment between two former colleagues, who came to it with the hope of inspiring thoughtful conversations, had suddenly become a quest. We had to answer just one question, but the more we chased it the more elusive it seemed: "How do we design *and* coordinate a global telecollaborative project to inspire dialectical discourse?"

This had initially compelled attention to technical matters. If you can't solve the riddles of how to send and receive messages—via facsimile transmission, listserver, newsgroup, or carrier pigeon—then good project ideas are doomed to fail. Once we had settled upon the mailing list as our communication medium we could proceed to questions of design. Yet we quickly conceded that we'd never have complete control over the design or facilitation of the project. Nor did we want such control. We believed that true collaboration would lead to something more satisfying than anything we could devise or command, which meant allowing teachers to adapt exercises to suit their students and curriculum. Every time I send out a "Call for Collaboration" I'm awed by the thought that strangers "out there" may soon become acquaintances, then collaborators, and colleagues. Who am I to expect that an overworked, underappreciated teacher treated like a *paidigagos* will take a chance on our work-in-progress? Thus, while it's essential that we begin with a clear purpose, we must also allow for the adaptations and idiosyncracies that breathe life into an otherwise sterile design, giving the project a unique personality.

While I wasn't aware of it at the time, since I had not encountered her work before banging my head against the telecollaborative wall, *Utopian Visions* began as a blend of the three primary genres that Judi Harris has identified: interpersonal exchanges, information collections and analyses, and problem-solving projects (Harris 1998). We wanted students to gather information for category reports, engage in interpersonal exchanges in their follow-up e-mail and personal visions, and work toward problem-solving as they discussed possible solutions to contemporary problems in their respective municipalities. All of this, mind you, was to occur while allowing teachers the latitude necessary to adjust the project to their particular curriculum and students.

What we discovered in the first two iterations of this project, and in every other telecollaborative activity we've undertaken, is that a project's design is never enough to ensure success. This is no grand revelation for the classroom teacher who knows what it's like to prepare a "great lesson" or set up an elaborate simulation, then watch it suffer the abuse of uninspired students. This is, however, the reward for thinking about a curriculum as a container rather than a tool, privileging the material over the students. So while the integration of a telecollaborative project into one's teaching must begin within preexisiting curricula, it's critical that the creator-coordinator not stop there. We must go beyond the technology and project designs to fundamental concerns of human communication. Unfortunately, most of the research we encountered while conducting these trials had focused upon groups that spoke the same language, which helps explain their neglect of "communication" problems in global, telecollaborative activities.

From what we could gather, some things were simply taken for granted, particularly by educators more interested in the Internet as a container and telecollaboration as the collection and exchange of information. Such activities assume communication with distant peers will occur, without necessarily making it a priority. It was important to keep this in mind when pondering ideas about telecollaboration in the classroom, including Judi Harris's suggestions for "organizing and facilitating telecollaborative projects." While she may have intended it as a checklist, educators accustomed to rigid curricula could interpret the following sequence as a strict recipe:

Step One: Choose the Curriculum-Related Goals

Step Two: Choose the Activity's Structure

Step Three: Explore Examples of Other Online Projects

Step Four: Determine the Details of Your Project

Step Five: Invite Telecollaborators

Step Six: Form the Telecollaborative Group

Step Seven: Communicate!

Step Eight: Create Closure (Harris 1998, 82–94)

Despite our ignorance of Harris's work when we started, the nature of telecollaboration forced us to attempt all of these tasks save one (it wasn't possible to "explore examples of other online projects" in Malaysia during the pre-Web days of the early 1990s). What's most significant, however, is that while the "steps" imply a prescribed order, the recursive nature of telecollaboration frustrates a strict formula or sequence. What's more, anyone thinking in terms of a "things-to-do" list for telecollaboration would be well advised to elevate the penultimate step, "Communicate!," to privileged status. Disillusioned students and noncommunicative educators had brought the dirty little secret of poor reciprocity to our attention. What we couldn't determine, however, was whether or not dialogues failed because of differing expectations, poor access and connectivity, linguistic and cultural barriers, or a number of other variables. What we did know, however, was that researchers like Nicholas Burbules were right about the fragile nature of dialogue in education as well as our motivation for attempting it:

Every form of dialogical engagement can fall into patterns that become antidialogical [...] Debate can become an argument; inquiry can become an obsessively narrow, ends-driven endeavor; conversation can become a meandering chat that leads nowhere important or interesting; instruction can become manipulative. We engage in dialogical approaches not because they are methods guaranteed to succeed, but fundamentally because we are drawn to the spirit of equality, mutuality, and cooperation that animates them. (Burbules 1993, 143)

While such statements are reassuring, reminding us that genuine dialogue is difficult to create or sustain, they offer small consolation and few solutions. For that, we must continue our classroom trials and professional conversations. Perhaps Lowell and I suffered unrealistic expectations, but we were determined to raise the level of online discourse rather than lower our standards. What, precisely, was our definition of a "successful" dialogue between students? How would we know this phenomenon when we saw it? Quite simply, we envisioned dialogues that stimulated *further* dialogue—which demanded, of course, thoughtful inquiry, sustained research, and continual reflection. We wanted students to learn from one another through shared labors, thoughtful conversations, and mutual respect. Instead, we witnessed many of the "antidialogical" behaviors that Burbules described in the previous passage. Though disappointing, this pattern helped us acquire an intuitive understanding of dialogue's value, as well as the sadness of its failure, for reasons we were just beginning to articulate:

... the failure of dialogue pertains primarily to damage done to the fabric of the dialogical relation itself: what cuts the discussion short, what preempts certain areas of investigation, or what silences or overwhelms certain points of view within it. If the value of dialogue is in facilitating the possibilities of future conversations, then interactions that inhibit those possibilities must be seen as signs of failure. (Burbules 1993, 144)

Indeed, this is *how* dialogues fail, but it doesn't explain *why* they do so. The time had come to look carefully at the nature of online discussions, focusing a critical eye not only upon the quality of the project design and the efforts of participants, but also upon the media that facilitated this correspondence and the discourse practices that it fostered.

Divided by a Common Language

By now we knew the answer to our central questions wouldn't be found in commercial plug-and-play materials or the naive embrace of a "global village." How do we encourage students to strive for synthesis, analysis, and higher order thinking skills rather than cutting and pasting downloaded data? How do we help them engage in constructive dialectics rather than frivolous keypal exchanges or bitter flame wars? How, ultimately, do we design and coordinate global telecollaborations to inspire dialectics? Such questions demand a serious and sustained conversation, a dialectical discourse that electronic mail endangers even as it engenders.

From the outset I have wondered about the impact of telecomputing upon human discourse. This began with concerns about jargon seeping into my students' compositions ("Romeo and Juliet rarely interface . . ."), their reliance upon spellcheckers and preoccupation with font styles and other surface details that distracted them from content. None of that, however, worried me as much as the discursive habits I encountered in electronic mail. Perhaps because I had once been a journalist and had long been a writer of letters on a standard Olivetti typewriter, I cherished traditional correspondence. Letters were small gifts that one sent off in a package called an envelope to a friend or relative. The act of writing was often a demonstration of one's affection. Of course, there were many types of letters, but implicit in them all was concern for "communication" with the recipient. We were responsible for our words, especially written ones, and we'd even pay for transmitting a single one via telegram.

Yet, what is electronic mail? Is it written or spoken discourse? By which rules—those of the informal, spoken word or those of the written, formal word—should it abide? As a letter writer I was inclined to transfer the conventions of written discourse that I had learned from Strunk and White—personal salutations, capitalization, paragraphs, et al.—to this new medium (1979). However, this was clearly not the way that cyberwriters spurred on by the likes of *Wired* magazine approached their e-mail. How was I to teach communication skills to adolescents when would-be authorities offered the following advice?

When we say "screw the rules" we encourage you to do the following: Welcome inconsistency, especially in the interest of voice and cadence. Treat the institutions and players in your world with a dose of irreverence. Play with grammar and syntax. Appreciate unruliness. (Hale 1996, 96)

I could be wrong, but I doubt this advice will inspire thoughtful online discourse. Imagine the consequences if adolescents follow such counsel, acquiring these discursive habits before they're initiated to a telecollaborative project that asks them to respect others' opinions and engage in healthy dialectics. How do we prevent self-aggrandizing fools who spread the gospel of irreverence and unruliness from destroying communication—and educational endeavors?

Among other bits of wisdom, the compilers of *WiredStyle* encourage a departure from the convention of identifying acronyms like FBI, FCC, or NSA in an article's first reference. Imagine what this contributes to the discourse of a "global village." While coordinating telecollaborative projects I often remind students not to assume their audience will decipher acronyms pertaining to a particular school, culture, or region, since we lack a common frame of reference. Thus, I ask schools to identify their *Utopian Visions* reports by the name of their municipality, not an acronym. After all, what does ISKL (International School of Kuala Lumpur) mean to DMPS (Des Moines Public School) or AISB (American International School of Budapest) mean to CEDI (Centro de Desarrollo Integral Arboledas)? To assume that anyone should know what those acronyms signify reveals individual provincialism or institutional myopia at best, cultural imperialism at worst. Apparently the *Wired* stylists haven't given much thought to the impact of irreverent, unruly correspondence in global discussions, nor upon human interactions in real life, particularly among adolescent 'Netheads.

In global telecollaborative projects we are a people divided by a common language. In some instances we are adults with fifty years' experience of one language conversing with adolescents coming to it as their second or third language. We are native speakers corresponding with nonnative speakers. We are speakers of dialects ranging from North American variations to the British, Australian, South African, Indian, Singaporean, and Malaysian versions. And yet, some unenlightened, twentysomething editor who thinks the island of Manhattan is the center of the universe has the temerity to advocate unruliness online? "Treat the institutions and players in your world with a dose of irreverence." What admirable foresight. Only people who've failed to consider what life might be like after age thirty can offer such breezy counsel. The rest of us ought to know better.

Beyond Simplicity : *Utopian Visions '97*

Unfortunately, "knowing better" isn't enough. As educators, we search for ways of "showing better." Our ability to influence "'Netiquette" and online discourse seems to shrink with each day. The phenomenal growth of newsgroups and chat rooms on the World Wide Web means that many adolescents engage in hostile discursive practices before they're introduced to educational telecomputing. As any composition teacher will tell you, helping students overcome bad writing habits has never been easy, but the consequences are much greater when the unskilled writer's audience shifts from a single mentor to a global audience. Are we equipped for such a shift? Not really. Just because students are writing online doesn't mean their language skills are better, just more visible. Raising their awareness to this ought to be the starting point of any telecollaborative activity.

In the midst of *Utopian Visions '97*, a far more complicated version of the project and a harbinger of things to come, I found myself confronting language barriers and discursive practices on a daily basis. Eight schools on four continents completed applications to participate; only three of the faculty coordinators were native speakers of English. The majority of student participants were nonnative speakers of English. Yet, English was our *lingua franca,* something that piqued the interest of participants in Kuala Lumpur, who came to the project while studying the topic of "language" as part of the International Baccalaureate's Theory of Knowledge curriculum. Though their contribution was short-lived, their personal visions raised several important questions with respect to language, communication, and media:

A world not restricted by the barriers of language would be ideal. We shape everything we know in the form of words, but what if we could enter a whole new dimension of expression? One in which we could express abstract feelings and put them into a coherent form of communication? We would be able to accurately explain what it is to love or BE loved, or understand how a blind person feels in his/her world of darkness; how a deaf person feels in his/her world of silence. We would no longer have to "step into other people's shoes" to be able to know how they feel, instead we would understand them from an outside perspective. Then again, this is only an impossible vision, without the uniqueness of our own feelings, the world would not be as interesting and diverse as it is today. (Maya H., ISKL).

Ideas such as these helped me realize a significant flaw in our approach to the *Utopian Visions* project, a flaw that granted privileged status to a secondary concern. Despite our best intentions, Lowell and I were guilty of thinking more about technological devices than human interactions when we created one of the research categories. We had conceived of the Communications reports as discussions of the technology and media through which humans corresponded, rather than the medium of a language itself. I tried to convey this realization, and its profound implications, in my response to the ISKL contingent:

Date: Tue, 8 Apr 1997
From: R. W. Burniske
To: UV Mailing List
Subject: Dialogues: Kuala Lumpur/Personal Visions/Communications

Dear Scholars at the International School of Kuala Lumpur:

Thanks for your thoughtful insights on language and "communications." You've raised several issues which apply to us all, from the role of language as a medium within your class and municipality, to its significance *within* a medium of communication: in this instance, the Internet. I wondered if you had discussed how the English language shapes your thoughts as individuals and your relations as a group, given that half the members of your group, including your instructor, would consider English a second language (with Italian, Spanish, Afrikaans, French, Mandarin and Bahasa serving as alternative tongues). It's a wonder you can communicate at all! Your observations made me pause to consider, once again, what happens when groups like yours adopt English as a "lingua franca" to communicate with other ESL students, many of whom are new to the medium of telecommunications?

Given the complexity of language, a technology in its own right, the complications of software (derived from programming languages), and the limited bandwidth of computer networks, how do we manage to communicate through this medium, imperfect speakers (writers) and listeners (readers) that we are? For starters, I'd like to know what audience you had in mind while writing your personal visions. Were you thinking of your teacher? Were you thinking of students in Austin, Bangkok, Budapest, Cesky Krumlov, Des Moines, Jalisco, Verl and Ziezmariai? Or were you thinking of that nebulous audience known as "people on the Internet?" I ask because the idea of "audience" seems critically important to your discussion of language within the medium of telecommunications. Perhaps a syllogism will help (though I invite you to debate its terms and validity):

"Co-mmunication" requires "shared semantics."
Shared semantics require "shared experience."
Thus, co-mmunication requires "shared experience."

If true, this applies to classes such as yours as much as multinational corporations, listserv subscribers or any other "thought collective," yet we often forget the importance of developing "shared semantics" through "shared experience." We assume miscommunication results from poor language skills or personality conflicts when it may have more to do with the cognitive dissonance arising from different ways of "seeing" the world. As one of you observed, "We shape everything we know in the form of words. . . ." Indeed, but whose words do we employ? Which language? How does the process of "thinking in English" affect the way you see and experience the world? What metaphors do we adopt and how do they shape the way we think about things (ex: is the Internet an "Information Highway," "electronic frontier," or "cyberspace")? Do idiomatic expressions translate (ex. "You hold on, ah?" . . . "Off the light!")?

We assume people understand what is meant by co-mmunication, yet we privilege speaking skills and neglect to study how the listener's "experience" compares with the speaker's. Think how often we deceive ourselves, imagining we "understood" or we "had a good conversation" when we've merely constructed what we wanted to hear, the message which pleases our ears, rather than the message the speaker intended. Given all of this, isn't it naive to think people coming online will have the awareness to think about the form and content of their message, its impact on a global audience, let alone the ability to code that set of symbols so that the audience de-coding it will participate in a shared experience of shared semantics which enable communication? Can we embrace the cliche of a "global village" without considering the complexities of the language(s) shaping it?

What you could help me with, in this discussion of language and communication, is a question I confront on a daily basis as coordinator of this project: "How do we effectively communicate within an international, telecollaborative activity?" What we're all groping with here is the challenge of creating "shared experiences" among diverse groups—ones "divided by a common language," physical space and cultural differences—in the hope that we'll arrive at the shared semantics necessary for communication. I've never been to Budapest, Cesky Krumlov or Ziezmariai, so I don't share the "experience" of those places with some of our participants. However, I may share other experiences with those individuals, including discussions within this project. Perhaps mutual respect and desire are the chief prerequisites, ones enabling us to celebrate diversity rather than merely tolerate it. Certainly, speakers need to be considerate of their audience, without patronizing or abusing it; listeners, meanwhile, must pay attention to the speaker, resisting the temptation to dismiss a message because of prejudice against its messenger.

How do we effectively communicate within an international telecollaborative activity? The answer, I believe, lies more in the personal desires of the participants than the idiosyncrasies of language, the graphics of a Web site or fluidity of a listserv, message forum or other technical apparatus. The desire for genuine communication is what binds a "community of inquiry" such as ours, but not all participants possess it in equal measure. Indeed, some may not possess it at all, but if there's any hope for building "virtual communities" online or real communities offline, I'm convinced that communication lies at the heart of such constructions.

Thanks, again, for your good thoughts! We hope you'll share more of them in the coming weeks.

Sincerely,

R. W. Burniske
Project Coordinator, Utopian Visions '97

Communication in a telecollaborative project begins with clear and consistent terminology and a design that others can easily navigate. However, once the terms are established, the dialectics initiated, one must always remember the "LCDs" that technophiles often forget: "the lowest common denominators." Not all computers, modems, or language skills are created and distributed equally. Nor are project designs sufficient for successful telecollaboration. Above all, we must bring a strong desire for communication, beginning with a sincere commitment to the people who join our online community of inquiry.

Coordinating the Coordinators: *Utopian Visions '97–'99*

By now it should be apparent that there is far more to integrating the Internet into a curriculum than just pouring its contents into your classroom. This is not, nor will it ever be, "as easy as changing a light bulb." People who tell you differently have mistaken you for that fool who is easily parted from your school district's money. By the time we began *Utopian Visions '97*, the project had undergone further revision. The fundamental aim had not changed, nor the research categories, but we had lengthened the interval between reports to three weeks, providing more time for student dialogues. Lowell and I also discovered more time for our own dialogue, thanks to a move that placed us in the same time zone and country for the first time in half a decade. Shortly after the conclusion of *Utopian Visions '96*, I left the International School of Kuala Lumpur to begin my doctoral studies at the University of Texas, initiating further innovations and dialectical tensions.

Upon my arrival in Austin, John Slatin, the director of the newly created Institute for Technology and Learning, invited me to join his staff. I accepted the invitation and began working on a number of projects, including *Utopian Visions '97* and *Tx2K: The Texas 2000 Living Museum,* a Web-based project derived from the *Utopian Visions* paradigm (Tx2K, 1999). The complexity of *Utopian Visions '97–'99* would increase exponentially with the development of a Web site featuring databases for research categories, an interactive library, three online discussion forums, and two mailing lists (one for students and one for faculty coordinators). The introduction of more sophisticated technology, however, did not guarantee improved dialogues or learning. In fact, I worried that we would fragment the discourse, creating more disparate chatter instead of coherent and sustained conversations.

Nonetheless, as the online archives indicate, we enjoyed much healthier dialogues in the project's third iteration (http://uv.cwrl.utexas.edu/dialogues/index.html). There was a surprising equality in the number of category reports and dialogue messages (164 to 166) submitted through the student mailing list, indicating greater reciprocal correspondence among student readers and writers. What's more, conversational "threads" enjoyed greater longevity, revealing an effort to sustain dialogues, which helped students reexamine their claims and the assumptions behind them. Most important, the discourse inspired a greater blend of imagination and critical acumen, as the "invention" or "discovery" of questions often does. Consider, for example, the following message from a Lithuanian student to her peers in Germany, which came in response to their speculation about Recreation and Leisure in the year 2097:

You mentioned, that computers will replace the work so that people won't have to work any more. Theey'll [sic] be able to spend more time with their family or to travel. The question is: where will they get money from, if they aren't going to work any longer? I think they'll get bored soon. (*Utopian Visions*, 1997)

If we want students to interrogate information and conduct more scholarly investigations online, we must provide opportunities for meaningful inquiry and thoughtful dialogue. Was new technology responsible for making that happen in *Utopian Visions '97*? I don't think so. The biggest improvement came in the form of human commitment, which began with an application promising active participation in our community of inquiry. What's more, despite the new innovations, electronic mail remained the project's common denominator for the third consecutive year. Four of the eight participating schools lacked access to the Web; our electronic mailing lists provided their only medium for communication with distant peers. By now, Lowell and I had refined the project's design, internalizing it so thoroughly that we could articulate it more effectively. The technical logistics were also less of a mystery, which meant I could dedicate more time to the online discussions. As the project coordinator, a teacher without a class, I enjoyed nurturing the dialogues and watching them acquire a life of their own. In the process I discovered several critical duties for coordinators of telecollaborative activities, which subsequent experience with *Utopian Visions '98–'99* reinforced. I'll express them in terms of an earlier metaphor.

Plant the Seeds

Recruiting participants is more than just a matter of finding half a dozen volunteers. You want to find people who will collaborate, not just participate. This means identifying students and teachers who will make a commitment to the project, corresponding with other participants, encouraging dialectics, and doing far more than just submitting items to the listserver or Web site. As every gardener knows, not every seed will yield a healthy plant. The same applies here. The coordinator is responsible for planting an abundance of seeds, which means scattering the "Call for Collaboration" to educational listservers and the fertile soil of print and electronic media.

Cultivate

Though we might like to, it's best not to assume that potential collaborators know how to engage in dialectical discourse. Faculty coordinators must serve as models, cultivating dialogues by asking open-ended questions, demonstrating ways to weave threaded messages, and following guidelines. It's essential that coordinators alert one another to problems, sharing the many challenges that arise. I'm often dismayed to find that a group has disappeared from the mailing list without warning, only to hear two or three weeks later that a school holiday took them away. Cultivating dialectics requires consideration on the part of both speaker(s) and listener(s). We know this in face-to-face conversations; we need to learn it once more in asynchronous, online discussions.

Hoe That Row

Logistics will never take care of themselves. Even with all the new devices incorporated in *Utopian Visions '97–'99*, no automated responses or digital shortcuts could solve every problem. For instance, in 1997 the coordinators in Mexico had trouble joining our electronic mailing list. When asked if our listserver was faulty, because it rejected their efforts to subscribe, I requested a copy of the error message. What should I find? They had submitted the request *suscribir* to the listserver instead of "subscribe." I responded as best I could in Spanish, joking that we lacked a bilingual listserver and that they should try once more with the English verb instead of the Spanish. The following day they sent the request to *suscribe* instead of "subscribe," prompting yet another error message. Patience is a virtue at such times, and so is empathy. Had we relied upon an impersonal FAQ list (frequently asked questions), ignoring individual problems, I'm certain we would have lost potential partners, and frustrated many more. If they were willing to brave the challenge of communicating in a foreign language, they deserved personal attention and reassurance from time to time.

Meanwhile, I needed to teach participants discursive habits that would enable dialogues rather than sabotage them. This required a deliberate strategy and methodical implementation, beginning with the identification of messages. Through trial and error we devised a set of simple conventions, but they required a consistent and collective effort. If successful, they would help participants identify the source and content of e-mail messages, follow discussion "threads," and create personal databases for future reference. Much of this relied upon one of the simplest, yet most neglected, features of an e-mail message: the subject line. For each submission, participants employed one of five "message labels" to indicate the message genre, followed by keywords identifying specifics. For example, the subject line of a category report would read, "Reports: Municipality/Category/Year" (e.g. "Reports: Budapest/Arts/1897"). The other message labels would alert participants to the arrival of a "Dialogues" message, a description of "Participants," a submission to the UV "Library," or logistical matters for "Coordinators."

I feel strongly enough about the significance of "subject lines" to take a regulatory approach when I "hoe" this particular row. Otherwise, vague or ambiguous subject lines ("Greetings!") undermine the dialogues, enabling the misplacement or neglect of student work. Such was the case when one group identified their submission as a "Pollution" report, falling somewhere between the "Environment" and "Health" categories. After weeks of research, in-class discussion, and preparation of that report they were in jeopardy of receiving no reply because no one else had studied that "category"—and so no one else felt obligated to reply. These are not purposeful errors, just human ones. As such, they merit a human response. Without it, conversation may give way to chaos.

Irrigate

Showering participants with genuine praise is one of the coordinator's great pleasures. However, it's easy to neglect this duty if we become preoccupied with logistics. One complimentary note often has more impact than five cautionary messages reminding people how to identify reports or avoid common mistakes—essentially pointing out the error of their ways. I'm not advocating insincere flattery or messages that "damn with faint praise." I am, however, reminding tele-coordinators to bring a generous spirit to their work. This can be accomplished through short, private messages or public listserver submissions; either way, it remains an essential requirement for successful coordination.

Survey the Field

The coordinator's work is never done. We must monitor the "health" of individual plants, take note of dry patches, and beware of potential infestations. I make a point to send a private note to the respective coordinators every week, many of which go unanswered, but at least convey my concern for them. I also make public appearances each week in the respective mailing lists, one reserved for student "Dialogues" and the other for faculty "Coordinators." A brief question or response to another's message furthers the discussion and provides a model for others. Mental notes, I've learned, are seldom worth the paper they're written upon. Therefore, I'd advise coordinators of telecollaborative projects to make a checklist of their duties, helping themselves anticipate responsibilities that a "catch as catch can" approach might neglect.

Weed judiciously

It's an ugly, yet necessary job. I do not enjoy it, nor do I neglect it. In every telecollaborative activity there's the potential for weeds to grow in the garden you've planted and cultivated so diligently. What will you do when a student sends a rude message to one of his counterparts? Bring the project to an abrupt ending, or approach this as an opportunity for learning? What action do you take when students begin using the mailing list as a personal chat channel? What if a coordinator misunderstands directions? The project coordinator must be prepared for such occasions. They *will* occur. The myopic individual wrings his hands, claiming this proves the Internet is evil. Those with foresight, however, will anticipate them, confronting problems to teach participants what is appropriate and what methods encourage human communication rather than discourage it.

In every telecollaborative project that Lowell and I have organized I've witnessed volatile exchanges of one kind or another, as well as some embarrassing scholarship, inappropriate language, and questionable taste. In each instance I felt it necessary to address this with the students and faculty involved via "private" e-mail or, whenever possible, face-to-face discussion. If the behavior persisted, I took it to the more public forum of the mailing list to call attention to it in a general manner, responding firmly, and reminding everyone of the project's fragile nature. As yet, we've not had to abort a project due to "irreverence and unruliness," but given the counsel students receive from "wiredstylists" and the kind of discourse that some MUDS, MOOs, and chat rooms inspire, faculty coordinators should be prepared to confront online misbehavior just as they do classroom disturbances.

Enjoy the Harvest

Easy to say, yet so hard to do. One of the best pieces of advice I received as a young teacher came from a mentor who said, "Always find something positive to say about their work, even if it's to praise their penmanship." Alas, with the advent of the word-processor, the language arts teacher lost that opportunity. Nonetheless, at least once every week coordinators should make a point to thank someone for their contribution to the discussion. It sets a collegial tone, reminding participants that an online community of inquiry relies upon the kindness of strangers. Considering all the obstacles that must be overcome—technological, curricular, linguistic, cultural, and more—it's hard not to marvel at the dialogues that *do* take place. The least we can do is to thank those who have offered their time, energy, and intellect in a charitable and humane fashion. Students often emulate this and begin thanking each other for a report or reply. The caveat, of course, is to avoid disingenuous praise; look for something genuinely positive and applaud it, rather than focusing on what's going wrong all the time.

Tools 'R Us

> Now, what I want is Facts. Teach these boys and girls nothing but Facts. Facts alone are wanted in life. Plant nothing else, and root out everything else.
>
> Dickens (1967, 1)

A telecollaborative project clearly challenges conventional curricula and pedagogy. What's more, if we think of a project such as *Utopian Visions* as both a "container" and a "tool" we realize that it simultaneously presents the static quality of an archive and the dynamic qualities of a classroom discussion. Despite its relatively stable structure and half a decade's evolution, no two iterations of *Utopian Visions* have been alike, for each was flavored by the personality of its participants and contemporary events. Consequently, as the project coordinator I cannot predict what will happen from one year to the next. Though I may try to anticipate extremes and mitigate the chaos, I couldn't have predicted that *Utopian Visions '98* would be composed entirely of novices, some of whom struggled to participate despite technical difficulties while others dropped out of the project without explanation. Nor could I have foreseen the way that NATO's intervention in Kosovo would disrupt *Utopian Visions '99,* prompting participants in Estonia, Lithuania, and the United States to dismiss the project's guidelines for an emotional discussion of dystopian realities.

All of which prevents me from speaking about telecollaboration—from design to implementation and coordination—in terms that would've pleased Dickens's insufferable schoolmaster, Mr. Gradgrind. What are "the facts" with respect to telecollaboration? What lessons might we draw from the evolution of the *Utopian Visions* project? Perhaps one more agricultural analogy will help. Every gardener knows that tools can be used as weapons. The difference is often just a matter of how one holds the tool—or employs it. The Internet presents both a container and a set of tools, but if we stare too intently at the surface of that container we may lose sight of the tools' potential for both good and evil.

Modern attitudes toward education and educators leave much to be desired, yet one hopes we've made progress since Mr. Gradgrind uttered his infamous creed more than a century ago. There's evidence to the contrary, however, which means we must continue arguing for a departure from curricular structures and pedagogical practices that fail to question "facts," challenge authorities, and stimulate higher order thinking skills. Information may interest or entertain a child, but it makes a fleeting impression unless we provide opportunities to construct meaning from it. As a number of educators and philosophers have observed, information is not knowledge, nor is knowledge wisdom.

Knowledge is private, while information is public. Knowledge, therefore, cannot be communicated; only information can be shared. Whenever an attempt to communicate knowledge is made, it is automatically translated into information, which other learners can choose to absorb, act upon and transform into their own knowledge, if they so desire. (Harris 1998, 59)

To acquire knowledge, and wisdom, students need far more than information from a container, or skills with a tool; they need inspiration, patience, imagination, and dialectics. In short: they need to realize their humanity. When it comes to educational telecollaboration, meanwhile, educators need courage and discretion, the former to fly from curricular labyrinths, the latter for restraint.

Without this dialectical tension, the delicate balance between personal vision and community expectations, there's small chance we'll ever "fly halfway between the two" extremes of personal whim and curricular stagnation. If we cannot strike that balance we're destined to flap our collective wings, admonishing our children like Daedalus, only to witness another fall or prevent their flight altogether. After all, Icarus had "access to information" and the skill to fly from his labyrinth. What he lacked was the knowledge that technology can fail and the wisdom to realize there was no safety 'Net.

6

The Global Suburb

Lowell Monke

The very structure of our technological civilization prevents us from communicating in depth with the native peoples.
Thomas Berry (1988, 181)

We have now worked our way through the evolution of the Utopian Visions *projects. Each of them taught us a number of specific lessons about using telecollaboration in the classroom. It is now time to move on to consider some of the broad issues that cut across these and other Internet projects.*

One of the major educational attractions of the 'Net is its global nature. Utopian Visions *eventually enabled our students to communicate with peers from many different parts of the world. This we assumed to be one of the clear benefits of our continued collaboration.*

In this chapter we will examine that assumption and in the process confront two of the mantras of educational telecommunications—the development of multicultural awareness and citizenship in the "global village." These are surely to be counted as benefits of using the 'Net in schools. Or are they? Once again we find that this technology is the bearer of many unintended consequences.

Marshall McLuhan is generally credited with coining the term "Global Village." He certainly popularized it (McLuhan, 1964). McLuhan believed that electronic communication would eventually so connect all cultures of the world that the sense of both time and space would become compacted (McLuhan & Powers 1989). This contraction of the world would result in the development of a pervasive sense of village life writ large—the planet would begin exhibiting the characteristics of a small town, with all of the close-knit qualities that this metaphor calls to mind. McLuhan himself actually was not so sanguine about this prospect as many of his disciples, who used the pastoral,

nostalgic image of village life, where everyone had a place and everyone looked out for everyone else, to promote the development of a global communication network. Still, McLuhan did see many benefits arising from the shrinking of the planet, one of which was the greater tolerance for hitherto incompatible cultures. Starting close to home, he predicted that, "most Americans will be able to tolerate many different thought systems at once, some based on antagonistic ethnic heritages" (McLuhan & Powers 1989, 86). Just how this tolerance would be managed psychologically or socially he didn't make clear, but he was optimistic that, contrary to homogeneous conditions in most traditional villages, cultural diversity would continue to thrive in the global one.

Neither Buddy nor I set out with any intentions of putting McLuhan's predictions to the test. Yet as one project led to another and certain patterns began to emerge, I couldn't help but wonder if the kinds of communities we encountered in cyberspace were what McLuhan had in mind.

East Meets West in the Looking Glass

Our first telecollaborative effort, *Project Utopia,* produced two visions of the perfect society: Fredonia and Yamagata. The former title paid homage to freedom, the central value articulated by American society. The latter, drawing on the traditional emphasis on aesthetics in some Eastern societies, worked off of the motto "Happiness is Beauty, Beauty is Happiness." Clearly, there was potential to explore the confrontation between very different worldviews. It didn't happen. Instead, each group described remarkably similar utopias: governments that were democratic; economies that exhibited strong centralized controls; a heavy emphasis on environmental protection (recycling was big in both utopias); free education and health care; and further development of high technology. Indeed, though there were certainly subtle cultural differences that could be teased out of the two documents, they were so similar that one of the students wrote in her evaluation, "It got to the point where there was nothing left to discuss, and the interest level was hard to keep up" while another student got the idea that, "Through this project we learned the ideals of the other cultures. But obviously, most people's ideas will be somewhat similar."

It wasn't long after the conclusion of this project that I attended a workshop led by one of the early pioneers in applying the Internet to learning in the classroom. I was struck by an example she gave that echoed the observation of that last student. She had recently worked with a group of fourth grade students in North Carolina who shared information about their lives with students in Alaska. "What struck these students most," the woman said, "was that students in Alaska eat at Pizza Hut just like them." The point she was making, which met with general audience approval, was that such exchanges are often valuable not

so much for discovering the cultural differences in people from different parts of the world but in helping students see the similarities.

Had it not been for the experience with *Project Utopia* I might have been tempted to ridicule an observation based on such superficial similarities. But after more thought I realized that this 'Net guru and the high school student were both onto something important, though I don't think either of them recognized just exactly what it was. Telecollaborating students do learn that they have a surprising amount in common with children from other cultures, and in fact, that all cultures are far more similar than they are different. They learn this for the simple but generally obscured reason that the cultures of students who have access to the 'Net, regardless of where they are in the world, share a common techno-culture that subsumes whatever local culture may exist. This is not to say that all technological societies are the same. In many ways each local society retains some of its peculiar customs. But when it comes to the major issues of conducting our life and business activities at the global level, which is the level at which more and more of our lives and business is being conducted, these customs are increasingly irrelevant.

For some observers, this is a change to be applauded. Michael Dertouzos, head of MIT's Laboratory for Computer Science, looks at what he calls the "cultural veneer" of an "Information Marketplace" imposed by the new digital communication technologies and sees it as a peacemaking trend.

This thin but universal cultural layer may help overcome polarization between nations that demand ethnic cohesiveness and others that strive for diversity. . . . A shared cultural veneer arising from the Information Marketplace might offer people a chance to retain their tribal identities while reaching out to share a universal experience. (1997, 283)

Others, with a somewhat more critical view of technology, see a less utopian outcome. Jacques Ellul, the French sociologist on whose work much of the analysis of technological society is founded, agrees that industrialized societies can adapt to the imperatives of new communication technologies, but the "tribal identities" they might retain will not be of much value:

It is just that each culture is made obsolete. It lives on under the technical universal but no longer has any usefulness or meaning. We can still speak our own language. We can read the poets and great writers. But all this is simply an amiable dilettantism. The astonishing thing is that what is fully achieved with all this is the judgment of the nineteenth-century middle class that art, literature, the classics, poetry, etc., are simply a matter of pleasure and distraction and bear no relation to serious matters. They are pleasant whims when important matters have been settled. (1990, 144)

The important matters to which Ellul refers are those political, social, and economic issues that govern our public lives. These matters tend to be settled

more and more according to the values on which the technological society operates and proliferates throughout the world. George Ritzer, who calls this proliferation "The McDonaldization of Society," names four fundamental values of the technological society: Efficiency, Calculability, Predictability, and Control; all of which he lumps together under the title Rationalization (1996). What struck me about both Fredonia and Yamagata was that while the idealistic principles of freedom and beauty both tend to lead to some very messy social consequences, the societies these students proposed were both extremely well-ordered, that is, rational. Rather than welcome the internal contradictions of a society based on individual freedom or the inefficiency of one based on the glorification of beauty, they "solved" the dilemmas we face today by constructing a rational structure that to a great extent denied the very values on which their societies were nominally based.

I don't want to be too harsh in my judgment of two groups of high school students who surely saw much less significance in what they were doing than I have from the distance of several years. To observe that their societies were both rational is not to find fault, but merely find evidence of Ellul's and Ritzer's claims. And, in any case, it is not my intention to argue here the relative merit of such a worldview (you probably already have a hint of what that argument would be from chapter 2). What I want to stress here is not the kind of views these students displayed, but that they were so much alike. At the time I passed it off as simply a missed opportunity for exploring cultural pluralism. Three years later a blunder I made during *Utopian Visions '96* helped me to recognize that it was more than that.

The Case of the Lost Continents

Utopian Visions '96 was the first project in which we asked students to submit a personal vision of utopia. It was also the first project that included a Web site. The Web site was actually an afterthought, proposed by one of my students as his major project in my Advanced Computer Technology class. The class wasn't otherwise involved with *Utopian Visions '96*, but the student was willing to design a site that would archive every bit of correspondence that took place during the project. So we put him to work.

By the time he had completed the structure of the Web site most of the personal visions had already been submitted and distributed via the listserver. There were over a hundred of them and separating them all out of the messages in which they had been sent (most schools had collected and sent them together in one or two messages), copying them, putting appropriate HTML tags on them, and uploading them to the Web page was a monumental task. My student enlisted the help of two others from the class to help with this part of

his project. I reminded all of them to be sure to cut out all of the lengthy e-mail headers that accompanied the messages. It never occurred me, or them, that in doing so we were also deleting the only indication we had as to what school the students came from. It wasn't until after all the personal visions had been uploaded to the Web page that I discovered the error. Anyone reading the essays wouldn't know where they came from—and neither did we.

After considerable head scratching (and much silent cursing of their teacher I'm sure) the students decided they would have to go back through the listserver messages and match them up with the ones on the Web pages. Again I gave them what I thought was sage advice: take a quick look at each Web page message you are trying to match. Since these are visions of a perfect society you should at least be able to tell which continent the student came from. See if it reads like something an American would write, or a Japanese or a European. If they could have done this, it would have cut their search considerably. They couldn't. But then, they were all midwestern high schoolers who had never set foot outside the country. I had traveled all over the world and lived on three continents. I figured it wouldn't take me long to spot different cultural orientations. So I tried. I was embarrassed to discover that I couldn't do it either. The writers had come from Australia, Asia, Eastern and Western Europe, and North America but on the vast majority of their utopian visions they had left no cultural fingerprints. There were individual differences aplenty, but the core values that guided these idealistic messages seemed to have no geographic markers.

Perhaps this is an indication that the world really is beginning to sing in perfect harmony. If so, then the global village envisioned by McLuhan has indeed arrived via the electronic telecommunications grid. But I think there is another explanation for this homogeneity of telecollaborative youth—one that conjures visions not of a global village but something more disturbing.

The Virtual Empire

In choosing as his metaphor "Global Village" McLuhan obscured just what Ellul made clear—that our tolerance for diversity of cultures would grow out of the impotence of local cultural mores to actually govern people's lives. All cultures are granted entrance into the electronic village, but only if they first dump their own governing traditions at the village's cultural landfill (or hide it carefully in their homes). In fact, rather than a global village, the qualities engendered by the global communications grid more closely resemble those of the gated communities that are becoming popular in affluent suburbs in the United States. Like those exclusive residences, the community life that has sprung up within that grid is more reminiscent of the self-justifying clubbiness of the far-flung colonials of the British Empire that was still flourishing just a century ago.

That the 'Net exhibits this kind of cultural exclusivity is not at all obvious to either children or teachers, and is certainly not included as a topic in 'Net curriculum guides. In fact, at first it seems ridiculous to suggest that the 'Net helps erect barriers between people. The culture of the 'Net is, by its nature, inclusive, freely available to all. The very structure of the 'Net is designed to thwart efforts to stymie the flow of information. But even this assertion betrays a technocentrism that equates "freely available" to freely available to anyone with a high-speed modem, computer, electrical outlet, and private phone line. Anyone who has traveled extensively in third world countries knows that this excludes the vast majority of the world's population. Those who live in areas of the world, including the third world, who have access to the sophisticated equipment needed to participate in the global community of the Internet lead a very different, and for the most part, separate life from those billions who do not.

I'll use my own experience to illustrate. The Ecuadorian students who attended Academia Cotopaxi when I taught there, like those enrolled in most private international schools in poorer countries, came from the society's upper class. They were comfortable relating to the children of international business people and diplomatic corps who filled out the population of the school. Indeed, these Ecuadorian citizens had much more in common with students from other international schools, or students from Des Moines Public Schools for that matter, than they did with Ecuadorian young people living just twenty miles outside of Quito, who attended schools without indoor plumbing, much less an Internet connection, or a computer, or even a telephone. This lack of technologically advanced facilities in the school environment is typical of both the high Andean and Amazon basin indigenous groups. But it is not simply a matter of impoverishment.

These are nontechnological cultures, and they exhibit not just different lifestyles but entirely different ways of thought and living from that of the students who attend the exclusive private schools in Quito. Many still live where electrical lines have not yet reached, guided by traditions that predate the Incas. If it is cultural diversity one seeks, it is under their thatched roofs that one should look, for there exists a way of life and thinking that most American children (not to mention adults) do not understand, and may only vaguely be aware exists. Yet it is not this culture that one encounters through telecollaboration. It is the affluent students from Academia Cotopaxi (which is now one of the few k–12 schools in the country with Internet access) who convey their impressions of life in Ecuador to other similarly influenced techno-elite children around the world, just like it is the affluent techno-elite children at the International School of Kuala Lumpur, rather than the children of the Sarawak tribe, who convey their impressions of life in that part of the world. This global network of techno-haves reinforce each others' impressions that they live in a homogeneous thought-world, comforting each other that life is familiar shades of a single color and leading Internet gurus to extol the virtue of the 'Net as a means for discovering commonalities among "all" people of the world. The irony of this sort of technologically engendered "homogeneous multiculturalism" is, of course, that the similarities being discovered are those that high technology itself has spread.

The New Iron Pot

One of the consequences of homogeneous multiculturalism on the 'Net is that it tempts us to ignore the imperialistic qualities of the developing global electronic grid. Dertouzos tells of chairing a panel on global communication at a conference for CEOs of the world's largest companies. Among the panelists were Rupert Murdoch and Michael Spindler, then CEO of Apple Computer. At the end of the session Dertouzos was handed a handwritten question from the audience. It was written by the famous violinist, Yehudi Menuhin. Menuhin asked, "When are all these new technologies finally going to let us hear from the voiceless millions of this earth?" (1997, 284). Dertouzos admits that "No one of us could tackle the great violinist's question" (284). But that didn't dim his optimism. No wonder. Within two pages of acknowledging Menuhin's challenge, Dertouzos predicts how easily all of these voices will eventually be heard:

The Information Marketplace, with its powerful force of electronic proximity, can help us *all* reach a more common understanding through widespread sharing of modest daily activities. We will visit museums together; attend plays and sporting events and street demonstrations together; chat next to virtual water coolers together; play games, bid at auctions, pursue romances, and obtain degrees together—much of it internationally. (286) (emphasis added)

Think about how many of those virtual activities cited above would make sense to an Iban tribesman in Sarawak, or even an elder of a Navaho Indian tribe, and it will become instantly clear that this techno-utopia is one in which cultures without water coolers simply do not exist. As Ellul observes, "When these technocrats talk about democracy, ecology, culture, the Third World, or politics, they are touchingly simplistic and annoyingly arrogant." (1990, 29)

What this bit of blinkered mentality illustrates is that the answer to Menuhin's question is probably "Never." But then, Menuhin was asking the wrong question. Providing "equitable" access to the currently dispossessed is neither an answer to the problem of ethnic strife nor a means of empowerment to indigenous people. As Jerry Mander's *In the Absence of the Sacred* (1991) and Stephen Hill's *The Tragedy of Technology* (1988) make depressingly clear, nontechnological societies cannot use electronic communication technology without changing the way they think, the way they act, the way they live—in other words, without abandoning their traditional cultures. This is what Thomas Berry is talking about when he says that the structure of technology itself is what prevents us from communicating in depth with native peoples. Just as it was impossible for eighteenth- and nineteenth-century settlers to understand the native Americans' unpossessive, sacred view of the land, today it is impossible to communicate through high technology with societies whose cultures are founded on unmediated human interaction. They are locked out of the global conversation, not able to enter the electronic gated community until they have traded in their "backward" ways of thinking and communicating for the more upscale, modern, expensive one.

This inaccessibility certainly isn't a new development. Children in the United States have long looked at pictures and movies of exotic places and peoples and learned bits and pieces about those cultures without being able to communicate with them. What is different today is that the 'Net connects children to those exotic locations (or near enough to be taken as such), and presents the illusion that even in these distant lands all people pretty much think alike. When a group of students from Uganda joined *Utopian Visions '99,* even I had to fight off the *National Geographic* images that were conjured in my mind, and constantly remind myself that the teacher and students I was conversing with were not the remote villagers of travelogues but city dwellers with considerable knowledge of Western ways and a more than adequate command of written English.

The illusion that the good folks we meet in our Internet projects represent all, or even much, that is Uganda, or Ecuador, or Malaysia is not only ill-founded but dangerous. For not only is it likely that thousands of ill-prepared telecomputing teachers are unwittingly deceiving their students about the characteristics of nontechnological cultures associated with these lands, the spread of the global communications grid seems to be playing a big role in exterminating them. We know that culture is tied closely to language. The University of Bristol Center for Theories of Language and Learning (1995) has reported that "According to reliable estimates, half of the world's six thousand languages will become extinct in the next century. Furthermore, two thousand of the remaining three thousand languages will be threatened during the century after next." Certainly the spread of the 'Net, which has increased the demand for the use of regional, national, and global languages like English, Spanish, and Japanese to conduct its business, will contribute mightily to the extinction of these local languages.

Long before the Internet arrived on the scene, Ellul pointed out the inevitability of its effects on nontechnological cultures:

Technicians have not willed this outcome; no one seeks consciously to destroy a civilization. This is simply the proverbial collision between the earthenware pot and the iron pot. What happens, happens, despite the best possible intentions of the iron pot. (1964, 124)

It may well be that the destruction of the high Andean and Amazon basin cultures is inevitable, along with the Iban of Sarawak. If so, then the answer to Buddy's question of whether we can integrate without annihilating is a resounding "No!" The longhouse may live on, but only as a meaningless museum piece, much like the floating reed communities of Lake Titicaca that I visited in Peru, where the reed "dwellers" motor out to the floating beds before dawn, just ahead of the tourists. In both cases, the physical artifacts will rapidly become empty shells of a culture that no longer gives direction to the lives of the local people, for whom they are now only necessary to draw a wage.

But it is fair to ask, so what? These cultures are tiny, and seem very far away from us and, thus, their survival may not have any significance for our lives.[1] If we think about it carefully, I think we will find that the idea that these nontechnological cultures are so remote as to be insignificant is, in itself, another deception created by the same compression of space that I discussed in chapter 4. The Amazon rain forest is far closer physically than Russia, yet when students from Moscow exchanged yearnings for nuclear disarmament with children in California in 1991, it was seized upon by telecomputing advocates as an illustration of how significant the shrinking of distance between cultures can be. Yet it is just this psychological compression of space between techno-have children that makes the nontechnological cultures, and the environments in which they live, seem even more remote, and their survival less relevant, even though it is the extension of this compressing technology itself that is a primary cause of their demise.

All of this is happening at the same time that we hear social critics claim that the thought-world of the indigenous, nontechnological societies is precisely what we need today to "reorient the consciousness of the present occupants of the North American continent toward a reverence for the earth, so urgent if the biosystems of the continent are to survive" (Berry 1988, 184). It is ironic that concern for the environment is a consistent theme in each iteration of the *Utopian Vision* project, yet those who perhaps have the most to show us about how to live at peace with the biosystem are excluded from the conversation.

The point that I am trying to make is not that nontechnological societies possess a better way of life than ours. What I want to get across is precisely the argument that proponents of cultural diversity make when pushing Internet projects: that diverse views strengthen our civilization, that they help us in our pursuit of truth in precisely the way Buddy describes in talking about the "indispensable opposition." What a jolt to the minds of Pat Ramsey's students it would have been if a group of Sarawak or even Navaho elders could have participated in Project Utopia and articulated their vision of a perfect society. Of course, their offspring might one day be able to do just that (indeed, may be doing it now), and through the Internet. But it is likely that what they promote will be only a consciously reconstructed remnant of a way of life that was once as unquestioned and all-encompassing as our techno-culture is for us today. Their arguments will be undercut by the very fact that in order to enter our dialogue they have had to use our cognitive tools and, therefore, to a great extent, compromise their traditional way of thinking.

The Gated Mind

None of what I have just said should be taken to imply that there are no cultural differences between, say, the Lithuanian and Mexican students who have participated in our projects. The differences are smaller and less easily revealed than we may have anticipated, but they remain differences all the same, and like the small but meaningful differences between family members, they still lead to misunderstandings and conflicts. So perhaps we might yet have hopes that the 'Net, in at least connecting all the members of the techno-family, could help us to overcome some of the alienation and misunderstandings that result from these smaller, but very real, diversities.

That's a more modest and reasonable position, I think, and the *Utopian Visions* projects seem to have generally moved students toward that goal. Each year student evaluations of the project include comments like this one from Verl, Germany:

We learned something about the history and present situation of our town/region. We could compare our informations and situations to all the other participants. We got closer to the opinions and dreams of pupils from all over the world.

It's that last sentence that makes telecollaboration such an attractive educational vehicle. Like no other medium, it allows us to go over, around and through the physical barriers that separate us. Yet if we recall the ecological character of technologies, we shouldn't be surprised that this overcoming of physical barriers is accompanied by the erection of other psychological ones, and it is the psychological fences that ultimately must be torn down to achieve tolerance for cultural differences. These mental barriers are even more difficult to deal with than the physical ones because they are invisible. Rarely do we see just how high and dividing they are. We may not even recognize where they have been erected. And if we don't we may find that telecollaboration does little to help students embrace diversity where it matters most—within their own communities. In fact, it may be that the 'Net not only keeps the nontechnological peoples of the world out, it can help lock our students inside even smaller psychologically gated communities. Again let me draw on one of my own painful experiences to explain.

Throughout my collaboration with Buddy, I taught in a unique school. Central Campus provides special programs that cannot be supported at the five high schools in the Des Moines school district. From vocational programs like Auto Body Repair to business courses like my Advanced Computer Technology class, lots of small programs are offered to students who spend half a day with us and half a day at their home school. Central Academy is an accelerated program for gifted and talented students within Central Campus. The Advanced Placement Economics class that Mike Schaffer teaches, and which participated in the South African Project, fits into that program. Until recently, interspersed among the Academy classrooms were the English as a Second Language (ESL) classes. Des Moines has, for a variety of reasons, become a popular final destination for refugees and immigrants from all over the world. The ESL program has exploded in the district and Central Campus is the first stop for most high schoolers trying to learn English. Even though the program is a revolving door, moving students to their home schools full-time as quickly as possible, there are constantly more than 200 ESL students attending Central Campus.

One day, near the end of the *Utopian Visions '95* project, I happened to be standing outside my room, just down the hall from the doors going into an AP Language Arts room and an adjacent ESL room, when the bell rang to end classes. I watched the two groups of students emerge from their rooms, walk side-by-side out the narrow twenty-foot corridor that spills into the hallway, turn the same direction, and walk to their lockers, many of which were directly opposite each other in the hall. From the time the doors opened until the time the halls were cleared I never saw anyone from one class talk to a person in the other class. Indeed, to the Language Arts students the ESL students seemed more like obstacles to navigate around than interesting people to engage.

I don't blame the students for this, and I don't want to paint them as callous snobs. They were merely doing what all students do in a large school: associating with their friends, learning to let the mass of humanity flow by. But what really caught my attention was that most of the volunteers I was working with in the *Utopian Visions '95* project were among the students emerging from the Language Arts class. Here we were exchanging ideas about cultures with students on the other side of the planet and it had never dawned on them (or me, for that matter) to merely turn their heads ninety degrees and introduce themselves to students from Bosnia, Somalia, the Sudan, Russia, Mexico, the Czech Republic, and half a dozen other nations. The disjunction unnerved me. But the hardest slap to my pedagogical face was the realization that I had never before even thought about the real and present people who attended the ESL program as valuable contributors to multicultural learning. Instead I had looked to the 'Net and the disembodied text arriving from people none of my students would ever meet.

Why had I let this happen? Put aside for a moment the possibility that it was just my own stupidity (subsequent discussions with other teachers uncovered only one, the always innovative Mike Schaffer, who was helping his students connect with ESL students by inviting them into his classes as guest lecturers). To teach within shouting distance of Bosnian refugees, or as students to walk every day down the hall with them, and yet never even think about engaging them in discussions about their homeland, indicated to me a psychological barrier that had its foundation built on something far sturdier than mere feeble-mindedness.

The Benefits of Blindness

Face-to-face interaction always carries some emotional risks. Stepping across the hallway to introduce myself to someone I don't know takes a certain amount of courage. What will the reaction be? Rejection? Incomprehension? What is there to talk about? Given that I will see that person nearly every day for the rest of the year, what will the long-term consequences be? Do I really want to strike up a relationship with someone who is new to the city, has a poor command of English, may not share any of my interests? What if the person decides to become more of a friend than I want? Besides, that person looks different and acts a little odd. All of these concerns are the common inhibitors of young people in any social circumstances. They are merely heightened when dealing with strangers from strange lands. In most cases the thirst for knowledge will not overcome these fears and aversions. But all of these inhibitors tend to be muted over the 'Net. The implications of saying "hello" to someone in cyberspace does not carry all the psychological baggage that approaching someone in person does. It is much easier to disengage a relationship in cyberspace and therefore emotionally safer to start one. There is much less investment of oneself since there is much less of oneself that is present on the 'Net.

All of this has long been known. It is often restated in a more positive way as a means for overcoming social inhibitions and injustices. The common anecdote at educational technology conferences is how the shy girl, the homely boy, the minority, the disabled youth overcame the typical prejudices and his or her own inhibitions on the 'Net. Edwin Taylor and Richard Smith express this sentiment in observations of online physics classes they have conducted: "The medium is largely race-neutral, location-neutral, status-neutral, age-neutral, income-neutral, disability-neutral, and would be gender-neutral except for the clue of first names" (1995, 1093).

To a great extent this is all quite true. But what neither Taylor nor Smith nor any of the other promoters of the 'Net in education dwell on is just how this social egalitarianism is achieved in human terms. Actually, it's fairly simple—just make sure that the participants cannot see or hear each other. All of those neutralities would evaporate if the people involved had visual and aural contact. Thus, the lack of bigotry displayed in some online communication is accomplished not through the elevation of human sensibilities but by the amputation of human senses. Are blindness and deafness the means by which we wish to teach our children to suppress (rather than overcome) bigotry? Is it a great benefit of the 'Net that we cripple our children in order to spare them the trauma of colliding with social injustices? To what extent does this out-of-sight-out-of-mind approach to teaching tolerance actually foster tolerance in face-to-face relationships, where the issues of race, age, status, gender, etc. cannot be hidden behind an electronic wall? And, finally, what does this say about the evolution of our concept of education, when in order to reveal the world to students intellectually we willingly conceal the full humanity of those with whom they learn?

What I witnessed in the hallway that day has made me wonder just how much of whatever cultural awareness students learn over the 'Net gets transferred to their here-and-now, face-to-face social relationships. Does the 'Net encourage tolerance of real people who are different from ourselves or merely a sort of easy, inconsequential tolerance for distant, disembodied intellects that we don't have to confront in our hallways, in our streets or in our own neighborhoods? I once heard a minister refer to a common malady he called "The Missionary Syndrome." He described it to me as the condition that sometimes exists in churches where the members cheerfully give large donations to help those in need halfway around the world, whom they perceive as hapless victims of ignorance and poverty, but refuse to give a dime or a minute of time to help the needy in their own communities, whose human foibles they know all too well. Whether the analogy is accurate or not, it seems clear that the walls that form around our students' minds in school are not necessarily brought low by blowing on the horn of the Internet.

Communities That Aren't

What we seem to have encountered here is a paradox (one of many that swirl around the educational uses of the Internet). On the one hand, the 'Net helps people like Buddy and myself bring young people of somewhat diverse backgrounds together in an attempt to further their understandings of a wider range of possibilities that humans possess. On the other hand, the 'Net seems to have a fragmenting, isolating effect, producing what David Shenk, in his book *Data Smog*, calls "A Nation of Lonely Molecules." He claims that "the Net encourages a cultural splintering that can render physical communities much less relevant and free people from having to climb outside their own biases, assumptions, inherited ways of thought" (1997, 125). Because there is so much opportunity to communicate via the 'Net, the trend toward insulation from those physically around us, which began with the radio and became problematic with TV, has reached new dimensions. More and more we are able to draw up around us psychological walls that keep us apart from those physically close, while we commiserate at a distance through the 'Net with only those who share our narrow interests.

Teachers are not immune. After the incident in the hallway I began making some sporadic attempts to change the situation I had observed—to find a way to bring the cultural perspectives of these new Americans to the attention of the other students at Central Campus in some systematic or project oriented way. I found that trying to overcome the structural and psychological barriers of a highly segmented curricular system that narrows people's interests rather than broadening them proved to be overwhelmingly frustrating. Some of the causes of that frustration were similar to those Buddy has already mentioned in chapter 5 and will take up again in more detail in the next chapter. They are important enough that I will look at them from a different perspective again in chapter 8. But for now what is pertinent is to acknowledge that when I finally got around to asking myself the same questions I asked others, I found myself answering in much the same way. The walls that I would have to beat down were so thick, and the expenditure of energy required to do it so great, that I found all kinds of reasons to retreat to my room, plug into the Internet, and start discussing another online project.

There is a comfort we get from relating to like-minded souls, even if they are halfway around the world. It is, I believe, one of the dangerous seductions of the 'Net for educators. Isolated as we tend to be in our separate rooms, telecollaboration can serve as a convenient means of escape from the frustrating, difficult, but critical responsibility of breaking down both curricular and social barriers within our own school communities, of developing the qualities of tolerance and compromise through face-to-face dialogue on which healthy communities rely. As Shenk argues:

There is a great danger here of mistaking cultural tribalism for real, shared understanding. . . . A pluralistic democracy requires a certain amount of tolerance and consensus, rooted in the ability to understand a wide variety of perspectives and agree on common questions. In this country, we increasingly speak very different languages and different dialects of the same language. We share fewer metaphors, icons, historical interests, and current news events. Bill Gates' celebrated "asynchrony" is but an eloquent way of saying that in our new electronic world of endless communication options, we are "out of synch" with one another. (1997, 127)

Even as the Internet contributes to the destruction of cultural differences determined by physical place, it facilitates the growth of a new sort of cultural divergence—this one established by our own mental space. Though there are undoubtedly benefits to be gained from both trends, I am not hopeful about the consequences of purchasing familiarity with far-off lands with an increased sense of estrangement from our own.

My own weakness for out of synch communication, contrasted with Buddy's and my attempts to raise the level of tolerance and increase the ability to understand a wide variety of perspectives, illustrates the internal contradictions in this technology's relationship with the educational community. We encounter two forces working against each other: one profoundly human, attempting to bring diverse peoples together; the other, a product primarily of a communication technology that overwhelms us with information and an accompanying bureaucracy that gives us little room to maneuver, lures us into cubicles of special interests and like minds. Unfortunately, the second force is aided by a third one—the computer itself, which I have found can shrink the cubicle until there is room for only one. One final experience from another project illustrates how this happens.

The Media Matter, which Buddy will detail in the next chapter, was the first project in which my Advanced Computer Technology students participated. In some ways it was a success, but I was surprised at the resistance my students showed to communicating with students in other parts of the world. Most of these students were new to the 'Net and I expected a high level of excitement, at least for the opportunity to get online. But these were not the same kind of academic minded students I had worked with before—most of them found the computer the most, if not the only, interesting thing about school. As the project progressed their resistance grew until finally, after one student suggested that the students "might" be more interested in communicating through the Internet if I would just let them write "fun stuff" about themselves, I confided in Buddy:

[I]t interests me that my students are so into computers and so disinterested in telecommunications . . . What does that mean? I don't know. It sure seems strange. At the same time, they are asking me if they can check out software manuals to take home to read at night. Yuck! Tell me what is going on.

Buddy's response was quick and frighteningly accurate. His comments reminded me once again of the challenge posed to us by the computer.

I think McLuhan had the answer to this 30 years ago. Guess what it was? The myth of Narcissus. The story goes like this: a beautiful boy breaks the hearts of many a girl, letting them give chase, but never catch him. One day, one of the girls calls upon the gods to punish Narcissus for his cruel rejection of her love.

You know the rest. He comes to a clear, calm little pond and bends over to take a drink. But before he scoops his hands into the water he sees the most beautiful image he has ever encountered. The word "narcissist" has come to mean "one who loves himself" and yet, the ironic thing here is that Narcissus had NO CLUE that he was in love with himself. He lacked "self-knowledge." He repeatedly reached his hands out to the water to try capturing that gorgeous image before him. Thus, the gods—in typical Greek fashion—meted out punishment to fit the crime.

Let's apply this to your kids' fascination with the computer. They "think" that what they are in love with is this "image" that is "new" and "beautiful" and unlike anything else they've ever encountered. And yet, what they are really infatuated with is their own image, reflected in that screen. The computer is yet another "extension of humanity," and as those lacking self-knowledge, the essential initiation to the self, looking into it they fall in love with THEMSELVES. Need proof?

Consider:

-Are your kids more interested in seeing my kids' reports on the listserv or their own?

-Are your kids more interested in content or style of the letters they've written?

-That student who "just wants to write fun stuff"—is that because she wants to learn or because her vanity tells her she could look so much more beautiful if you'd let her flirt online?

-Are your students more interested in producing documents or Web pages?

-Why are so many people creating Web pages, anyway? (and why are they always telling everyone to look at their Web pages?).

McLuhan, a former English teacher, answers the future by looking at the past. I'm indebted to him for that. I think the answers to so many of our questions rest in stories like Ovid's Metamorphoses (the most brilliant collection of myths I've encountered, told as one continuous narrative in almost seamless fashion). The text is about all the strange "Metamorphoses" which are described in Greek mythology. And what are we facing now, other than a strange metamorphosis of our world?

Gotta close, but let me give you a chunk of McLuhan, to answer that question of yours:

> The Greek myth of Narcissus is directly concerned with a fact of human experience, as the word Narcissus indicates. It is from the Greek word narcosis, or numbness. The youth Narcissus mistook his own reflection in the water for another person. This extension of himself by mirror numbed his perceptions until he became the servomechanism of his own extended or repeated image. The nymph Echo tried to win his love with fragments of his own speech, but in vain. He was numb. He had adapted to his extension of himself and had become a closed system. (McLuhan 1964, 51)

Now then, might all the frustrations you've had with your students not be comprised in that final sentence? Have they not "adapted to the extensions of themselves and become a closed system"? It's up to us, as educators, to open them to others, to pull Narcissus's head away from the pond. If not, our students may face the same fate as Narcissus, who sat regarding that extension of himself until he withered, and died.

b.

Probably nothing in our correspondence over the years has had such a profound effect on me as that message. It went to the core of explaining the isolating influence of the computer that I had noticed in so many of my students over the years. It was as if Buddy had gotten inside their heads, or almost. Only one piece seemed to be missing, which I tried to supply in my response, along with what has continued to serve me as a primary justification for our work:

. . ."Closed system" is the essence of what these students are attracted to. I think it is not just narcissism in all cases, but that certainly contributes to some of them. It is also a refuge from the insane uncertainties of their personal lives in some cases. Think about being a teenager today and wouldn't you find the unemotional, deterministic character of the computer attractive in comparison to all the chaos that most of them cope with at home, on the streets and even in school? Combine the two ideas—narcissism and security—and I think we have a pretty good foundation for the irrational draw of the computer. And an even stronger justification for the kind of work we have been doing. The two topics, Utopias and Media, can be used as vehicles for drawing students attention to these very issues—maybe leading to real self-awareness as opposed to the ersatz kind of unconscious self-worship. I'm still not so sold on using telecommunications to do the investigations as you are, but it is better than not doing it at all . . .

Later,

Lowell

Are these accurate insights into the effects of computers on kids? Could the Web really be a modern day metaphorical reincarnation of Narcissus's pond? Talbott argues that the computer, more than any other tool, embodies our thoughts, our tendencies, our conscious and unconscious choices. It is such an expression of ourselves that "the one sure thing about the computer's future is that we will behold our reflection in it" (Talbott 1995, 32). In *Life on the Screen* (1995) Sherry Turkle observes the enormous popularity of MOOs and MUDs among college students and notes that many of these students use the simulations to test alternate personas, trying on new identities much as they would clothes in a store. What does this phenomenon indicate if not an absorption with one's "image" and a confusion between that image and the student's inner essence, which seems to have retreated so deeply within that it no longer beckons young people toward it? Does their infatuation with what takes place on that flat screen condemn our students to such a superficial sense of self that they can't look beyond its shallow image-making power into the depths of their own souls? Have we indeed developed an environment for our youth that more than anything else serves the culture of narcissism that Christopher Lasch (1979) called to our attention at the very moment the desktop computer arrived on the scene? If so, what does it mean that we are leading our children Pied Piper–like to its very edge?

Expanding the Mind

We are faced with a situation in which even as the world seems to be opening up to us, our minds are, in important ways, narrowing down. The 'Net, in supplying far more information than we can hope to cope with, furthers this trend by encouraging us to shuffle off to our own special interest groups. This is an effective way to increase expertise in small intellectual arenas, but it contributes little to the enlightenment of youth. Indeed, it discourages the development of an understanding of "The Big Picture" that young people need to be good world citizens.

We confront an unsatisfactory choice: walk away from the pool of cyberspace, knowing that its conforming yet fragmenting, connecting yet isolating influence will roll merrily along without us; or continue to labor in our small corner of the 'Net, trying to transform this tool into a means of building common ground among young people, even while in the larger sphere it pulls the common ground out from under our feet. It is both a frustration and a motivation: knowing that in a sense we have chosen to work in the belly of a beast, we feel an urgent need to reach as many youth as possible with opportunities for shared discourse, "something we desperately need to support our pluralistic culture" (Shenk 1997, 129). One of the reasons Buddy and I have chosen to pursue the theme of *Utopian Visions* is because it consciously focuses on the big picture, drawing students' attention away from their narrow interests to wrestle with, or at least acknowledge, the massive complexity of a pluralistic society.

Engaged Globally, Committed Locally

The 'Net encourages us to turn the populist political maxim of "Think Globally, Act Locally" on its head. We act globally, but as long as we stay physically in one place we cannot escape thinking parochially, if not altogether locally. As a consequence we find ourselves locked within the digital walls of a gated community of techno-haves without really being aware of it. What we have tried to do with the *Utopian Visions* project is turn this outward looking medium back on itself to help the world citizens we are charged with educating investigate the physical places in which they live. We hope that through that process they will come to appreciate the value of place itself in their lives. For *Utopian Visions '96* Buddy sent many of his students out into the Malaysian community to do their investigations. For *Utopian Visions '97* several of my students started their research by visiting the Iowa State Historical Society. We now try to get all of our participants to focus on their *municipalities* rather than their nations, not just to prevent overlapping contributions but to encourage students to pay closer attention to the actual place in which they live. How successful we have been is difficult to judge, for the effects of place, like those of cyberspace, are subtle and often indirect. But the experience I had with my own students in developing our 2097 report has raised some hope among all the doubts. In trying to predict where Des Moines was headed in the next 100 years a multitude of issues surfaced. Many of these issues grew out of the research done for the two previous reports of 100-year historical periods ending in 1897 and 1997, respectively. Throughout the four hours we devoted to discussing the direction our report would take, two large issues nagged at the students: what would happen to Des Moines in comparison to the rest of the United States and the world, and how would all of the different factors we had studied influence each other. Everything revolved around local place and complexity.

The conversations were frustrating, confusing, and even at times heated, because they dealt with *home,* the most significant place in a young person's life (and, by the way, a term that has no significance on the 'Net except as a qualifier for "page"). My students found that they couldn't help but relate their local environment to the larger, less controllable happenings of the world around it. They discovered, for example, the very thing we had missed two years earlier when the investigation had been nationally oriented: the remarkable cultural impact of the influx of immigrants into the Des Moines community. This getting at the big picture through a focus on the local, personal conditions of life made the investigation of society much more real than the abstract musings of *Project Utopia* or the many simulations that are served up to students both on the 'Net and via CD ROM.

Not only did the students become more aware of the impact of the varieties of cultures that had emigrated to Des Moines, but the ESL program that first called my attention to our earlier failure reemerged in a remarkable way as well. One of my participating students had been an ESL student just a few years before. His perspective as an immigrant from Vietnam had a strong effect on the direction our 2097 report took. But I am convinced that the influence he wielded was not based simply on the fact that he once lived in Vietnam (there were several other immigrants in the class), but because of the way he had conducted himself in association with the other students in the class for the better part of a year. His ideas and opinions had gained him considerable respect among his classmates due to his presence in their lives, his integrity, his work ethic. When he found that his experiences in Vietnam were applicable to our study the other students gave great weight to what he said. He represented a different culture to my students, but his effect on them could never have been so strong if it had not been carried to them through his character, something impossible to reduce to bits traveling across mere electronic pathways.

All of this is a matter of not only acting locally but of making a commitment to understand the local, personal context as well. The multicultural benefits of acting globally through the 'Net are, as I have tried to argue, mostly illusory. The physical village we live in is the only one we can truly know—and it is our responsibility as teachers to help our students come to know it well. If we can do that, then they will have a foundation, a real home, from which they can reach out to the rest of the world. Without that comprehension of their own community our students will have no basis on which to pass judgment on the ideas and customs they encounter in their online activities. Indeed, they will have no judgment at all. Instead, they will find themselves adrift, molecules floating in cyberspace, and we shouldn't be surprised if many of them seal themselves up into closed systems—the gated communities of the digitized mind.

And the Message Is . . .

In his book, *The Global Village* (1989), McLuhan predicted that any medium pushed hard enough will implode on itself and begin pushing us in exactly the opposite direction we intended. It may be that we have already pushed telecomputing too hard, for in terms of multiculturalism and the creation of a utopian global village it seems to be moving us away rather than toward our goals.

McLuhan, like Postman and others I have cited in this book, viewed the media as a governing force in our lives, independent of the content carried by it. That's the message in the aphorism "The medium is the message." But what that view represents is, as I said before, one side of a paradox. In sociological terms it represents the side of structure, the way in which our environment, in this case telecomputing, imposes its imperatives upon us. It is, obviously, the side that fascinates me and to which I too attribute a great deal of influence in our lives and in the way children learn. But we must not ignore the other side of the paradox, the side that issues from our own intentions and decisions—our agency. This is the side that Buddy so often and so stubbornly pushes back at me. It calls into play our human will and our conscious efforts to impose it on our environment. It is what we make of our tools in contrast to what they make of us. It is, in the end, a faith in human freedom. This too must be a powerful and important ingredient in our telecollaborative efforts. It is what gives hope and meaning to working in the belly of the beast, for it presupposes that we can impose, to some degree at least, our will on this medium. It supports our belief that we can use it to enhance some multicultural awareness and perhaps contribute to a more humane, tolerant society. It is the assumption on which we can take up the banner to fight against a school structure that strangles meaningful learning and that finds fulfillment in pedagogical victories no matter how small. In the next chapter Buddy will provide ample evidence of one such struggle, and human agency in all its gritty, often painful dimensions will be given full expression.

In many ways, trying to resolve the tension between structure and agency has shaped the personal dialogue and online projects that Buddy and I have shared over the years. I am greatly concerned that we are in danger of being swallowed by the structural imperatives of the medium, to be overcome by a technological system that has become essentially autonomous (Winner 1977). But I do not feel the situation is hopeless. If we come to know what the real challenges are, what the real barriers to understanding are, and what the limitations of these tools are, we may be able to use them more effectively than they use us. I'm not at all sure of that. But we must hope that the kind of effort we are making can accomplish something neither McLuhan nor the Greek myth tellers had considered: pull our students through the looking glass in order to help them develop meaningful relationships with the people, things, and events that make up their own communities.

7

The Media Matter

R. W. Burniske

... how nice it would be if we could only get through into Looking-glass House! I'm sure it's got, oh! Such beautiful things in it! Let's pretend there's a way of getting through into it somehow [. . .] She was up on the chimney-piece while she said this, though she hardly knew how she had got there.

Lewis Carroll (1983, 9)

Pulling students through the looking glass of a computer screen may prove more difficult than we imagined, particularly if they hardly know how they got there and why they stayed. As always, the first step is greater awareness of oneself and the world. Educators may, however, find it difficult to speak to such issues or guide their students' initiation until they've gained an understanding of this new medium and its impact upon those who enter it. Such understanding seldom comes easily, but it remains our best hope for discovering the influence of telecomputing upon our children, schools, and communities.

Toward that end, this chapter focuses upon a single telecollaborative project, attempting to convey "what goes on inside" such affairs. It is difficult to approximate the experience of a global telecollaborative learning activity through print media. However, by reflecting upon the genesis and evolution of a single project, from its creation to the subsequent trials and tribulations, I hope to provide a clearer picture of what may still seem a rather mysterious process. This is neither a flattering portrait nor an unequivocal indictment of telecollaboration in the classroom. Instead, it is a determined effort to represent things as we found them, in one particular instance, rather than as we might have wished them to be.

Literature, Language, and Society

In August 1995, while teaching at the International School of Kuala Lumpur, I had the chance to teach an English elective entitled "Literature, Language, and

Society," which I inherited from a host of predecessors who made of it whatever they would. The course had undergone a number of transformations, from a study of gender in advertising to the "found poems" of print media; it was the only true elective in an otherwise prescriptive language arts program and, if the truth be told, invented primarily to enable seniors in need of a second English credit to fulfill the requirements for December graduation, though it habitually stumbled through a second semester with a change of students (and sometimes instructor). As a result, student expectations were rather low, as indicated by one student's response to a questionnaire issued on the first day: "I just want a fun class without much homework."

I had different ideas, though. To begin with, I questioned the title of the course.

"Which came first?" I asked in our inaugural session, "literature, language, or society?"

My students, ten males between the ages of fifteen and nineteen (whose first languages ranged from Bahasa, Mandarin, Spanish, Arabic, and German to English), had difficulty understanding the question, let alone its significance. However, when I offered one possibility, that society came first, followed by language, then literature and contrasted it with the theory that language was required to create a society, which in turn defines its literature, the students saw the importance of this chicken-and-egg inquiry. So we began with research on the origins of language, from sign language and body gestures to the story of English, word etymologies, and personal narratives concerning recollections of one's "furthest back word." I moved intuitively throughout the first month, trying a variety of exercises to spark interest in topics that many of them had never considered before. I knew, instinctively, that if I couldn't get them to ask questions, to think about matters which they routinely, thoughtlessly, took for granted, that the transition to telecollaboration and a study of media would produce little more than unexamined platitudes. So I tried a variety of exercises, hoping to excite their collective imagination:

- We shared photographs conveying a significant personal story, attempting to "read" the images without annotations, before hearing the author's explanation of the document.

- We studied Vladimir Nabokov's short story, "Signs and Symbols," about a young man whose "referential mania" caused him to attach meaning to everything he encountered. This led to journal reflections on the myriad signs and symbols that a single street in Kuala Lumpur imposes upon its "reader" and the acts of interpretation required of us every day.

- We attended foreign language classes, each of us observing a language we didn't speak, noting facial expressions, body language, recurrent sounds, and the "culture" of that language community. We then shared observations to discuss what all languages have in common.

- We engaged in role playing activities to examine signs, symbols, and language in a social context. In one session, for instance, students adopted roles—from fireman to pyromaniac, convicted arsonist to pyrophobe—and simulated a town meeting that discussed a proposed ordinance increasing the number of fire extinguishers in public meeting places. I placed a fire extinguisher in the middle of the room and encouraged reaction to this "symbol."

This sampling from the first month of the "LLS" course demonstrates the pedagogical variety and experimentation that many teachers bring to their classes. While the technophobe fears the integration of technology will annihilate the humanities (and the technophile sees no problem with that!), I look upon this as another opportunity for open-ended inquiry and dialectical discourse. Certainly, the combination of technology and a humanities curriculum produces something new, but the introduction of networked computers does not mean all other resources and pedagogical strategies suddenly vanish. Let me emphasize, then, that the first month of this course did not involve computers for more than word processing or research in the school library. In fact, I was in no hurry to leave traditional, face-to-face discussions for online conversations. Before we undertook telecollaborative activities I wanted to establish healthy discursive practices, ones inspired by a Socratic method of teaching and respect for open-ended inquiries. That did not stop once we moved to a computer lab or began our study of the Internet as a medium; rather, it simply adopted new forms, allowing an integration of the technology without annihilating our purpose. This is not to say that technology had little impact upon this classroom and all who entered it. However, rather than hold technology at arm's length, as a threat to the humanities, or embrace it as a panacea—looking for excuses to use it at every opportunity, I sought to make it both a means of communication and a subject for critical inquiry.

Challenging Rhetoric

Throughout those initial weeks I drafted various designs for a telecollaborative project; I wanted to investigate emerging issues concerning "literature, language, and society," particularly as they manifest themselves in the media. At one point we examined, in discrete fashion, the typed script, audio presentation, and videotape of a documentary film depicting the collapse of the Tacoma-Narrows bridge in 1941. For the first time, several of the students understood what I meant by the "technology" of a printed page and significance of the "writing space" that different media establish (Bolter, 1991). They could also sense the importance of such insights, which contradicted the claims of media critics like Neil Postman, who identified the problem of "public discourse in the age of show business," but saw little hope for solutions:

The desperate answer is to rely on the only mass medium of communication that, in theory, is capable of addressing the problem: our schools. This is the conventional American solution to all dangerous social problems, and is, of course based on a naive and mystical faith in the efficacy of education. [...] It is the very principle of myth, as Roland Barthes pointed out, that it transforms history into nature, and to ask of our schools that they engage in the task of de-mythologizing media is to ask something the schools have never done. (Postman 1985, 162)

I respect Postman's views, and think they're an important contribution to public discourse, yet I found this passage both demoralizing and demeaning. I wondered if he were serious, or simply posturing. Was he losing faith in education or trying to revive moribund discourse by prompting a response? Who was Postman talking about, after all? For years, I had demanded that students enact Shakespeare's plays before watching video representations of them and resisted the temptation to show cinematic interpretations of novels because they overwhelm the literary experience that I wanted my students to have. Why was a man who encouraged a generation of teachers to think of teaching as a "subversive activity" now sounding so defeated and resigned? The more I thought about the media the more I realized the need to teach students how to analyze its psychological and social impact. Why couldn't schools—that is, *students and teachers*—"engage in the task of de-mythologizing media" and subject theories of communications theorists like Postman to critical analysis as well? The answer to that rhetorical question lies as much in the prescriptive labyrinths of our curricula as it does in the limitations of classroom teachers. As discussed earlier, the innovator must learn to circumvent the curriculum, lest a device constructed as a guideline should become a straitjacket.

So while I respected Postman's views, I felt compelled to challenge his rhetoric, which contributed to a polarized discussion of computer technology in education. Setting hype against hysteria merely drowns the more thoughtful voices in an impassioned sea of hyperbole. I had witnessed plenty of the former while attending the National Education Computing Conference in Baltimore, Maryland, in June 1995. On several occasions I winced at the gushing, uncritical presentations of technology in education. However, I was equally put off by reactionaries chanting the impotent mantra of latter-day Luddites ("Refuse it!") without investigating matters for themselves (Birkerts 1994). From the vantage point of a humanities teacher living in Kuala Lumpur, a city where the government continues to employ civil servants to censor unwanted print materials, access to the Internet was both singular and salutary. I enjoyed the novelty of rapid correspondence with friends in the antipodes, as well as access to information that government censorship previously denied. Yet, how could I convey that to people in North America who looked upon the Internet as just another form of television, perhaps an even more pernicious form? More important, how could I inspire my students to think for themselves, conducting an experiment right there in the school's writing lab that might help them explore some of their generation's definitive questions? I wasn't overly concerned with their answers to those questions. The first step was to simply awaken their curiosity, lest they forfeit their place in public debate because they failed to see the need for it.

As far as I could tell, from my position within an Islamic country in Southeast Asia, far too many people were segregating disciplines and adopting divisive postures; not enough were attempting to integrate technology and the humanities while assessing its impact. This produced the polarized discourse on the topic of computers in education. On one side, we had the reactionaries telling us to ignore something that simply wouldn't go away. On the other, however, we had technophiles speaking with missionary zeal about a "paradigm shift" that would transform our lives. While I admired their enthusiasm I was less impressed with their efforts to articulate new classroom paradigms. For one thing, how could bright, innovative people adopt such awful terminology? "Computer-based" education made it sound like they were schooling machines—or at least thinking of computers more than humans—while "computer-enhanced" seemed uncritical, as if any use of the computer were an educational "enhancement." Here was a movement in search of a modifier. Some might prefer "computer-assisted," conjuring images of robots while conferring more power to computers than humans, but I preferred placing emphasis upon the human beings behind the machines. We're talking, after all, about electronically supported, pedagogical tools, tools designed by and for human learners. The transition from slate chalkboard to LCD panel was a difference in both degree and kind. The computer was a medium through which educational activity occurred, but also the medium shaping the activity; thus, "computer-mediated" education sounded most accurate, and most in need of study.

This wasn't a matter of finding Truth somewhere between two extremes. Indeed, the truth may have transcended this political tug-of-war, hovering beyond the realm of petty debates. Nonetheless, there was much at stake. The advocates needed funding; the opponents feared for their (professional) lives. I could, at this point, have adopted conventional methodology: introduce students to the respective positions, stage an in-class debate pitting affirmative versus negative on a terse resolution, assign a research essay, and pretend we had settled the matter. But I've been there, donned that, and suffered for it. That approach inspires an educational charade, a game in which students and teacher pretend they're learning something when, in actuality, neither side takes any risks, questioning personal beliefs, expressing doubt, or testing ideas in a larger forum. Instead, both student and teacher drag their respective bias into the classroom, reciting beliefs they haven't fully examined (including the origins of those beliefs), arguing in rather strained, competitive terms, before taking their unexamined beliefs with them, along with the conviction that they're right, and their opponents are misguided fools. So much for public discourse.

And yet, what discursive models did my students have to emulate? Malaysia's constitution, as it stood then, mandated election victory for the United Malay National Organization (UMNO), the ruling party to which Prime Minister Mahathir bin Mohammed belonged. Meanwhile, political rhetoric in the West had deteriorated to a point at which televised authorities held forth, broadcasting views that support the interests of Big Business without giving much thought to their impact upon children and schools. How else might we explain the way in which political leaders promoted technology in education, supporting phenomenal expenditures without proof that it made any significant difference in learning? Is it any wonder that students don't know how to engage in public discourse? Is it any wonder that latter-day Luddites don't feel it necessary to conduct a thorough examination of hypertext and telecollaboration before rendering judgments? This makes for amusing "sound bites," but amounts to little more than playground antics.

The integration of technology and the humanities is both significant and daunting. Telling adolescents to "refuse it" does as much to satisfy their curiosity about technology today as it did to satiate their desire for premarital sex and reckless driving a generation ago. Meanwhile, embracing the technology with the idea that one's pedagogy will immediately benefit from "computer-enhanced" methods, is equally foolish. So I suspended judgment and challenged myself and my students to engage a series of troubling questions, not the least of which is one that haunts me still: *Is it possible to integrate technology without annihilating the humanities?*

Razing the Blind(er)s

> "We become what we behold."
> "The tools we shape, shape us."
> "The medium is the message."

Some truths we hold as self-evident. The rest merit skepticism. All of these maxims beg investigation. Unfortunately, despite their rebellious attitudes, adolescents often embrace an idea without subjecting it to critical inquiry. From their earliest comments I could tell that my students may have looked at the *what* of news reporting, but had seldom considered the *how* or *why* of it. This inspired some vague notions for a telecollaborative project, but nothing that I could fully articulate. I wanted to examine ideas ranging from William Blake to Marshall McLuhan, testing their accuracy while discussing their relevance to modern media. Yet, I confronted a "chicken-and-egg" question of my own. Should I design a project, then see if colleagues around the world were interested, or should I first survey the field to solicit interest, then hope for collaboration? I split the difference, sending out a "call for collaboration" on the electronic mailing list that I had previously used, before I even knew what the project would entail. I hoped to find a kindred spirit with the courage and energy to try something new. The mailing list seemed a sensible starting point, since it might attract virtual colleagues with whom I had established some rapport and credibility in previous telecollaborative projects:

Date: Sun, 27 Aug 1995
From: R. W. Burniske
To: Multiple recipients of list <jaring!isklproj>
Subject: THE MEDIA MATTER

Greetings from the tropics!

This is a test of the "isklproj" listserver. Those of you who subscribed to our last project, "Utopian Visions '95" might be interested to learn that it was awarded a 1st place prize in the Int'l Society for Technology in Education's annual contest.

Lowell Monke and I were invited to the NECC '95 conference in Baltimore, where we presented an overview and shared samples of student work through a Powerpoint presentation. Many thanks to all the school coordinators and students for their good work throughout the project. We're indebted to all of you!

And now, isn't it time we started something new? We're in the process of drafting a project entitled, THE MEDIA MATTER. Its aim is to help students become more critical readers of the news media and share perceptions with other students around the globe. If you'd like to know more please contact me directly. Or, if you're inundated with start-of-the-new-year errands then just stay tuned to this mailing list and a project description will be coming your way.

Best of luck with the start of the new academic year!
R. W. "Buddy" Burniske
ISKL Humanities Department

The Creator's Conundrum

To appreciate what "goes on inside" a telecollaborative project one must understand the fundamental anxieties that attend their creation. For such endeavors to be truly "collaborative," after all, the creator must find a colleague willing to share the labors. Consider the courage required to design a project that depends upon virtual strangers scattered around the globe. Why would a teacher who enjoys a good classroom atmosphere and relative autonomy risk losing that for such experimentation? And what of those who answer the "call for collaboration." Why should they take a risk, perhaps compromising their curriculum to participate in something created by a distant colleague they had never met or worked with before? Clearly, this requires a leap of faith from both sides. Once more, recruiting project participants made me feel like I was inviting everyone in Kuala Lumpur to attend a party at my house. What's the best way to arrive at a happy medium in telecollaboration? How could I make sure that *someone* showed up while limiting the number of uninvited gate-crashers? Setting limits may prevent the latter, but one still needs to disseminate a "Call for Collaboration" to ensure the former. With that in mind, I submitted the following "call" to several educational listservers, including this one for teachers in South America.

Date: Mon, 28 Aug 1995
To: Multiple recipients of list <OASIS>
Subject: THE MEDIA MATTER
INTERNET PROJECT SEEKS PARTICIPANTS
"THE MEDIA MATTER—A Communications Study"

Querido Subscribers to OASIS/AASAA:

Greetings from Malaysia! I've recently designed a telecommunications project which I'd like to begin in mid-September. Perhaps you, or one of your colleagues, would like your students to participate in this project, tentatively entitled,

"THE MEDIA MATTER—A Communications Study."

Why? Well, for one thing, telecommunications has inspired plenty of hype and hysteria of late. And wouldn't it be nice to study email, Internet and all the rest as they relate to other forms of media? Think how valuable it would be for your students to study how a medium "shapes" a news story, considering everything from newspapers and magazines to radio, television and the Internet.

Essentially, *The Media Matter* is both a declaration and an invitation. We'll ask secondary school students around the globe to monitor news stories, ask how (and why) the media can become their own message, and "consider the source." We're open to any-and-all disciplines and/or extracurricular activities, from Language Arts to Journalism, Theory of Knowledge/Philosophy to Computer Sciences and more.

There's no catch to any of this.
No hidden fees, chain letters, or software upgrades required! ;-)

All that IS required is a desire to expose your classroom to the world and your students to global communications. If this sounds like JUST ANOTHER PROJECT then consider the following from a renowned educator and communications" theorist:

". . . we have been slow to acknowledge that every extension of speech—from painting to hieroglyphics to the alphabet to the printing press to television—also generates unique ways of apprehending the world, amplifying or obscuring different features of reality. Each medium, like language itself, classifies the world for us, sequences it, frames it, enlarges it, reduces it, argues a case for what the world is like . . ." (Neil Postman 1988b, 32–33)

Here's an opportunity to question the hype and hysteria of mainstream media! Along the way, we might just help students argue their OWN case "for what the world is like . . ." Help us, and your students, subject the media to the kind of scrutiny they deserve.

For more information, please contact:

R. W. "Buddy" Burniske
International School of Kuala Lumpur
e-mail: buddyb@iskl.po.my

By now, the reader should discern the labor-intensive qualities of this endeavor. I marvel, in retrospect, at the sheer determination of these documents. What reason did I have to believe anyone out there would take interest? I knew, from fourteen years' experience in schools, that many humanities teachers would not be able to participate because of prescriptive curricula. So I wasn't surprised to hear no responses from a teacher of English or Language Arts. Nor did I hear from anyone in social studies. Or journalism. Or Theory of Knowledge. Cause for worry? I suppose. Yet, if I'm honest, I must confess to having an ace-in-the-hole: Lowell Monke. We had discussed the possibility of trying a project like this, but never actually moved from vague conjecture to a project description. If I could persuade Lowell to give it a try I figured the differences between the media in Kuala Lumpur and Des Moines would provide students with ample opportunities for dialectical discourse. So I drafted a project structure, with a statement of intention, and sent them to Lowell. I feared curricular restraints would prevent collaboration between these teachers of English and Computer Studies this time around, but Lowell's reply was as swift as it was emphatic:

Date: Sun, 27 Aug 1995
From: jaring!ACAD.DRAKE.EDU!LM7846S
Subject: Climb every mountain, Swim . . .

To: budjack@tropics.pc.my

Buddy,

How could you even think of doing this one without me? Actually, I'm a little miffed. I recall a year ago I suggested something similar to this, though directed more towards technology in general, and was rebuffed for proposing a college level philosophy course. Ah, but that was before Postman got under your skin.

Seriously, I like the project a lot because you did what I never worked out (and what made my idea unworkable for high schoolers): you found a way to make an abstract investigation concrete. It is a lesson I have had a hard time learning, but see as the key to nearly all learning now.

I haven't had time to work through all the nuts and bolts of the project (I think there may be a problem with how to relate the disparate topics to each other) but I definitely want to be part of it. I am not going to offer it to other teachers at CA, I am going to do it with my own class. Until we get Internet access for participating teachers (should come around November) I am not going through the frustration of trying to work with volunteers and shuffling messages back and forth.

Tonight I will take a closer look at the particulars and make some recommendations tomorrow night. When are you sending out the feeler? If you have a few days yet, let me take a look at that too. For some reason a cursory reading didn't grab my attention like the actual project outline did. Keep in mind your reaction a year ago. What seems obvious to us, what seems to be a major factor in society to us, is not even at the level of consciousness for most of the rest of the world. [. . .]

Lowell

Questioning the Unquestionable

It's hard to explain the significance of such messages to the uninitiated. It represents something that we need to consider more deeply: the need for faith and commitment among faculty who engage in telecollaborative learning activities. Lowell's faith in this enterprise, in me, was enough to encourage the final push. It was reassuring to know that we'd have the opposing views of media in Malaysia and the United States to feed our dialectical fires. Would it be enough to justify the use of computers and the Internet? Would my students, and Lowell's, learn more because of a telecollaborative project than they would by simply studying local media? I wasn't sure, but how would I ever learn if we didn't take a chance?

Unfortunately, I couldn't spend as much time recruiting participants as I would have liked. I was teaching five courses, most of them with twenty students or so; the LLS course, 20% of my teaching load, was consuming a disproportionate amount of time. More chilling, though, was the thought that I might lose the thread of the LLS course if I divided my attention too much, worrying that nobody would show up for this "party" of mine. So I let the call for collaboration circulate, and focused upon my own classroom. What was it that I wanted to do? What did I want these students to investigate? For one thing, I wanted them to challenge cultural platitudes, ones that, in some cases, they had already heard, but never considered deeply. Like any veteran English teacher I despised clichés, and cringed whenever I heard students employ someone else's words or phrase without pausing to consider its meaning. I wanted my students to stop doing that, but I also wanted them to test their ideas beyond the parameters of one isolated classroom, school, and country, parameters that sat like provincial blinders, limiting their field of vision. Even though my students had traveled extensively, some moving to a different school and country every year of their lives, their social milieu of expatriates from the diplomatic and business communities, families atop the socio-economic ladder, often fostered the homogenized perception of the world that Lowell identified in the previous chapter.

This worldview, which they saw little need to examine, manifested itself, curiously enough, with respect to television. When I informed the class that I didn't own a television, hadn't during my four years in Malaysia, they were incredulous. One boy simply refused to believe that anyone could live without a television. I asked why this was so remarkable and he shrugged. He couldn't articulate a reason; he simply maintained that such choices were "just plain weird." Others explained that they could understand living without television if one lived in a shack without electricity, like those outside the school gates, but that it made no sense for someone with the financial means and supporting infrastructure. What interested me about their response was the unequivocal nature of it. There was, to their minds, something absolutely WRONG about my decision not to own a television. They were particularly outraged in light of my two children, ages five and eleven, whom they described as "deprived." I asked them if they would say the same thing about my decision not to own other appliances. I didn't, for example, own a fax machine or a telephone answering device. Did they find that odd? Did they think it deprived my children of some inalienable right? No. So why was the television so special? Why was it "weird" not to own one? They were stumped. When I asked if they didn't see something strange in this, an implicit social pressure which coerced their participation in a particular medium, their favored reply was, "You're the one who's being antisocial."

My antisocial behavior was suddenly rewarded with a flurry of inquiries concerning a telecollaborative project that was still mostly a fiction in my head.

It was time to get serious about the project description. A postponed delivery was sure to make interested educators wonder about the credibility and competence of the project coordinator. So I began with questions about the media, about our assumptions, and proceeded from there. I was guided, more than anything, by the desire to debunk a few myths. Just three weeks after the school year had begun, and I had launched the newest version of the "Literature, Language, and Society" course, I posted the following project description on the "isklproj@jaring.my" listserv and distributed it to all interested parties. Mind you, my school still didn't have a Web page, our server was often down due to tropical thunderstorms, and my connection to the Internet was via tenuous SLIP connection at home. I was in no position to ask for more than communication via electronic mail:

THE MEDIA MATTER: A COMMUNICATIONS STUDY

Welcome! Thanks for your interest in "The Media Matter." The choice of *double entendre* for project title is deliberate, for not only do we believe "media matter," but we're also inclined to think "something's the matter with media." This project has grown out of concerns about media, from print to electronic, and a desire to scrutinize them. Epithets such as "information highway" and "cyberspace" are currently popular, but what lurks behind such clichés? How important are the signs, symbols and methods of the media culture, which students must learn to "read" if they're to become informed, thoughtful citizens? What makes a source of information reliable? How does an audience distinguish between information and propaganda? Ultimately, how does one extract Truth from a pile of hype?

I. OUR AIMS: In general terms, here's what we'd like to accomplish:

* Help students become "critical readers" of disparate media sources and information.

* Create a community of inquiry via the newest medium, the Internet (while also subjecting telecommunications to close scrutiny).

* Investigate how, and why, a medium shapes a message, and what is required for an audience to properly "decode" those messages.

II. APPLICABLE To: Students aged 14–19, from all disciplines/extracurricular activities. Participating groups may be large or small, gathered within an organized body or brought together specifically for this project. We'd be delighted, in fact, to have an eclectic mix of students, from Language Arts to Journalism, Theory of Knowledge (TOK) to Computer Sciences, and more.

III. THE STRUCTURE: Students will choose ONE News Story to study through the course of a week. The choice of "News Story" is left to the discretion of students (and teachers) at participating schools; however, the full group must focus upon this story. The class should then subdivide, allowing students to specialize in one medium, thereby gaining "expertise" in one of the following:

1. Newspapers (local, national & international)
2. Magazines/Tabloids (local, national & international)
3. Radio (local, national & international)
4. Television (local, national & international)
5. Telecommunications/Internet (newsgroups, listservs, email, etc.)

Confused? Then imagine this: A class of 15 pupils chooses "Hurricane X" as their News Story. They divide into 5 trios, with each trio specializing in one of the media listed above. The trios study all of their medium's reports on Hurricane X throughout the week. Then, they prepare a "Media Report," providing the contributors' names, ages & nationalities.

IV. MEDIA REPORTS—these documents, carefully drafted and revised, should provide:

a) Primary Sources—Description of sources (Name, language(s) employed, local/int'l distribution? public? private? conservative? liberal? daily? weekly? monthly? etc.)

b) The Medium's Message—"Objective" report: Quotes, dates, placement of story in the medium from day to day (Lead story? Page 6? Editorial? Morning/ evening news? Special bulletins?).

c) Story Development—How did the story "evolve" during the week? What did the medium focus upon? What did it neglect? What tangents arose? Repetitions? Patterns? Errors?

d) Assessment—Strengths/weaknesses of this medium's "reportage." What "bias" did you detect? Frustrations/surprises/satisfactions of those studying through THIS medium. Was it possible to determine the veracity of this medium's messages? If so, how?

Each group of "experts" will file a report of 500 words or less. We ask that all teachers take note of the word limit and hold students to it. This will mitigate "information overload" as well as teach valuable writing skills. (Note: Five Media Reports of 500 words each will produce a 2,500-word "School Report"). Please, be succinct!

V. SCHOOL REPORT—GUIDELINES

When completed, the "Media Reports" should be collated to form one SCHOOL REPORT. To limit confusion, send all five Media Reports as one file. Identify the file as: SCHOOL NAME/REPORT #. Thus, the students at the International School of Kuala Lumpur will compile five Media Reports, collate them as one SCHOOL REPORT, and entitle it: "ISKL/REPORT #1." All School Reports will be submitted to the "project listserv" for dissemination.

School Report Schedule:

September 15 = Report #1 (Focus: One Local or National News Story)
September 22 = Responses/Questions to Report #1
September 29 = Report #2 (Focus: One International News Story)
October 6 = Responses/Questions to Report #2
October 13 = Report #3 (Focus: Local/National or International Story)
October 20 = Responses/Questions to Report #3
October 27 = Final Reports—Analysis of "The Media Matter"/ Project
Evaluations

**Please Note: This schedule is designed to allow time for reflection and e-mail correspondence between students. Let's all work toward more than biweekly "data exchanges." The follow-up responses are just as important as the School Reports. Please encourage students to ask questions, clarify statements, and generally engage in a responsible "community of inquiry."

VI. STARTING POINTS—While we hope this structure is helpful, minimizing the chaos of listserver communications, we do NOT want to dictate the terms within your classroom. We'd ask that you observe report formats, guidelines, and dates, but beyond that feel free to experiment and share classroom strategies with all of us. "The Media Matter" is, after all, both a declaration and an invitation. Perhaps the following will help initiate classroom discussions:

"What is information? Or more precisely, what 'are' information? What are its various forms? What conceptions of intelligence, wisdom, and learning does each form insist upon? What conceptions does each form neglect or mock? What are the main psychic effects of each form? What is the relation between information and reason? What is the kind of information that best facilitates thinking? Is there a moral bias to each information form? What does it mean to say that there is too much information? How would one know? What redefinitions of important cultural meanings do new sources, speeds, contexts and forms of information require? Does television, for example, give a new meaning to 'piety' to 'patriotism' to 'privacy'? Does television give a new meaning to 'judgment' or to 'understanding'? How do different forms of information persuade? Is a newspaper's 'public' different from television's 'public'? How do different information forms dictate the type of content that is expressed?"—Neil Postman, *Amusing Ourselves to Death* (1986, 160).

"Looking At" and "Looking Through"

This is where the trouble begins, both as a project coordinator trying to over-come inertia, and as a reflective educator, trying to convey "what happened" long after the project's conclusion. There is a significant difference between "looking through" a telecollaborative project and "looking at" it. In the midst of a telecollaborative project, a distributed learning environment that takes on a life of its own, participants look "through" the filter of e-mail or Web-based discussions without much opportunity to step back and regard it from a critical distance. Afterward, however, what was dynamic becomes static, affording time to "look at" the project, but no longer providing opportunities to look through it as a living, breathing organism. This is when we must resist the temptation to cull greatest hits from an archive of e-mail messages, presenting yet another deceptive success story.

So while I might boast that I heard from educators in Africa, Asia, Europe, and North America, providing a list of the countries to reveal how global our reach had become, it would prove both disingenuous and irrelevant. Of far greater relevance is this point: in addition to teaching my regular classload, including an elective that I was inventing as I went along, commitment to this project meant accepting the weight of logistical concerns, corresponding with faculty who sent a one-line query and then disappeared, clarifying the project description for those who said they were eager to participate, but then, for whatever reason, opted out, as well as serving as catalyst for online discussions. Perhaps it wouldn't have been so difficult if I'd been part of a networked community, one in which colleagues might help with dissemination of the project and recruitment of participants, but I can only speak from my experience as one teacher, in one school, located in one country of Southeast Asia.

There was great excitement initially, the kind that attends the creation of a unique endeavor. We weren't following someone else's syllabus or program, we were inventing our own. Pick your metaphor: we were flying by wire, playing jazz, and conducting improv drama all in one. I wanted to convey some of this to our mailing list subscribers, while also requesting greater commitment as we neared the first exchange of reports:

Date: Wed, 6 Sep 1995
From: buddyb@iskl.po.my
To: Multiple recipients of list <ISKLproj>
Subject: Media Matter Participants

Dear "isklproj" subscribers:

We've had requests for project descriptions of "The Media Matter" from South Africa, Luxembourg, USA , Canada, Thailand, and more. Now, as we near the scheduled date for our first exchange of Media Reports (Sept. 15) it seems wise to find out just who will be participating. So if you're reading this and planning to participate in some capacity please send a note to the listserver indicating:

1) The Name of your School
2) City & Country in which the school's located
3) Class/activity involved
4) Estimated # of students and age group
5) Name of teacher/coordinator

For example, here's what ISKL's group looks like:

1) International School of Kuala Lumpur
2) Kuala Lumpur, Malaysia
3) English Elective: "Literature, Language & Society"
4) 10 students—ages 15–19
5) R. W. Burniske (teacher)

If you're feeling shy, overworked, or noncommittal, you are still free to "lurk" and submit an occasional quip or quote concerning "The Media Matter."

Regardless, thanks for your interest. We look forward to hearing from you!

Cheers,
R. W. "Buddy" Burniske
ISKL Humanities Department

Media Report #1: Local News

Within a week we received notice from the Maru a Pula School of Gaberone (Botswana), Hawaii Preparatory Academy (USA), and Central Academy of Des Moines, Iowa (USA), that they would participate in the project. I shared these confirmations with my students, who were struggling with a story choice, primarily because they couldn't find many news stories sustained for more than a few days. Following discussion one day, though, we settled upon the only "story" that we knew everyone could track through disparate media lenses for a full week, the only story playing on a daily basis in Malaysia: Prime Minister Mahathir. I was pleased with the students' clever solution to our initial problem, yet concerned that it introduced a new one. Under the Internal Security Act (ISA) of Malaysia one could be arrested for criticizing the government openly, particularly the prime minister. As expatriates, I reminded my students, we were guests in this nation, and could earn ourselves prompt deportation if we weren't careful with what we sent through the public forum of electronic mailing lists and newsgroups.

The point was well taken.

Given the nature of this project, and our collective need to accommodate both internal and external schedules, I wasn't surprised when none of the participating schools met the deadline for the first report. Extracurricular activities canceled my class session that day, which I announced through the listserver; meanwhile, a host of reasons made it difficult for others to finalize their reports. The following arrived the day after the deadline, revealing obstacles that our participants in Hawaii confronted, as well as a glimpse of the naivete many participants brought to their study of the Internet:

Date: Sat, 16 Sep 1995
To: Multiple recipients of list <isklproj@jaring.my>
Subject: HPA/REPORT #1

Note: HPA is a boarding school, and so the students have little opportunity to watch TV or listen to the radio. Therefore, we chose to concentrate our efforts on the Internet, magazines, and newspapers. Below are three student reports:

* * *

THE UNABOMBER: JR, Serena, Holliss, and Scott (Internet)

By far the most enormous and controversial source of information ever available to humankind, the internet, unsurprisingly, is teeming with opinions, facts, and questions about the infamous Unabomber. If you're looking for opinions about the bombings check out the newsgroups—in the past 2 months alone there have been over 700 articles posted to newsgroups about the Unabomber. Some have excerpts from the Unabomber's Manifesto complete with physiological analyses of every paragraph, others make predictions about who will be the next victim (obviously it's Bill Gates) many claim that they know who the Unabomber is or that he is their neighbor, and still others say they know where he grew up or who he worked for in his hometown (which is, beyond a doubt, Maine Township, IL).

Although Bill Gates being the victim of the next bomb isn't the only opinion about the head of Microsoft and the Unabomber on the Usenet, here is an excerpt from an 8/27 posting in sci.physics:

"perhaps the Unabomber *IS* Bill Gates (notice the resemblance?) That would definitely explain why Bill Gates was not Made An Example Of. What could possibly be a better way to wipe out all your potential future competition? And note the antitechnological bias of the Unabomber's notes: perfectly consistent with the relentless campaign by MicroSoft."

Here is another excerpt from a Usenet posting to comp.dcom.telecom on 8/29 regarding the Unabomber's name and place of birth:

"now they have decided—as I did sometime back—that the mystery person known as Unabomber had his roots here in the northern Illinois area. A few weeks ago, I expressed my belief, based on conversations with some net people, that Unabomber is a fellow whose initials are P.M.G. The 'M' stands for Michael . . . and the 'P' stands for Patrick."

In this 8/09 posting to comp.dcom.telecom the author claims to know who the bomber's father is and the name of his company:

"Further research has shown that if PMG is the son of GG, a fellow who had a construction/home remodeling business in those days, with a TAlcott-5 phone number at the office in Park Ridge, and a Vanderbilt-7 number at his home in Des Plaines, that he might well have had an affiliation with Northwestern University for a few years during the early to middle 1970's.

If it's facts you're after, the WWW is the place to go. Jump to nearly any major magazine, news service or newspaper on the Web and you'll be faced with a whole array of Unabomber articles and information. Unfortunately, so little is known for certain about the Unabomber that the data taken from these pages is usually based on either letters sent to the New York Times or San Francisco Chronicle from the Unabomber or have something to do with the FBI's Unabomber Page. [. . .]

The students in Gaborone chose to remain quiet observers in the first round. Meanwhile, students in Des Moines offered a critique of media reports on a "news story" that had dominated US media for months, while Malaysia's media paid it little attention: the OJ Simpson trial. Des Moines presented several insightful reports, but we were especially impressed by the newspaper group's effort to describe the evolution of a story within the story.

Greetings from Central Campus, Des Moines Public Schools, Iowa, USA. Good to see the contribution from Hawaii Preparatory Academy. Good stuff! We are the Advanced Computer Technology class, a business class at Central Campus. The class has students from all five of the Des Moines high schools and one student from a nearby suburb.

Here is our entry. We figured someone HAD to cover the U.S. media event of the year—O.J.'s trial—but we decided to concentrate on one facet that has just emerged, the controversy over Mark Fuhrman's racist statements and activities.

    * * *

NEWSPAPER: John R, Tom T

Detective Mark Fuhrman and the O.J. Simpson trial. This is based on *USA Today* which is internationally distributed and in the English language. The newspaper's coverage on the Mark Fuhrman issue is in a liberal sense and slightly biased towards Fuhrman. On the first day the article is on the first page and takes up about a page in length. It has the headline: "Fuhrman refuses to answer." The article is based on the fact that Fuhrman uses the "N" word and is a racist cop.

The pictures shown on this page are Judge Ito thinking and Mark Fuhrman on the stand with a blunt look on his face. The caption for Fuhrman's picture says "Fuhrman has denied using racist language."

On the next day *USA Today* has an article on page 3. The headline states: "Trial within a trial begins today—Jury's focus is directed to Fuhrman." It takes up the whole page. It focuses on Mark Fuhrman's "mini-trial." The prosecution is trying to filter out all evidence that points to Fuhrman's using the racist language. He is denying the use of racist language.

The next day, the article is on page 4 and is much smaller compared to the first day's headlines and article. It takes about half a page in width and length. The headline reads: "Defense targets Fuhrman with renewed fervor." The article focuses on the defense and their strategies concerning the Mark Fuhrman incident. It also has a picture, but of Johnny Cochran, one of O.J. Simpson's lawyers.

The following day in an article on the 4th page again the headline reads: "Simpson's majority-black jury hears tape of Fuhrman's Slurs." It is about the size of the 2nd article. It talks about how the Simpson Jury has heard the Mark Fuhrman tapes. There are a few witnesses including Kathleen Bell, who is saying that Fuhrman made racist comments. The story continues to downsize in the newspaper. The photo on this page is of Kathleen Bell at the stand, her arms stretched a little, answering a question. She looks to be speaking a little loudly as she answers.

The next day, the article is much smaller, and is again on page 4. The headline is "District attorneys made cops like Fuhrman." The picture shows Mark Fuhrman at the stand, with a blank look on his face.

This newspaper is not very biased in our opinion, very little could be detected. The story moved from first page to the 4th page within a week. The articles and headlines continued to get smaller as time went on.

What happened to it?

Did the newspaper lose interest in the story? Did the people lose interest in the story? [. . .]

Clearly, these students are looking closely at both the medium and its message, which leads to questions that will further their own investigation as well as that of their counterparts. Students at the International School of Kuala Lumpur, meanwhile, did their best to analyze the way in which the Malaysian prime minister was depicted in the respective media—most of which the government owns and operates. The students serving as Internet specialists demonstrated especially good judgment, tactfully broaching a sensitive topic in local news-group discussions. They submitted the following report to the project listserver on September 18, 1995:

* * *

ISKL INTERNET REPORT #1

A) PRIMARY SOURCES:

1) Newsgroups
news:jaring.general
news:jaring.members

2) Private E-Mail

B) THE MEDIUM'S MESSAGE:

The topic was Dr. Mahathir the PM of Malaysia. Information was gained through the use of newsgroups. The only internet service in Malaysia is Jaring. Although these newsgroups can be accessed by people all around the world, response was obtained only from Malaysian residents; as they know more about the PM's doings than do people located out of the country.

A Malaysian, that works as a financial controller for a group of companies based in KL, wrote:

"Well, I once had the opportunity to meet the man in person . . . All in all, based on the above occasion and general knowledge, I think he has a very sharp mind. He is also a shrewd politician (must be, I suppose, to be a PM. This also came from my boss who is fairly close to him). He has faults, of course, but overall a good leader . . . " Received 11th Sept. 1995.

The following excerpt is from a Eurasian student studying at Victoria Institution (Malaysia). It was sent as a response to a message we posted on the newsgroup jaring.general:

"In my opinion, the PM (Dr. Mahathir Mohamed) is a very good leader and puts the country before himself. Unlike other leaders, he is not afraid to criticize higher powers and will push other countries to do the right thing. He seems to be right about everything he talks about, and if a certain matter does not involve him, he will not intervene . . ." Received 8th Sept. 1995.

C) STORY DEVELOPMENT:

Our topic of study was not a "story" as such so it did not develop or change over time. But the ten people that e-mailed us, seemed to say the same things about Mahathir (PM) . So it seems that the PM's impression on the people is, for the most part, standardized. None of the people seemed to say anything negative about him. Since no one is perfect, we wondered if it was fear that drove these people to silence or maybe the fact that Dr. Mahathir has no flaws?! Since a lot of the media is controlled by the government, people are, or don't seem to be, as free with the expression of their ideas.

D) ASSESSMENT OF THE MEDIUM:

The Internet has been around for about 25 years and is increasing in popularity. According to THE ECONOMIST (July 1st 1995) in 1988, there were about 5 million "host" computers spanning the globe. Now there are approximately 20 million "host" computers around the world. Due to its increasing popularity in Malaysia, it is virtually impossible to get connected. And when you are connected, the SLIP connection is lost in about 10 minutes due to poor phone lines.

Since the communication is oblique, information contains bias. Thus this medium is open to distortion by the source. This makes it hard to determine who or what is a worthy source.

Report Written By:

Dave S: 17 year old Australian Student who has been at ISKL for 6 years.

John S: an 18 year old Australian Student who has been at ISKL for 4 years.

Creating Dialectics: The First Responses

While the reports showed promise, the most important feature of this project, as with its predecessors, was the opportunity for students to engage in dialogues. Without dialectical discourse this would quickly become just another routine, with students collecting information, analyzing it, and preparing a report. I sent participating faculty a note encouraging follow-up e-mail, essentially saying what I've just stated here. In class, meanwhile, I spent time with my students examining all of the reports, including our own. However, time was not an ally. I assigned homework that asked respective "media specialists" to critique their counterparts' efforts and submit a follow-up e-mail message to the listserver. To overcome inertia and model how this might be done, stressing the need for questions that prompt further reflection rather than defensive reactions, we composed a collective response to learn more about the media in Hawaii:

Date: Wed, 20 Sep 1995
To: Multiple recipients of list <isklproj@jaring.my>
Subject: ISKL Questions: Hawaii

Dear HPA,

We received your first media report and, while we understand your limitations with regard to TV and Radio, we wondered if you could answer a couple of questions.

What type of coverage do people get on the Hawaiian Islands? Is it from the States?

Are there local TV stations in Hawaii? Are there literally NO television sets on the HPA campus?

As for Radio, how many stations can you receive? Do they come from the mainland USA or stations in Honolulu? What languages are most commonly used in broadcasts?

We'd appreciate learning more about these media sources in Hawaii.

Thanks,
ISKL Media Matter Team

Just moments after we'd posted this message to the list one of our Internet specialists asked if he could post another, which he'd composed shortly after reading HPA's report. I was impressed with his careful reading of their report as well as the quality of the questions he raised about the Internet and their analysis of it. Here's what he posted:

Date: Wed, 20 Sep 1995
To: Multiple recipients of list <isklproj@jaring.my>
Subject: ISKL/Response1/Internet

G'Day everyone at Hawaii Preparatory Academy,

Some interesting points. First of all I did not know anything about the Unabomber. In fact, I had never heard of the person.

>.". . perhaps the Unabomber *IS* Bill Gates (notice the resemblance?)"

After reading this quote a question came to my mind . . . Who is the person that posted this message? Your report did not specify much about the posting. Wouldn't the person's background shed some light on where this accusation is coming from? For all we know this person could be the owner of Netscape (Microsofts' competitor) or maybe even the Unabomber himself.

>"If it's facts you're after, the WWW is the place to go . . . Unfortunately, so little
> is known for certain about the Unabomber that the data taken from these
> pages is usually based on either letters sent to the New York Times."

You said that the WWW was factual and that a lot of the "major" newspapers contain info on the bomber . . . Well if the majority of this info is sent in by readers and other people, how can we be sure that this info is true. I have found that when people see the words *TIME, NewsWeek* and *New York Times,* they say "This information is the truth." But how do we know this? How can we trust the source if we don't know them?

What is your Internet service like? as specified in our report, we can't stay on for more than ten minutes because we keep on loosing the SLIP connection! Hope to hear from you!

Dave S (apologies to Iowa; my partner is ill today—we'll send his response to your Internet report soon)

One of the more interesting developments in a telecollaborative project is the way in which participants interpret and adapt guidelines. Initially, one worries about structure a good deal, hoping it will minimize the inevitable chaos. If we enter such affairs with a truly collaborative spirit, however, then we must allow participants some room to maneuver within that structure, approaching various activities in a manner that suits their needs. The students in Iowa, for instance, chose to collate their questions, sending a collective document to the listserver for the simultaneous attention of HPA and ISKL students. I offer this document in its entirety because it demonstrates the kind of inquiry the initial reports prompted as well as the challenges such a message presents for those who wish to follow a particular conversational thread. Imagine, for the sake of simulation, receiving the following e-mail message, distributing it to a class, and asking students to reciprocate in some manner. How might they follow the subsequent dialogues?

Date: Thu, 21 Sep 1995
To: Multiple recipients of list <isklproj@jaring.my>
Subject: DMPS questions

Hi everyone,

We just got the set of questions from ISKL but haven't had a chance to read them yet. Yesterday we got together and talked about the issues brought up by your reports and put together some questions (and a few friendly criticisms) that came up. We decided to package them altogether this time but we are all going to respond to any other questions and comments individually. [. . .]

* Newspaper Group—Tom T, Mark A, Matt K

HPA Question/comment 1: I would like to see you focus more on how the story developed in the newspaper instead of the actual story. What happened to the story? Did it gradually get smaller? Did it go to the last pages or generally stay on the first page?

ISKL Question/comment 1: Are the stories ALWAYS positive on the PM? Is there anything that's ever negative?

ISKL Radio Question: Aren't the stories always arranged from least important to most important? Or is it just on certain important stories that this is done?

* Television Group—Tam N, Joe L, Josh B

International School of Kuala Lumpur, Malaysia:

I would like to congratulate all of you on a well written paper. I was so impressed by the quality of your work that I asked other people I knew to read the paper. And after they read it they were just as impressed as I was. Good Job!

Questions for the Television Media Group:

1. Why do you think the television media wants to censor the stories that the public view? Is it for good intentions or bad intentions?

2. Does the government have complete control over the Television Stations and/or TV Reporters?

3. Do you believe that if Malaysian people had satellite dishes and received other news reports, would it be totally opposite to what you are seeing right now?

Questions for the whole class:

1. In your opinion do you believe that the Media is lying to you?
2. Is Datuk Seri Dr. Mahatir Mohammed, in your opinion a bad and/or good leader by the way the media portrays him?
3. Do you believe that the rest of the general public in Malaysia shares your opinion about the Media and Datuk Seri Dr. Mahatir Mohammed?
4. In the United States the media always portrays our leaders as bad people which leads to unrest with the government, in Malaysia do you believe that the media portraying your leaders as good people leads to happiness with the government?
5. How big of an effect does the media have on the general population?

Hawaii Preparatory Academy:

—— We would like to thank you for your contribution to the project. Your report was both informative and entertaining. It is very neat to find out what someone else's views are when we are seperated by about 5,000 miles of land and water.

Questions for the whole class:

1. Our group was in charge of the television aspect of our media, what do you believe that your television media would have shown and/or said to you?
2. Knowing that the media printed the manifesto of the unabomber does this change your opinion on the Media?
3. How do you believe the unabomber is portrayed in the Media? Is he portrayed as a visionary or as a threat to society?

* Magazine Group—Chris T, Alex B, John R

Magazine criticisms and comments:

HPA Boarding School in Hawaii:

1. What are your feelings on publishing the Unabomber's statement in *Time*?
2. It was well written, but we feel that you should include your own opinions on the issue to fully understand the impact the media places on you.

International School of Kuala Lumpur, Malaysia:

2. What do you mean by, .". . always accompanied by a photo of him doing a good job"? Would you prefer that they show a photo of him in a negative aspect?
3. Has anyone ever thought that the riot predicted was incited by the Prime Minister himself?
4. Do you feel that the advertisements are a distraction to the issues at hand? i.e. Should all the ads be there?
5. We feel that you think your prime minister is far from the prophet that your media makes him out to be. Could your feelings towards the PM be just as biased as the media's due to the fact that they are your prime source of information.

General criticisms and comments:

1. Why do think that the pictures taken of Dr. Mahathir are never seen from behind and why they always place him in the middle? (possibly for security reasons?)
2. Why do you feel that the propaganda has already affected the reader's bias towards the story?

* Radio group—Ben H, Carla O, Melissa J

Radio:

All of the stories on the Unabomber were very interesting. Our main questions, though, are for the students who worked with the radio and television.

Our first question is for the students at the HPA boarding school. Why are the students not able to listen to the radio or not able to watch television?

Another question for you is, What exactly is a "Unabomber?" Explain in detail what a "Unabomber" is. I'm not speaking for everyone here, but I, myself cannot explain what a Unabomber is.

Our last questions go out to the students in ISKL. How long has your Prime Minister been in service?

What has the Prime Minister done to help your country since he began his term?

* Internet Group—Ken K, Mark L, Juan C

To: ISKL
Re: Internet
From: Central Campus, Des Moines, IA, USA

(hacker question)

Is the Jaring.general newsgroup available on the international Internet? On the access that I have to newsgroups, it would appear that they are arranged differently on Jaring. The colon made it impossible for me to access anything on there seeing as our newsgroups are arranged like news.general, or news.members. I was unable to find anything along the lines of "news:jaring.general" or even news.jaring.general. I even went so far as to search for any instance of jaring and several variations of it and couldn't find anything. I got the same results with Malaysia or "my," which is the country abbreviation that I've found on the ISKL addresses.

Explain what you mean by "Since information is oblique, the information contains bias. . . . Thus this medium is open to distortion by the source." Neither the meaning nor the justification of it is clear to us.

What WWW sites did you visit?

On any of the World Wide Web sites that I was on, I was only faced with the current issue of the publication, i.e. *Newsweek, USA Today,* etc. As far as newsgroups go, I don't think that anyone ever deletes those so it would be understandable if you found something from quite a while ago, but on Web sites, I haven't seen anything that keeps up all of the past issues on their server.

End of questions

The role of a project coordinator, at least as I perceive it, is to set the parameters for a project, recruit participants, and then encourage their efforts while gently admonishing those who missed the point somewhere along the line. Following the first reports I felt like a cheerleader, happy to see the group from Des Moines ask so many questions, yet hopeful that we could build upon these initial exchanges to enrich our study in the second round of reports. Clearly, a document such as this presented ample opportunity for dialogues, but it also introduced logistical challenges for those who wished to reply or follow the ensuing conversations. We were at a critical juncture, certainly, trying to establish healthy discursive habits and collaborative relationships. Students were keen to receive replies, but not nearly as eager to send them. With this in mind, I submitted the following message to the project mailing list.

Date: Thu, 21 Sep 1995
From: budjack@tropics.pc.my
To: Multiple recipients of list <isklproj@jaring.my>
Subject: Media Report #2—Sept. 29th

Dear Media Matter Participants & "Lurkers":

As planned, the 2nd round of reports for THE MEDIA MATTER should be submitted to the "isklproj@jaring.my" listserv on (or about) September 29th. That means selecting an INTERNATIONAL News Story now, if you haven't already, and studying it through the multiple media filters for the coming week.

In the meantime, feel free to continue the "dialectic" which the 1st round of reports initiated. Congratulations to all contributors, who had to overcome a good deal of inertia to file those 1st Media Reports. They seem to be gaining momentum with their follow-up questions. Let's keep the discussion alive!

To that end, I'd like to welcome the Maru-a-Pula School of Botswana, and the American International School of Luxembourg, both of which have subscribed to the list in the past week or so. We look forward to learning how & why THE MEDIA MATTER in southern Africa and Europe! I'd invite coordinators at the respective schools to send a brief note to the listserver, introducing your school and participants.

Cheers,
R. W. "Buddy" Burniske
Project Coordinator, ISKL

Media Report #2: International News Story

One of the lessons we've learned from telecollaboration is that students become far more engaged if: (1) their work elicits a prompt and personal reply; and (2) they have a clear sense of their audience. This is particularly challenging at the outset, when a limited bandwidth restricts student interaction to written words. This, too, explains our emphasis upon student dialogue, which is a prerequisite for developing relationships as well as an online community of learners. To further this effort, we invited participants to exchange digital photos just prior to the second report deadline, hoping it would help students "contextualize" messages by attaching faces to the disembodied messages coming from their virtual classmates. We discovered that it wasn't a good idea to send these by way of the listserver, since large graphic files had a tendency to clog our channels, but we continued experimenting with direct e-mail exchanges.

Meanwhile, the second round began with a pleasant surprise: a report from Botswana.

Date: Fri, 29 Sep 1995
From: (Maru a Pula School, Gaborone, Botswana)
To: Multiple recipients of list <isklproj@jaring.my>
Subject: Media Matter submission

Dear MEDIA MATTER participants:

This is the first report from the Maru a Pula School E-Mail Club. Maru a Pula is situated in the capital city of Botswana, Gaborone. This is our entry for the second deadline: an international news story. As we haven't managed to organise a large enough group of people, this report has been compiled by two sixth-formers and three first-formers. Therefore this will be a limited submission and not as comprehensive as the others.

From

Sanchita G. (12),
Ayesha K., Shakila K. (18),
Marwah Mohammed E. (12),
Harini M. (12)

* * *

We are concentrating our report on the only local daily newspaper, "The Daily News." It is a government financed paper that is bilingual—Setswana and English (the official languages).

This paper was chosen because all other local newspapers are weekly, and cover international events at their own discretion, if at all.

"The Daily News" does not cover international events on a daily basis either, although most issues do have an INTERNATIONAL section. The reports are all taken directly from Reuters or AFP (Africa Press) and show little continuity. They are also chosen selectively and the stories portrayed do not correspond with what has made headlines in other international press (e.g. South African newspapers, BBC, CNN—these are the capital's main sources of international news; rural areas do not have wide access to these).

Although the Media Matters Study is meant to concentrate on the media's portrayal of one particular story, we have found this difficult to do, because of the reason mentioned above—little continuance of media reports. This is true for national news as well. We decided to do a general overview on what stories they selected to report on. What we discovered was that the selection of news events appeared to be random.

Only one page per issue is assigned international news in English, while the Setswana international section covers approximately half a page. Since the international news covered is so limited, it would be expected that stories of particular interest to the Southern African region would be selected, but this does not appear to be so.

During last week, events in Bosnia were covered over two separate issues, concerning the suspension of NATO air strikes on the Serbs. These articles appeared in the editions of the twentieth and the 21st September. These articles were both from Africa Press. The unrest in Kashmir was also reported on in the same two issues, both from Africa Press again.

It is unfortunate that media sources in Botswana are so limited. The media field is growing though, with many weekly newspapers mushrooming (although of varying quality) and also monthly periodicals. For the time being, Botswana remains reliant on outside media sources, particularly South African.

It has been interesting for us to participate in MEDIA WATCH for the opportunity to observe comment on international media from students our own age.

Our online community was beginning to take shape. At this point, our circle of active participants included a private, international day school in Malaysia; a private boarding school for Africans in Botswana; a public school in the United States and a private, American boarding school in Hawaii. We had the makings of an interesting discussion. Nonetheless, there had been a few misunderstandings in the first round of exchanges. Some students complained the criticism they received was unfair or severe, others felt misunderstood, but for the most part the discourse was promising. This was an initiation to telecollaborative learning for many of the students; they needed both guidance and practice. With this in mind I posted several messages to the listserver, calling attention to distinctions between public and private messages. Lowell and I also reminded students to provide proper documentation, citing their sources so that we could verify one another's work and further our collective research. Finally, we called for more critical analysis of news *sources*, rather than summary of the news *story*, reminding participants of our purpose and the need for careful scrutiny of the respective media.

In the interim we sustained our first serious blow. Without warning, the faculty coordinator at Hawaii Preparatory Academy suddenly announced that they couldn't continue with the project. She claimed her students were more interested in building Web pages than participating in online discussions. "Please unsubscribe us," read one terse note. There was no detailed explanation. My requests for such were not answered. Worse yet, follow-up e-mail from students at ISKL and Des Moines to the HPA contingency never received a reply. This upset students at both schools, who felt their time and effort deserved at least the favor of a reply. I conveyed this via private e-mail, but never heard from Hawaii again.

Community of Inquiry

We moved on, turning attention to the second reports, an international news story. My students chose to look at the war in Bosnia, a story that the Malaysian prime minister kept in the news through outspoken criticism of relief efforts in the West. We were delighted to learn that students in Iowa had chosen the same story, providing a unique opportunity to compare and contrast media representations in two nations on different sides of the Pacific. E-mail exchanges continued, with students seeking clarification, or simply applauding each other's efforts. Critics of educational telecollaboration often dismiss anecdotal evidence of this kind. However, case studies seem necessary to "show" what we might otherwise "tell" in a detached, impersonal manner. What's more, qualitative evidence allows us to investigate two questions that we should ask of any telecollaborative learning activity: (1) How can one prove that students learned from each other? (2) Did the use of the Internet provide unique learning opportunities that participants couldn't have had otherwise? As a partial response, consider the following message written by a student who had received few responses to his media reports. Imagine what this document might mean to both its sender and recipients, and what it reveals about the potential for telecollaborative learning:

Date: Thu, 5 Oct 1995
To: Multiple recipients of list <isklproj@jaring.my>
Subject: Re: Media Matter submission

Dear Sanchita, Ayesha, Shakila, Marwah, and Harini,

I read your report on the Botswana media and found it very interesting. I am not studying the newspaper media, but instead I am looking at radio. I would be interested to find out what sort of radio media you have there. I have found some interesting things out about the radio media here in Malaysia. I have been looking at the way stories have been presented, what kind of stories are reported, and also comparing different radio stations. I have found that the local Malay radio stations are very different from some of the international ones, like BBC. I list some of these reasons in my media reports.

After reading your report, I was left with a question. In your report, you said concerning the stories covered in your newspaper:

"THEY ARE ALSO CHOSEN SELECTIVELY AND THE STORIES PORTRAYED DO

NOT CORRESPOND WITH WHAT HAS MADE HEADLINES IN OTHER INTERNATIONAL PRESS (E.G. SOUTH AFRICAN NEWSPAPERS, BBC, CNN—THESE ARE THE CAPITAL'S MAIN SOURCES OF INTERNATIONAL NEWS; RURAL AREAS DO NOT HAVE WIDE ACCESS TO THESE)."

I wasn't quite sure what you meant by this. Do you mean that they cover stories that are not covered in the major newspapers? What kind of stories do they cover? I'm interested to find out what you're having to deal with in terms of story coverage in that part of the world.

I hope to continue learning through your future reports about the conditions of the media in Botswana. I also hope to convey to you a sense of what it's like to deal with the media in Malaysia.

Sincerely,

Fred D. (American, 17 years old)

Such efforts were encouraging, for they moved beyond the petty rivalries that often develop when students are asked to critique one another's work. This student was disappointed that his reports concerning the radio were neglected. Instead of taking his frustrations out on others, however, he turned his attention to students in southern Africa to see if they could teach him something about his medium in that region. This spoke highly of the student's initiative, but it also revealed electronic mail's potential to support a collaborative learning environment. Lowell and I had demonstrated ways of furthering a discussion through questions and synthesis, rather than indulging the adolescent appetite for flippant, disrespectful remarks. As much as anything, we wanted to show how this medium could facilitate discussion and learning rather than shouting, competing, or insulting. It was important to let participants know their work was appreciated, and that if a response were delayed it should be interpreted as a sign of deliberation.

Date: Sat, 7 Oct 1995 12:30:04 +0800
From: LM7846S@ACAD.DRAKE.EDU
To: Multiple recipients of list <isklproj@jaring.my>
Subject: Second reports

Hi ISKL and MAP,

After getting our report off we started reading yours and are finding them very interesting. They have already raised some interesting questions in our minds. We are going to think about them this weekend and then we will write them down and send them to you on Monday.

—Des Moines Advanced Computer Technology class

P.S. Wednesday the whole Des Moines Register was on the OJ trial. Today there was one small article on page 6. Talk about fading fast!

Ultimately, we were trying to create a "community of inquiry." This would take time, and patience, but messages like the preceding helped establish good will and empathy. As they gained familiarity, we hoped that students acting as media specialists would feel more comfortable questioning one another, developing the trust necessary to "think out loud." Until we reached that point there remained the possibility that competitive debates, adolescent struggles to see who was "right" and who was "wrong," would disable this community, preventing it from seeking deeper understanding of complex issues.

Media Report #3: The Challenges Ahead

Unfortunately, a community is terribly fragile, and many things conspire against it. We know this from real-world experiences; the online environment often confirms it. The sudden, unexplained withdrawal of the HPA contingent had done considerable damage to our community of inquiry, raising the concern of reciprocity. Even the most committed participants were feeling the crunch of deadlines, while wondering if their efforts would meet with a reply or neglect. Within our respective schools there were the demands of midterms and extracurricular activities; within the project itself the timeline became a concern. Students complained they lacked time to read e-mail, write responses, and conduct research for their reports. It seemed wise to adjust the schedule and ponder a slightly different approach to the third reports.

Drawing upon the serendipity of the second report, and feeling as though our "global" discussion had shrunk to a bipolar one, I sent the following message to the listserver. I included "lurkers" in my salutation, hoping it might compel them to set aside pre-existing syllabi and join us. It was a shot in the dark, but one worth taking when we consider the nature of the Internet. Custom has taught us to think in terms of a project's beginning, middle and end, but telecollaboration may compel a new paradigm for "participation." Potential contributors might subscribe yet decide to "lurk" before they leap into public discussions. Once again, flexibility is essential if we're to accommodate diverse academic schedules, though how a community of inquiry evolves when latecomers join *in media res* is open to debate:

Date: Sat, 7 Oct 1995
From: budjack@tropics.pc.my
To: Multiple recipients of list <isklproj@jaring.my>
Subject: French Nuclear Tests

Dear Des Moines, Gaberone, and "Media Matter" lurkers:

I have a proposal for the 3rd report, an idea which evolved while I was reading the 2nd reports. First of all, how about if we postpone the report date a week, shifting the deadline from October 13th to the 20th? That will give us the coming week for the exchange of e-mail which is essential for cross-examination and clarification. Otherwise, we'll tumble into the trap of collecting data without pausing for reflection upon it.

If you're amenable to that, consider this: How about if everyone involved in the project studies the same news story, as reported in their country of residence, for Report #3?

The News Story: French Nuclear Tests.

This may present challenges, particularly if the French cancel future tests, but considering the importance of this event isn't it worth the trouble? If we cannot find information on the story from one medium then what does it say about that medium? Students investigating the "Radio," for example, should by now be asking what their medium has become in the past few decades: what was once a news medium now seems an adjunct to the music/entertainment industry. Why so much focus on pop music, talk shows, and advertisement on the radio? Why so little time devoted to news? What percentage of a given hour does the radio devote to news? What stories does it neglect? Why does it neglect this story, or at least give it less attention than other news sources? After all, what a medium leaves out of a story—or a news broadcast—may be just as revealing as what it broadcasts. So if a group can't find information on a given story I'd encourage them to analyze what their medium is doing while it's omitting that story. If the Des Moines' Register devoted all that time, energy and ink to the acquittal of a former football player last week what does it say about North American newspapers and their "consumers" if the Register neglected to report on events in Muroroa the day before Mr. Simpson's acquittal, where a government detonated a bomb apparently 50 times the strength of those dropped on Hiroshima and Nagasaki 50 years ago?

Consider this a rhetorical question. But *do* consider it!

Please give these proposals some thought. If you're agreeable, we'll postpone our 3rd reports until October 20th (but commit ourselves to a thoughtful exchange of email via listserv this week). Then, let me know if you'd like to study the French Nuclear Testing for the 3rd report. It'll provide a common story, focus our energies upon an "historic moment" and get us thinking about the consequences of this event upon our planet and all its inhabitants.

Regards to all,
R. W. "Buddy" Burniske
Project Coordinator

Lowell thought this a good idea, but reported rumblings on his side of the Pacific, from students more interested in their computers than the people at the other end of the network. We were now more than a month into the project, the length of time for many "units" of study in a high school curriculum, and the novelty had long since faded. Some of the would-be "dialogues" had become monologues. My students were discouraged with a general lack of response; the radio experts were especially annoyed, since they had received precious few comments and questions. Meanwhile, back in Iowa, an ominous cloud was gathering. I had just sent Lowell a private message describing the difficulties and disappointments my students expressed as we prepared for the third reports; I had also broached the idea of a fourth round of reports, focusing entirely upon advertising in media. His reply offers the kind of insight that educators need if they are to understand the challenges of telecollaboration. Introducing technology to a classroom is relatively easy; proper funding and technical support are all we need. Inspiring students to use that technology to communicate with others, to question and think critically, remains far more difficult.

From: LM7846S@ACAD.DRAKE.EDU
Date: Wed, 18 Oct 1995
Subject: Re: Media Matter
To: budjack@tropics.pc.my

Buddy,

We are having the same kinds of problems you are with the third report. But I am also having major attitudinal problems. I handed out your students' responses to our second report and the students read them with great interest (did we miss the television response? We didn't get one). But trying to get them to think about responding again was like dragging a whale across a desert. Yesterday I finally gave up in disgust—for awhile at least—because they also were acting the same way toward getting ready for the 3rd report (I had sent the newspaper students down to the library the day before and they had come back saying they couldn't find anything. So I went down with them, and the magazine people, and dumped stacks of newspapers on the tables and made them go through them— they found lots of stuff. But even the threat of a bad grade (I hate stooping to that) isn't getting very far anymore.

What seems very odd to me is the total lack of interest in communicating with others. When I point out that G'day is an Aussie greeting I don't even get a shrug of the shoulders. Not one student has ever expressed an interest in knowing who is who when I have shown them your picture. This seems very strange to me. Is it connected with the fact that they are content to sit and stare at their computer screens for 2 hours a day if I let them, and never say a word to the person sitting next to them? Is that why they sign up for my class?

Tomorrow I am going to try something radical—and very much against school policy. I now have Internet access through the network in my room. The students aren't aware of it because they don't have any software to access it at their stations. Tomorrow I am going to put Eudora on all the machines. I was specifically told not to do it by Information Management until they have generated a user agreement form to protect us against liability in case some student happens to read a message with the word "damn" in it. But the hell with it. Maybe if they can send messages directly (up till now they have to write something up, copy it to my computer, then have me sign them on through my Drake account and send it; such a tedious job that we send everything in bulk) they will perk up and find something to say.

I hate using the computer as a motivational device even worse than grades but then again it is a computer class, and it may just be that the present use of the technology is getting in the way too much for the students to appreciate what is going on. In any event, if the connection suddenly goes dead you'll know that the bureaucrats have hauled me off to the dungeon for reprogramming.

Let's see if I can get some life into my students before committing to an extension of the project. I love the idea of looking at advertising, and I think it would probably interest my students far more than irrelevant stuff like Bosnia, A-bombs, and racism. It is also so ubiquitous that the harder task here would be to sort out what is advertising and what isn't. Also, maybe when the haze lifts a little my cherubs will seem more cooperative than I am giving them credit for.

Lowell

Needless to say, I didn't share this message with my students. Nor did I feel compelled to recruit new participants. I was through with that. It was time to devote full attention to my own students. We read John Hersey's *Hiroshima*, discussed whether or not a nuclear bomb could be considered a "text" and conducted research to provide the school's Earth Club with online resources for its booth at the school's annual International Festival. My students found television and radio sources useless for this story, mainly because there hadn't been a nuclear test that week. Newspapers and magazines proved more reliable as archives, but by far the best source of information—offering everything from video clips of a previous test explosion to Greenpeace reports—was the Internet. Our Internet media specialists, who located an electronic petition for the Earth Club to circulate, submitted the following report:

Date: Thu, 26 Oct 1995
To: Multiple recipients of list <isklproj@jaring.my>
Subject: ISKL/ Internet/ Report #3

ISKL Internet Report #3

A) PRIMARY SOURCES:

WWW Sites

- http://www.peg.apc.org/~Freedom/ (Boycott French Goods)
- http://www.ozemail.com.au/~reed/hot/french.html (Background Info) http://www.oneworld.org/news/msf_report.html (Radiation Effects)
- http://130.102.169.38/bomb/ (We Protest)
- http://mosaique.oleare.com/ (Letter to Chirac)
- http://www.greenpeace.org/ (Green Peace Home Page)

B) THE MEDIUM'S MESSAGE:

The WWW sites above provided us with a variety of information on the French Nuclear Tests. These are just a few of the hundreds of Web pages that contain references to the tests.

"Look, we don't have to take this crap. . . ."—(We Protest)

This quote from an Australian site is against the tests and states that fact blandly. They also said "The Real Bastards are: . . ." and gave the postal addresses of President Chirac and other French officials around the world such as the French Ambassador to the United States[and] the department of defense in France. The Green Peace home page contained information on the nuclear tests in China and in the Pacific. Pictures, sounds and even a video clip of the first test were found along side links to other "cyber-polls" and related sites. The video clip that was downloaded was in the apple quicktime format. First a view of the control room. Then a panoramic view of the ocean (via helicopter), and then a side on of the explosion. The most interesting part of the clip was at the end when it showed a group of people relaxing by the ocean and applauding loudly as the test was a success. This video is made to show the French attitude toward these events. This event has given birth to many other sites that indirectly state an opinion on the tests. One such site called, "The Effects of Radiation" supplied all of the facts about the hazards of radiation. Another site suggested that all French goods be boycotted. It goes to show how different people around the world can make a difference.

C) STORY DEVLOPMENT:

The story development in this sense was minimal on the internet. Although, frequent updates of information, petitions and polls were visible over the two week period. The WWW site's main focus was the stopping of the tests. This was shown through setting up petitions and sites that allowed the user to send e-mail to president Chirac. This was one idea; to send an overflowing amount of mail (electronic and snail mail) to President Chirac and hope that they get the message.

D) ASSESSMENT OF THE MEDIUM:

Covering this news story on the internet proved interesting because of the enormous amount of information. With all of the polls, petitions and e-mail, it seemed like there was more of a difference being made on the internet than in the other media. So many people from all over the world, including France, signed the petitions to stop the testing. Although this does not seem to be making much of an impact on the French government as they have not shown any sign of stopping.

By Dave S & John S (Both Australian)

Among other things, this report indicates a more sophisticated "reading" of the news medium, despite its unmistakable enthusiasm. My worry, as always, was that such reports might not receive the kind of response they deserved due to the attrition we had suffered as well as the myriad distractions within our respective schools. Much to his credit, Lowell persuaded his students to submit reports as well as respond to the ISKL submissions. He had obviously impressed upon his students the significance of communicating with their distant peers (though he never offered details of how he made this happen!). Here is one example, a response to the preceding report, which reveals a more collaborative spirit, or at least curiosity, at work:

Date: Fri, 3 Nov 1995
From: lm7846s@ACAD.DRAKE.EDU
To: Multiple recipients of list <isklproj@jaring.my>
Subject: a-bomb internet

Dear Dave and John,

It would seem as though you found quite a lot more information on the French atomic bomb testing than we did. We used the Lycos search engine and found, within the last three weeks that is, one World Wide Web site and a few newsgroup articles that had since been deleted. We decided to stick to the single Web site that we did manage to find. But, if you recall, we managed to find a mountain of information regarding the occurrences in Bosnia.

I'm wondering what search engines you are using to find the information available on the Internet, or, more specifically, the World Wide Web. It makes sense however, that you would have limited access to information regarding

Bosnia, because Malaysia has taken sides in the issue. I would be interested in other methods you use to locate information as well.

Thanx!

Ken K, Mark L, Juan C

One shouldn't make too much of any single document, but certainly this one indicates greater awareness of Malay politics than the Des Moines students possessed a short time before, as well as a desire to learn how a counterpart conducted research. There is often a wide gap between what a teacher expects the student will learn from a particular project, and what the student actually does learn. In this instance, sharing information about more effective uses of a "search engine" may have helped these students in future research projects. Thinking about the media's influence in another country may have helped them reflect more upon its role within their own. I can't help wondering what we might have learned from students in France or Australia if they had participated in this research, using different search engines and keywords. Ultimately, this was the kind of collaborative learning we had hoped to inspire. Despite the frustrations, from premature departures to unrequited messages, the possibility of creating a thoughtful, online community of inquiry still seemed within our reach. Like Tantalus, we extended ourselves, trying to ignore the evidence suggesting that our reach exceeded our grasp.

Media Report #4 : Advertisements for Ourselves

From the outset, my students had demonstrated genuine interest in advertisers' use of media. As mentioned earlier, I pondered a fourth round of reports devoted to this topic and sent private e-mail messages suggesting it to other coordinators. There were no takers. Not even Lowell. So we had come full circle. What started as an English elective's discussion of "Literature, Language, and Society" and evolved into an online discussion, had now returned to the confines of that initial classroom. I gave my students plenty of freedom to investigate advertising, but still demanded that they submit reports to the listserver. Our counterparts in Iowa did not follow suit, but I stayed in contact with Lowell on a daily basis. Among other things, he complained that his students, who came to the course with the expectation that they would study computers, now resented the project, or anything that would pull them away from what interested them most: "computer applications."

What we faced was not a technological problem, but an institutional and cultural one. In-class discussions were essential for students to contextualize developments within the project, but conventional definitions and expectations presented obstacles to an interdisciplinary project of this sort. Students entered an English class with the expectation that they would read and write; students entering a computer applications course expected to spend their time with computers and software applications, rather than human beings at the other end of them. Perhaps this explained some of the "attitudinal problems" Lowell confronted. One can only speculate. It was disappointing to see them lose interest, however, since the Internet had allowed my students to break free of censorship in Malaysia, the confines of our school and expatriate milieu, to engage in a brave new discourse via this mechanism called a listserver.

Unfortunately, this was not the last of our disappointments. At the end of October, just as my students sent their third reports to the mailing list and I began preparing for the second semester's telecollaborative project, I learned that the "Literature, Language, and Society" course would not be offered during the second semester. My department head delivered the news. Students confirmed it, informing me that when they attempted to register for the second semester their counselor said the elective was no longer an option. Apparently, the high school principal canceled the course due to high enrollment in tenth grade English. In addition to "LLS" I was teaching four sections of English 10 at the time; enrollment in each of those sections had grown beyond the norm. Rather than offer the elective for a small group of seniors, or allow sophomores to fulfill their requirements by enrolling in the elective, the principal decided to cancel it and assign me five sections of sophomore English. I was dumbfounded to think a course could be canceled without consulting the teacher or his department head. Given the numerous trials, the challenges of developing a new course and experimenting with telecollaborative learning, this hardly seemed like professional courtesy, let alone encouragement for innovative practices.

Evaluating the Experience

To help them gain a sense of closure I required my students to produce two final pieces of writing: first, an essay speculating upon the "future" of their medium; second, a project evaluation. I hoped these exercises would allow them to evaluate their respective news media as well as this new medium for communication and learning. The essay compelled everyone to learn proper bibliographical notation for e-mail and Web sites. The evaluations, meanwhile, provided valuable insights about student experiences in new learning environments. I posted my instructions on the project listserver in the hope that we would hear from some of the other participants as well. Recalling the dispute between Aesop's Lion and Man, I've selected the following evaluations to demonstrate a range of student responses. The first evaluation suggests that this activity had little impact upon the student, though one might wonder if the repeated denials reveal an accurate assessment of the project or a portrait of the adolescent as a "closed system" suffering the symptoms that Lowell described in the preceding chapter.

Date: Thu, 23 Nov 1995
From: lm7846s@ACAD.DRAKE.EDU (Lowell Monke)
To: Multiple recipients of list <isklproj@jaring.my>
Subject: Evaluations (2) DMPS

FINAL EVALUATION—MEDIA MATTER PROJECT

Joe L
16 years old
American (Dutch Descent)
United States of America
Central Campus, Des Moines, Iowa
Home School: East High School, Des Moines, Iowa

Biggest Thrill / Frustration: My biggest frustration is that ISKL and DMPS did not have a chance to really debate/talk about what we found in the different media's and how much the government can play in any country's media.

Favorite Quote: My favorite quote from all of these reports came from the Hawaii Preparatory Academy's Internet report on the Unabomber. The quote was "Perhaps the Unabomber *IS* Bill Gates (notice the resemblance?)." I liked this quote because it shows how people have a right to say what they feel, or Free Speech.

Research: I believe that the research we came up with didn't influence us very much because I believe that we all had certain feelings about the story's before the media even got involved. What I am trying to say is that the you almost always have your mind made up from the first time you see a report and very little can change the way you feel.

Social Awareness: This project did influence me because it showed that no matter how far apart people are, we all tend to act in the very same ways. I learned this because the Malaysian media treated stories very similar to the way American media treated the same stories.

Media Perceptions: This project really hasn't changed the way that I look at the media. I have always felt that the media is just trying to get ratings and that is all they care about. The media doesn't care about good news because the people want to see how many children are killed in Bosnia everyday or how much racism affects our everyday lives and consequently the media reports on the negative aspects of the world.

Telecommunications: I don't believe that the Internet really affected my learning because you could get the same information over the telephone, its just that the Internet is allot cheaper. I believe that the strengths of the Internet are in the way it allows people around the world to communicate at very low costs. But the weaknesses of the Internet are that you can't see who you are talking to. All you receive is a typed message that could all be lies or nothing but truth, how are you to tell. But if you were talking face to face with someone you could tell when someone was serious. My recommendations to make this project better is to expand the due dates for the reports, and maybe get a telephone conversation from one class to the other so you can get a real feel of who you are corresponding with.

Parting Words: The news media has definitely advanced over the past years and has now become a major part of people's lives because it provides them with information on the events that may change their lives.

Every dog shall have his day, and Aesop's Lion deserves his say. So here's the rejoinder to this evaluation. By no means an unequivocal endorsement of tele-collaboration, this evaluation does at least consider the influence a new medium may have upon individual learning, rather than holding it at arm's length, denying its impact. Note, for example, the writer's perceptions of how the public nature of a listserver influenced his writing process and how the project as a whole challenged his preconceptions.

Date: Wed, 29 Nov 1995
From: LLS_1@iskl.po.my (LLS 1)
To: Multiple recipients of list <isklproj@jaring.my>
Subject: ISKL/Evaluations/Muri

MEDIA MATTER EVALUATION

a. Nasrul M.
b. 15 years old
c. Malaysian passport (Canadian mother, Malay father)
d. Malaysia
e. International School of Kuala Lumpur

One frustration for me was the level of participation. If the four schools that participated all submitted at least three reports, more discussions may have come out of the project. I felt that most of the discussion for us at ISKL, was within our classes. It would have been more interesting for me dealing more with people outside KL.

"There are many other smaller newspapers, but I get the feeling they exist simply as a business venture (advertising money) rather than for serious news coverage. All the papers mentioned here are privately run."—Ayesha K, MAP, October 13.

I selected this quote more for what it might imply than for what it's saying.

Extending what is said, stop and ask yourself if newspapers might eventually be renamed "advertising mediums" rather than "news mediums."

Upon starting the MEDIA MATTER, I had a faint expectation that the study would cause my views on media to be super-critical. Before, I used to read newspapers for news, and considered them an official source. I accepted what I read as fact because of society's "established" standards; that newspapers are current, up to date, accurate and reveal what is important. I've discovered otherwise.

Social awareness? I've now realized that newspapers are one of the local politicians primary tools for "advertising." In Malaysia, ministers (political) are plastered all over the newspapers, they are quoted, cited and often used as publicity gimmicks for opening ceremonies. I am also more aware of the limitations and the powers of the different media. The Internet for example, can become just as influential as TV. "Someone can manipulate the reality I'm getting on-line more easily than they can manipulate the reality I get face-to-face." What happens when you start to rely on specific newsgroups, servers, and listservs on the Internet for information?

To me, "global village" involves everybody being closer to each other through different telecommunication media. Thus bringing individuals "closer" creating the so called "village." The term used to be part of the media hype to me, and I let it set in without thinking. I never really thought about some possible consequences of "global village," where people begin replacing many real world experiences with electronic ones; just as TV has done since it's creation.

Email and Internet: telecommunications medium for learning? I found that writing things for the listserv and writing the same paper for a class assignment completely different. I felt 100% more pressure to write clearly when I do things to be emailed, than when I write an essay for my English teacher. The medium through which my writing is read, changed my writing.

For the most part, I agree with the launching statement ("The Media Matter"). I also feel that the project has been successful, helping to scrutinize media, and decode it to find the truth of the matter.

Ciao,
Nasrul

Finally, I offer an antidote to the frustrations of faculty coordinators. Granted, Lowell offered this insight early in the project. However, in many ways he suffered as much frustration as I did, so it helps to return to our former positions, and look about, judging the distance our students traveled in just two months' time. This is not a definitive answer to our most troubling questions with respect to educational telecollaboration. Was it really worth the trouble? Did the students need the Internet to learn these lessons? Those questions remain open-ended, and certainly must be revisited. However, it seems critical that we also revisit moments such as these, lest the problems we encountered blind us to the lessons this community of inquiry learned, and the manner in which they learned them.

From: LM7846S@ACAD.DRAKE.EDU
Date: Mon, 18 Sep 1995 07:41:11 -0500 (CDT)
Subject: images
To: budjack@tropics.pc.my

Buddy,

As I watched my students wrestle with this topic it dawned on me that these kids have probably never been asked to think in this way before. It was like trying to teach a 15 year old how to shoot a basketball when he has never seen a game played and never touched a ball of any type before in his life. It was almost comical at times (in a pathetic sort of way) to listen to these people edge toward critical analysis only to constantly slip back again. It must have felt to them the way a really difficult book on philosophy feels to me—I think I'm starting to understand what is going on and then it slips away again and I'm confused all over. Some of them really tried hard, but without the repetitions over several years, effort alone isn't going to get you too many baskets. This is why I say that no matter the quality this is a very good exercise. It is truly a beginning for my kids, and if I can just keep that door to the gym propped open for awhile maybe they will return occasionally and pick up the ball on their own.

Modern Problems, Modest Proposals

I'm still not sure I accomplished what I set out to do: describe what "goes on inside" a telecollaborative project. I've offered glimpses of the course from which this project originated, the thinking that informed its design, the worries and struggles—both in class and online—but I've *not* conveyed the whole story. To do so would require a book-length manuscript or a hypertext document presenting all the participants' viewpoints. Obviously, students and coordinators in Kuala Lumpur and Des Moines are most thoroughly represented in this account, as they were in the project. I believe that representation is fair and accurate. I wish we could say more about the reaction of participants in Botswana and Hawaii. Unfortunately, we never received evaluations from either. Were they dissatisfied with the project? Was it too demanding? I'm not sure. For a time I worried that something had offended them, but there was never any message to that effect. The students in Botswana had a tenuous connection and participation was limited to an after-school activity. The HPA contingent, meanwhile, may have gotten precisely what they wanted out of this project: exposure to the first round of reports and e-mail responses to their work. It was unfortunate that they did not reciprocate, but their actions were beyond our control. Virtual learning communities are by their very nature unstable and vulnerable, relying upon strangers who may enter a telecollaborative activity with the best of intentions, yet discover they haven't the time, nor interest, to fulfill their initial commitment.

While mystery shrouds the perspective of participants in Botswana and Hawaii, I can offer a more detailed discussion of one community's reaction. I speak now of the International School of Kuala Lumpur. As mentioned earlier, the Internet allowed me to perforate the censor's walls within Malaysia, a country that until late 1995 prohibited ownership of satellite dishes and permitted the broadcast of three state-controlled television channels. Unfortunately, the 'Net did not resolve problems with respect to the "acceptable use" of telecommunications in my classroom, problems exacerbated by the school's lack of an official policy or classes addressing 'Netiquette. Rather than wait for such things to evolve I created my own. Much to their credit, my students were extremely cautious in posting items on Malay newsgroups and the project listserver. They were mindful of Malaysia's Internal Security Act (ISA), which prohibits publication of derogatory remarks about the government and its officials. Ironically, Malay censors never interfered with our study, but a high school administrator did.

Here was proof that networking a school does not necessarily open minds to new pedagogical models or curricular innovations. Ultimately, the real struggle for teachers who wish to integrate technology in a meaningful, individual manner stems not from technical apparatus, but the conventional beliefs and traditional routines of a community and school. These beliefs not only resist innovation, but often wish to annihilate the dialectical tension they create. Innovators should anticipate resistance from three prominent sources and prepare to defend their innovations. Here are some of the more common concerns and a few modest proposals for handling them.

Student Resistance

Despite their youth, and seemingly open dispositions, many high school students have a surprisingly low tolerance for alterations of the status quo—in everything from classroom dynamics and assessment to school traditions (prom, senior privileges, etc.). They may dye their hair a different color every day, but seldom accord the teacher and school the same kind of flexibility. Neither my students, who entered *The Media Matter* through the door of English, nor Lowell's, who entered through computer studies, were comfortable with this as part of the academic "discipline" that led them to it. My students thought we spent too much time on computers; Lowell's felt there was too much time devoted to writing. In both instances, the conventional definitions predisposed students to think this integration was an annihilation, and that it was inconsistent with their expectations and the school's curriculum. I conveyed my concerns with the "technology" of a curriculum and the ways in which that machine, designed to aid students and teachers, often became the driving force within schools, dictating far more of the program than it should. Unfortunately, this did not persuade my students that the course description in the high school handbook was accurate. Next time, I'll begin with that description and challenge the conventions from the very first day of class.

Parental and Curricular Resistance

Parental concerns, despite their legitimacy and good intentions, often dictate curricular realities more than they should. For example, due to policies beyond his control, Lowell's students were never granted "official" access to e-mail accounts through the Des Moines Public Schools. That hindered student dialogues considerably. Yet, such are the consequences of restricting student access in an effort to protect them from the evils of the Internet. This exposes the flaws of an "Acceptable Use Policy" that lacks an educational component. Draconian rules and outright censorship seldom teach students how to behave responsibly, whether they're driving cars or surfing the Internet. With respect to computers in education, school curricula initially emphasized "keyboarding skills" and courses in "computer applications" or programming. However, now that the technology has diffused throughout the curriculum, we must address its social and ethical dimensions as well.

Certainly, we need to offer children guidance for telecomputing, but acceptable use policies, as presently conceived, are legalistic and threatening when they ought to be instructive. What schools ought to do, in concert with faculty representatives from all disciplines, is develop a "CyberPilot's License" program that provides a more robust "computer literacy," teaching what is meant by the *responsible* use of computer technology by drawing upon precedents established in response to technology of another kind. I invite readers to visit an online prototype for such a program, which I've initiated at the Cyberpilot's License Web site: <http://www.cwrl.utexas.edu/~burniske.cpl>

When adolescents misbehaved with automobiles half a century ago few people proposed banning cars from local streets or schools. Instead, they introduced a new program to the school curriculum, one that would help students learn how to use this technology appropriately. In a master's thesis completed at the University of Texas in 1951, at a time when schools were just beginning to design driver education programs, one graduate student examined various proposals, noting that studies concluded "human factors—wrong attitudes, bad habits, lack of skill, and ignorance—account for the majority of (automobile) accidents" (Betley 22). This study reached two conclusions: first, that students who "received driving instruction in high school have fewer accidents than comparable groups of nontrained drivers"; and second, "as driving instruction is improved and made available to more students, young drivers may avoid substantially more than half the normally expected number of accidents" (24).

Unfortunately, it wasn't until the Highway Safety Act of 1966 that driver education actually became a component of federal standards for state highway safety programs. In this regard instruction on the appropriate use of the Internet must depart from its predecessor, for we should not delay its implementation. The analogy between automobiles and computer technology, manifested in the rhetoric of the "Information Highway" and "Infobahn," invites extension of this metaphor to help students learn how to rev up "search engines" without harming themselves, fellow drivers, or the society-at-large. What's more, such a program should address the fundamental anxieties that undermine this new mode of transportation and communication. There are serious issues to consider as schools help students merge with Internet traffic, but tossing litigious policy statements at students, without teaching them what those documents mean, is irresponsible. The implementation of a *CyberPilot's License* program would encourage a more thoughtful integration of technology into existing curricula, enabling educators to play a proactive role rather than a reactive one.

The *CyberPilot's License* program should be designed, like driver's education, to address not only the skills necessary to operate this machinery, but the attitudes and behaviors that promote healthy practices. In *Hot Rod,* a mid-century book about automobiles in America, Henry Gregor Felsen offered insights that speak as forcefully to "cyberpilots" today as they did automobile drivers then:

Those young drivers have learned to drive. They can operate a car all right, and make it go as fast as anyone else, but they haven't learned the one most important factor in driving—the proper attitude. (Felsen 1950, 50–51)

Critics of this proposal may consider it an unnecessary encroachment upon academic curricula. Others will quarrel over the appropriate place for it within the curriculum. Both responses, however, perpetuate myopic and evasive stances. We cannot dismiss "Netiquette" as irrelevant, banishing it to the null curriculum. Nor can we allow disputes over its proper place in the curriculum to stall its introduction. As currently designed, few computer science courses give "Web ethics" more than a peripheral glance. Meanwhile, humanities teachers complain they already have too much to do, too little expertise with telecomputing, to accept such responsibilities. However, emerging technologies blur the distinctions between disciplines, compelling simultaneous instruction of skills, and the responsibility inherent in their exercise. "Computer ethics" must, therefore, be an integral part of *any* class that uses computers—and a prerequisite for *computer literacy.*

The *CyberPilot's License* will be no more panacea for the abuse of computer privileges than driver's education has been for the abuse of an automobile license. However, such a program will help schools create an acceptable use policy that makes a meaningful contribution to their curriculum. The program should provide in-service opportunities for faculty and elective courses for students, introducing the terms and technology, ethical issues attending them, and the rights and responsibilities of cyberpilots. Upon completion of such a course, *not before,* students would acquire signed letters of consent from legal guardians, assuming responsibility for their online actions. This would address the legal and parental concerns that defendants of current acceptable use policies cite, yet employ an acceptable use policy as an instructional tool rather than a vague threat.

In essence, this proposal asks that we reinvigorate school curricula through the marriage of emerging technologies with the traditions of rhetorical education. One of the most eloquent advocates of such a synthesis is Richard Lanham, who reminds us that while computer literacy has encouraged an "extraordinary convergence" in university curricula, it also has the potential to displace a central fixture of the humanities curriculum. If allowed, the consequences will extend well beyond schools:

Once you abolish rhetorical education, then you must ask, "How then, do I teach decorum. What else do I use for my behavioral allegory?" Property? Stuff? And what about the teaching of language? Once it has become simply instrumental, the clear, brief, and sincere transmission of neutral fact from one neutral entity to another, it loses its numinosity and then its power, as our present literacy crisis attests. If you pursue only clarity, you guarantee obscurity. And people lose their vital interest in language, as any composition teacher can attest. The "literacy crisis" is not only a social crisis, a crisis of instructional leverage, of educational policy, although it is all of those. It comes from the repudiation of the rhetorical heart of Western education, and its linguistic and behavioral education in decorum. (Lanham 1994, 83)

It is difficult to speak to these issues, and articulate proposals like the *CyberPilot's License,* without sounding self-righteous or hysterical. However, I have been turning this over in my mind as a graduate student, teacher of undergraduates, and parent of high school and elementary students for some time now. The convergence of those viewpoints motivates the suggestion of a *CyberPilot's License* program as a progressive measure, not a reactionary one. To succeed, it must bring human concerns to the foreground of computer literacy, encouraging a thoughtful approach to technological narratives without neglecting human narratives. That basic tenet is our best hope for ensuring computer technology serves humanity, rather than humanity serving technology.

Faculty and Administrative Resistance

When I began these telecollaborative experiments it was evident that they upset a number of colleagues. One of the more poignant moments came shortly after our first exchange of electronic documents during *Project Utopia*. As I relayed the news of this event to members of the English Department one colleague snapped, "Well, you seem excited. What about the students?" The implication, as unmistakable as it was uncharitable, was that innovative teachers care more about their innovations than their students. Perhaps only the students can answer this charge, though it requires listening to their evaluations of online learning activities and taking those evaluations as seriously as we do The Curriculum. Even this, however, will not resolve traditional boundary issues, ones manifested by colleagues who wondered out loud why an "English teacher" was spending so much time in the computer lab. Initially, I interpreted faculty resistance to telecollaborative projects as a fear of change, a crippling anxiety that clings to the status quo because it's easier to maintain old methods than invent new ones. However, there are far more complex, underlying issues here, including the matter of self-preservation, which I'll return to momentarily.

As for the administration: the tendency toward central authority remains antithetical to a dynamic community of inquiry. The de-centralized, distributed learning that takes place in a telecollaborative learning activity runs counter to the centralized, administrative hierarchies within our schools. That hierarchy enabled the administrator in this instance to terminate a course without consulting the teachers it would affect. Certainly, the lack of a teachers' union is significant in this story, but so is the lack of respect—and courage—that betrays itself in the delivery of a message through department heads and counselors. Neither I nor my department head were consulted; we were merely informed that a "decision had been made." This led to a bitter e-mail exchange with the principal, who claimed ignorance of the "changes" that I had made to the course syllabi—as well as plans for a telecollaborative project in the second semester. This response came despite a formal observation from the assistant principal in the first week of the course, at which time I presented a course outline for the semester and year. The response also rejected counterproposals, such as admission of students from "regular" English courses to fulfill graduation requirements through the elective. That, I was told, signaled a significant departure and couldn't be implemented until the Curriculum and Instruction committee reviewed an official proposal. Certainly, innovators must work within the curriculum, satisfying requirements that support the credibility of the institution, but the institution needs to create structures that remain flexible enough to accommodate innovative ideas and unique opportunities.

This episode speaks volumes about schools where teachers wish to innovate, but confront an administrative hegemony hiding behind inflexible policies. The teaching profession, and all who hope for progressive educational reform, must not tolerate myopic authoritarians, particularly at a time when new technologies demand more pedagogical experimentation. If nothing else, this incident reveals a fundamental conflict between the rhetoric of innovation surrounding new technologies—which policymakers eagerly embrace—and the conservative nature of schools, which perpetuate traditional learning environments and standardized curricula. I was comforted by the knowledge that telecollaborative exchanges allowed my students to put forth questions, and ponder answers, long before a media critic or high school principal told them what to think. Several students protested the cancellation of the course and helped petition for its reinstatement. I shared those petitions with one of the high school counselors, who matter-of-factly informed me that there was no such elective in the second semester's schedule. I had to admire this elaborate Catch-22: not enough students had preregistered for the course the previous March—before I had inherited the class and constructed a syllabus—so it had to be canceled; once it was canceled, without my consultation, students couldn't enroll because no such class existed.

What's Going on Here?

I didn't intend such a lengthy account, but trying to describe what "goes on inside" a telecollaborative project is like trying to describe what goes on inside a life. For every instance one may sight, every anecdote one may deliver, there is an opposing instance and countervailing tale. However, there are also patterns that emerge, and one of the most pernicious of these is a lack of respect for what "goes on inside" classrooms. Telecollaborative projects are an extension of those classrooms, activities that could empower both students and teachers by enabling them to push beyond the confines of a particular place—if school structures and authorities will allow. As a result, the life of a telecollaborative project does not reveal itself in a simple, chronological fashion; rather, it requires a hypertextual narrative, one that emanates like the concentric circles from a pebble tossed into a pond. This analogy is useful, but it breaks down; with telecollaboration you never know what shores those circles will reach. I certainly didn't anticipate the following, which came my way less than a year after The Media Matter—and the course that gave it life—were shut down:

Date: Thu, 5 Sep 1996
From: Kathy Kothmann
To: Buddy Burniske <burniske@babbage.cwrl.utexas.edu>
Subject: Congratulations!

Hi, Buddy!

It is my pleasure to notify you that your entry to the SIG/Tel Telecomputing Contest, *The Media Matter,* has been selected as a Winning Entry. There were many excellent entries again this year, but twelve activity plans were selected as winning entries, and yours was one of these exemplary entries. Eight others were selected for honorable mention.

You will be receiving written notice by regular mail shortly from SIG/Tel President Chuck Lynd.

All twenty Winners and Honorable Mentions will be recognized at the Tampa or Monterrey SIG/Tel Meetings during Tel-Ed '96, December 6–7; and NECC '97 in Seattle, Washington, June 30-July 2. Likewise, all twenty projects will be published in TIE News (SIG/Tel's publication) and also on the ISTE Web site: http://www.iste.org

All winners and honorable mentions are invited to present your projects at both Tel-Ed '96 and NECC '97 in SIG/Tel's Exemplary Projects sessions. More information about this will be forthcoming.

Important: SIG/Tel would like to send a formal press release to your school, local newspaper, etc. Would you please email me the name(s) and address(es) of folks to whom you'd like to have the formal press release sent.

Congratulations again!
Kathy Kothmann
SIG/Tel Past-President

Indeed, there's irony to spare in this story, which is a variation on an all-too-familiar theme. As such, it illustrates the challenges classroom teachers face as they integrate technology into their classroom. A computer network is one medium, and a curriculum another. We must not overlook this. Administrators and public policymakers are fond of the term "integration," yet oblivious to the idea that integration implies a quiet annihilation *of that which came before.* This, too, is why educators resist change, particularly the kind that technology has wrought. Self-preservation inspires their resistance, for they realize a change of pedagogy implies a subtle change of oneself. Innovative educators cannot succeed without stretching the parameters of school policy, prompting controversies along the way. In my final months as a high school teacher I often wondered how schools would reconcile the push for "technology integration" on the one hand with policies supporting rigid curricula and standardized tests on the other. Perhaps my own naivete made me see this in terms of dialectical tension, setting the possibility for radical, pedagogical change against the demand for a conservative, standardized curriculum. I still believe that tension exists, but confess I'm increasingly fearful of the possibility that a rigid curricula and its supporters will simply adapt technology to serve their limited and limiting purpose.

So I'll speak as a classroom teacher one more time. I'll argue for a more enlightened approach, saying that we must not allow the integration of networked technology to annihilate debates over school policy, which means giving classroom practitioners more voice in such matters. Marginalizing classroom teachers, treating them like automatons programmed to fulfill rigid policies, impoverishes our schools one classroom at a time. Ultimately, who really loses in a situation like the one described in this chapter? The principal had his way, using his power to utter a *fait accompli* that he would undoubtedly defend as the most effective and efficient solution to a problem. There was no room for negotiation. No need to investigate alternatives. Who loses in such situations? The classroom teacher? Not really, for career educators learn how to subvert from within, making the curriculum itself a subject for critical inquiry. Ultimately, though, students will lose, forfeiting opportunities to learn whenever the censor's hand represses an idea, silences a teacher, or terminates a provocative course.

The media matter.

Oh yes, they most certainly do, but so do the words and images they transmit, the spirit that shapes those words and images, and the human beings who give expression to that spirit.

My students could have learned that lesson without a global, telecollaborative project, but I doubt their study of "Literature, Language, and Society" would have been so compelling. Nor would their teacher have learned as much about efforts to control the media within their school and community. And that, after all, is what led us to the telecollaborative looking glass in the first place, inspiring far more than "a fun class without much homework."

8

In Dreams Begin Responsibilities

Lowell Monke

...the range of one's responsibilities must be commensurate with the range of one's actions.
Joseph Weizenbaum, Early MIT Computer Science Pioneer (1976, 261)

For an innovative teacher like Buddy, dealing with an inflexible school bureaucracy can be a nightmare. Compared to the intransigence he faced, my situation at Central Campus was a dream. By 1995 my class had somehow taken on the character of a perpetual pilot program among the technology decision-makers in the district. Though officially no students were allowed direct Internet access for another three years, all of my supervisors carefully averted their eyes as I went about my business of experimenting with student e-mail and Web pages.

A dream it was, but one in which I also sensed a dark and threatening presence. I knew that if something went wrong, anything at all, it was my neck that was in the noose. A bad case of PR paranoia had paralyzed my district's attempt to develop a student use policy, and although all of my supervisors were anxious for me to experiment with the Internet, it was also clear that I was walking a telecommunication high-wire without a legal or professional net. One slip, one public scandal, and my program and I would take a long fall. Ironically, the opportunities of telecollaboration had put me in a tenuous position that forced me to reconsider my fundamental responsibilities as a teacher.

There are hundreds of books on the market today (not to mention Web sites) that list thousands of opportunities for using the Internet in the classroom. There is no need to recount them here. There is, however, a disappointing shortage of thoughtful literature devoted to discussing the sobering flip side of opportunity—responsibility. Perhaps this is just a reflection of a larger trend in our society: We have become preoccupied with liberties, and little concerned with the self-discipline that is its ethical companion. In education we have developed a consumer ethos in which we believe that whatever is desired ought to be made available (Solnit 1995),[1] with little or no thought given to the deeper consequences of our choices. The 'Net is, in this respect, a global department store, and the only responsibility that the educator-as-consumer recognizes is to help her students become discriminating shoppers.

I believe our responsibilities as teachers should go far beyond making appropriate choices in the cybermall. Each of the topics we have taken up in this dialogue has, in one way or another, involved a reexamination of the responsibilities a teacher has in light of telecollaborative opportunities. And, in turn, it is by examining those responsibilities that we can find some guidance in dealing with the many difficult issues that telecollaboration raises. In this chapter I want to turn our attention directly toward those responsibilities, hopefully in a more systematic way than I worked through them with my own students. I will discuss six different teacher responsibilities in a telecollaborative classroom. This is, to be sure, an artificial convenience, an examination of isolated threads that in reality weave through each other to form an intricate tapestry. However, by isolating these responsibilities and considering them from inside the classroom outward perhaps we can stitch together the larger context of telecollaboration in the classroom. The threads of responsibility I wish to explore are: to students, teachers, schools, communities, the world, and the truth.

Our Responsibilities to Our Students

As teachers, our primary responsibility is the educational welfare of our students. This simple statement is not as universally accepted as we may suppose. Certainly to others outside the teaching profession—parents, administrators, the business and civic communities—there are responsibilities that compete with it. Each of these groups, commonly referred to by that degrading economic term "stakeholder," tends to either see the welfare of the student as synonymous with their sphere of concern or relegate it to less than the primary priority. Too often the efforts of each interest group to influence the learning process results in students being reduced to objects, serving the interests of others, at the expense of their own personal and group welfare. One of the teacher's most important responsibilities is to sort out the various claims on her students and find ways to address them while making sure that the students' own needs are met first.

Administrators, parents, school board members, and business people seldom acknowledge a teacher's responsibility for mediating the pressures brought to bear on young people. The factory model of education introduced to American education at the turn of the twentieth century has, by the beginning of the twenty-first, gradually reduced the role of the teacher to merely the assembler of academic parts (Apple 1982), charged with carrying out the dictates of a management system that has little or no contact with the actual individuals whose lives they control. At the same time the students themselves have been aggregated into a community or national "resource," a faceless mass whose value is gauged not by the intrinsic worth of the humans who make it up, but by their present or future relationship to the various sectors of the existing society. Thus, a responsible teacher to an administrator is one who internalizes the goals and policies of the school and sees to it that students learn within those parameters. To the business community a responsible teacher concentrates on developing the skills that will allow the students to contribute to the profitability of corporate enterprises. To the community of parents a responsible teacher will instill the parents' values in their children and prepare them so that their knowledge will result in high SAT scores, a strong GPA, and a good attitude toward further schooling or gainful employment. A "model" teacher is one who can meet all of these responsibilities and still be popular among her students.

Of course, there are many dissenters in all ranks from this objectifying view of students in our schools, but the general operating premise tends to be one in which students serve someone else's purpose rather than their own. And this is what sets it at odds with what I see as the teacher's highest responsibility: to recognize that each young person is an individual, with intrinsic worth, and with personal and academic needs unlike any other; that each group of students creates a unique dynamic that must be addressed on its own terms; that the needs of both the group and the individuals in it may not coincide with what others farther removed from the classroom believe is in the interest of some abstract image of a mass student body; and that the teacher is one of the few persons in a position to help each student and group decide how to respond to those pressures. Thus, it should be the teacher's role to determine how to work with the students in his care. It is a responsibility we in the teaching profession have, in many cases, been forced to relinquish, some of us more reluctantly than others.

My experience with Buddy tells me that he will relinquish his claim on that responsibility when they throw dirt on his coffin. It is this sense of responsibility that was one of the major driving forces in his efforts to engage many of his students in telecollaboration while in Malaysia. Through telecollaboration he was able to liberate his students from what he recognized as the chokehold of a deadening curriculum and the information desert of a censorious political regime. Seen through his eyes, a responsibility to his students provoked an embrace of telecollaboration in order to meet their particular needs.

The contrast between Buddy's concern and the obligation I felt to reduce my students' overexposure to the high-tech information flow here in the States illustrates that this sense of responsibility is situated in a specific context. This, of course, points to one of the major problems with individual responsibilities: they don't always lead different people to the same conclusions. There is no way to codify responsible actions; no way to turn it into a technique that can be taught in a staff development course or a teacher preparation class. It is not something we can generalize. And that in itself is one of the most important features of being responsible first and foremost to our students: It personalizes the learning process; it invigorates the teacher-student relationship; it transforms teaching from mechanical cookie-cutting to organic discourse. That is one of the reasons this book has not been about techniques: *Techniques are methods that can be applied in general.* And there is very little that is general about a particular student or even group of students. The computer is rapidly making it clear that anything that can be applied *in general* doesn't need a teacher worthy of the title to apply it. To ignore this is to invite into the primary and secondary levels of education the same kind of digital diploma mills (Noble 1997) that are beginning to proliferate at the university level. Our unique role as teachers is determined through our relationship with our students, developed through the specific context of our shared situation. It takes into account all of those external pressures mentioned earlier, but transforms them according to the needs of each student and the dynamics of each group with which we work.

This is why I do not buy that popular aphorism I mentioned earlier and still hear at every computer conference—"Get the sage off the stage to be the guide on the side." I have no problem with getting the sage off the stage. Good teachers stepped down from the podium and started mingling with their students long before the computer came along. But relegating the teacher to being merely a guide denies the crucial responsibility I have just described. First, it implies that there is no place in the classroom for adult wisdom (what is a sage but a wise adult?). This is an incredibly antieducational, generation-gap promoting attitude. Second, and more important, it reduces the student-teacher relationship to a superficial, impersonal level. A guide is a hired hand who takes clients on a tour, showing the way, providing information, and even giving advice. She can lead her clients into an adventure and make sure they get back out again. All of these attributes of a guide are also important characteristics of a teacher or a parent or mentor. But in each case the role of guide is not deep enough or personal enough to fully describe the needed relationship (nor is the term "facilitator," which lacks in the same way). This is because the guide/client relationship is essentially a service/consumer relationship. Once the tour is over, the relationship is too. This turns learning into a commodity and the guide herself becomes a tool, contracted for a purpose that is defined by the commodity being pursued.[2] Both the teacher and the student suffer under this arrangement. They are constrained by this relationship from drawing on their full range of human capacities. A guide isn't expected to help the adventurer fit her experience into the rest of her life. A guide isn't charged with developing experiences that are meaningful in the context that the adventurer brings to the tour. The adventurer cannot expect a guide to care deeply that her experience grows out of a unique past or that it must somehow be integrated into her journey toward an uncertain future. Moreover, life is not a tour, and education is not a guided tour—it is the development of a human being in relation to the rest of humanity and the world.

The teacher as guide only serves to reinforce the degraded view of learning that Buddy and I have been striving to overcome. Yet more and more I hear people talking about students being consumers of education, about children being the clients of the school and the community at large being the aforementioned stakeholders. "The guide on the side" fits this commodified notion of education and nowhere is it applied with more frequency or verve than in the telecomputing club.

Perhaps I am overreacting to a term innocently used in a metaphorical sense to fit the virtual-travel nature of the 'Net. But I have learned from Buddy that words themselves often say more than we think they do, and we have to be very careful how we select them. Our responsibility in working with students in tele-collaborative activities demands a term that evokes a much deeper commitment that a teacher should have to his students. I would like to revisit the farm just one more time to suggest a word my dad used to describe his responsibility to the land he farmed: stewardship.

Stewardship of the land meant to my dad not just guiding the land to profitability, but caring for it, nurturing it, enriching it—committing his effort to its total welfare (even, at times, at the expense of profitability) so that when it passed out of his hands it had not only been productive, but was just as fertile as when it passed into them. In an era given over so heavily to utilitarian values, it is difficult to explain the kind of reverence and respect for the land's integrity that was implied by this sense of stewardship. I think it had a lot to do with an intuitive acceptance that the land was not just an object to be manipulated to produce certain measurable outcomes, but rather a rich, often obstinate partner whose potential bounty only testified to its intrinsic worth. This recognition of the land's inherent value, and its inseparability from the life of the farmer, called forth a sense of responsibility to protect and care for and enrich it, not just take what it could produce. With the advent of large-scale mechanized farming much of that sense of stewardship has decayed, as the land is viewed more and more in terms of inputs and outputs, a mere container of cash crops. The large-scale mechanization of schooling has had a similar effect on the relationship between teachers and students. Buddy's experiences testify to, and my own experiences in five different school systems corroborates, this commodifying trend: For all the high-minded talk of individualized instruction, school children today are mostly treated as objects (perhaps individual objects) on which we as teachers apply techniques (our cherished "methods") in order to assure certain inputs that, if the mechanism works as advertised, will effect certain measurable outcomes. The ultimate end, of course, is a product, marketed to colleges or employers according to quantified specifications that differ little from those used to sell stereos or automobiles, and the success of which indicates to the taxpayers just how smoothly the machinery is functioning.

Putting students on the 'Net will do nothing to improve this situation; indeed, I am convinced it will accelerate the trend (recall Buddy's discussion of Classroom Connect's "Internet-in-a-box" resources) unless it is accompanied by a profound change in consciousness among teachers concerning their relationship with their students. "Guide on the side" won't do it, for it encourages us to treat both the activities and the students as objects apart from ourselves, rather than subjects with whom we enter into an ongoing, deeply human relationship. Stewardship implies just that kind of approach. Becoming good stewards won't solve all of our pedagogical problems but it might at least get us started in the right direction. The following describe a few of the issues that a sense of stewardship might call to our attention in working with our students on the 'Net.

Finding the Person Behind the Words

One thing we have found over and over in our work is how easy it is for students to forget that there is a living, thinking, feeling human being behind every message they read and every e-mail address to which they write. To say that we have a responsibility to assure that our students are courteous in their online communications is merely to state the obvious. Any good guide will encourage good manners. Good stewardship has to go beyond that—to help our students examine why it is that courtesy is such a difficult quality to maintain in online exchanges. The causes are neither obvious nor certain, even to an experienced teacher. But then, our task is not to provide the answers to these questions so much as engage our students in serious thinking about them.

In this case, if we don't help our students reflect on this particular characteristic of electronic communication we risk letting them slip into a pattern of merely "conversing with words" (Talbott 1995, 221). This happens when the sense of a person at the other end of the wires fades away and the conversation is conducted between the squiggly figures that show up on the computer screens. Talbott points out that with each new development in the mechanical conveyance of communication, "the word has increasingly detached itself from the human being who utters it" (Talbott 1995). Consider the student cited in chapter 4 who wrote in his Project Utopia evaluation that he liked this form of communication "because you don't have to worry about consequences that a statement can make if you know the person." He understood that conversing with just the words of another person lowers the demands on civility. In his own personal, unsophisticated way he was merely echoing the *Wired* stylist Buddy condemned in chapter 5 who so brazenly advised cyberwriters to "screw the rules."

When the writer's conception of the reading audience is reduced from engaged human beings to abstract objects, much like the characters he manipulates on his computer screen, then what reason is there to treat them with respect or civility? If we won't take the time, or don't have the capacity, to empathetically envision another human's reaction to our text, then why care if what we say makes sense to them or honors their efforts to understand?

Empathy, the ability to stand in anothers' shoes, is crucial for communication. It is difficult to develop in young people in any circumstances, but is particularly problematic (though crucial) in an environment as fragmented as the Internet. How do our students develop their capacity for empathy if so much of their time is spent in front of electronic screens absorbing and producing abstract, detached words and images? If we want our students' written communication to "screw the rules" and, by implication, screw the reader, then I can't think of a better way to facilitate that attitude than to simply turn them loose on the 'Net. If, on the other hand, we want our students to seek common understanding with others, then one of our most important responsibilities is to help those students, whenever possible, to reconnect those detached words to the human beings who write and read them.

Getting to Know Our Relationship with the Medium

A good guide is highly knowledgeable about the terrain she leads her clients through. A good steward possesses not only a wealth of knowledge about the terrain but senses its deeper relationship to the human beings who work it. For the teacher leading her students into computer telecollaboration this means not only having some expertise in using the medium—what nearly everyone concentrates on—but understanding the character of the medium as well. This is a much more difficult task, for it doesn't just require hours of experience online. It requires, in addition, hours of reflection and study about that experience. I tried in chapters 2 and 4 to stress that computers and computer-mediated communication are tools that have their own impact on students, apart from the content and processes that we bring to them. If the teacher doesn't at least partly understand the influences these powerful tools have on people, then she is leading her students down a blind alley, whistling her high-tech curriculum in the dark. Certainly one of the purposes of this book is to provide the thoughtful teacher with at least a small flashlight and the knowledge that there are enough dangers out there that she had better keep searching for a larger one.

Developing a Telecomputing Ethic

Fears of the dangers lurking in cyberspace has generated a new kind of document in schools: the acceptable use policy. This is one of the stickiest concerns for schools and for some, like mine, a nightmare to devise. I stated in the introduction to this chapter that until 1998 the Des Moines Public Schools suffered from a debilitating case of "PR paranoia" in this regard. Why was this? In the fall of 1995, just before I received my unofficial approval to let my students have direct access to the 'Net, I sent the following angry message to Buddy in response to his suggestion that my students develop a Web page for *Utopian Visions '96*. It offers a sense of my impression as to why we were having so much trouble:

Excellent idea! Only one problem (bite your tongue, now)—administration. All of my students' computers are networked to the same Internet connection I use, but to date the administration (district, not Central Campus) refuses to allow them any access at all. They have had the fear of God put into them, literally, by all the religious right fanatics around here who will sue our socks off if one child sees a bare breast or reads the word "bestiality" on a listserv list. So rather than risk offending the purity police we sit here unable to teach students anything firsthand about a resource that is at our fingertips. Is this a great country or what? And your kids complain about government censorship. Here we have voluntary censorship.

It may have done my antibureaucratic spleen good to vent it on cowering administrators scared to wake up in the morning and find that our Web site has been trafficking pornography all over the globe. It turns out that I was painting the issue in much bolder, more exaggerated strokes than it really was. In fact, the Internet committee was also toiling with a more laudable concern. It had chosen not to do what so many school districts have done in the last several years in their rush to get students online: take the boiler plate appropriate use form designed by the ever helpful Classroom Connect and slap the district name in the appropriate places. Rather, this group wrestled mightily—perhaps too mightily—with the competing issues of control and freedom, along with the always burdensome concerns for public relations and legal liability.

Still, the trouble my school district encountered in their conscientious attempt to devise a viable authorized use policy is another instance, I believe, of attempting to generalize what ought to be personalized. There are just too many variables involved. This is one reason I think Buddy's proposal for a Cyber Pilot's License makes good sense. Given our faith (shared, I would hope, by the larger community) in the ability of education to spawn good judgment, requiring a training course at a particular stage of a student's academic career would seem only logical. The form and content of that training could be much more elaborate and comprehensive than any user agreement form. Furthermore, because it could have built into it an exploration of ethics, 'Netiquette, and other issues described here, the training course itself could go a long way to fulfilling some of the responsibilities I describe in this chapter.

Digging Deep

If the teacher has a responsibility to dig deeply into the character of the 'Net, it is also her responsibility to see to it that her students use the 'Net in a like manner. In *The Gutenberg Elegies* Sven Birkerts asserts that the computer has accelerated a course that reading has been on for centuries: "the gradual displacement of the vertical by the horizontal—the sacrifice of depth to lateral reading" (1994, 72). Birkerts notes a trend that most of us who use e-mail and read online text should have no trouble recognizing:

In our culture access is not a problem, but proliferation is. And the reading act is necessarily different than it was in its earliest days. Awed and intimidated by the availability of texts, faced with the all but impossible task of discriminating among them, the reader tends to move across surfaces, skimming, hastening from one site to the next without allowing the words to resonate inwardly. The inscription is light but it covers vast territories: quantity is elevated over quality. The possibility of maximum focus is undercut by the awareness of the unread texts that await. (1994, 72)

And what is the outgrowth of this shallower wading into reading waters? According to Birkerts it is precisely the loss of what I judged in chapter 2 to be the highest purpose of education:

We are experiencing in our times a loss of depth—a loss, that is, of the very paradigm of depth. A sense of the deep and natural connectedness of things is a function of vertical consciousness. Its apotheosis is what was once called wisdom. Wisdom: the knowing not of facts but of truths about human nature and the processes of life. But swamped by data, and in thrall to the technologies that manipulate it, we no longer think in these larger and necessarily more imprecise terms. In our lateral age, living in the bureaucracies of information, we don't venture a claim to that kind of understanding. Indeed, we tend to act embarrassed around those once-freighted terms—truth, meaning, soul, destiny. . . . We suspect the people who use such words of being soft and nostalgic. We prefer the deflating one-liner that reassures us that nothing need be taken that seriously; we inhale the atmospheres of irony. (1994, 74)

When I brought this issue to Buddy's attention in the middle of *Utopian Visions '95* he responded in a way that I think illustrates the responsibility I'm referring to here (for easier reading I've removed the characteristic ">" in front of the original sections and inserted our names where the voice changes; keep in mind that this is all from one message sent to me from Buddy—with his text inserted into my original message—which is why he gets the last word).

Lowell: There are so many phrases that catch my eye from other contributors that raise red flags, and my students don't seem to see any of them. Birkerts tries to make the case . . . that the electronic media flattens knowledge compared to literature. We substitute a wide ranging knowledge for depth of understanding.

Buddy: Yes! I see this even in my colleagues! Hell, Lowell, I think it explains why "extra" curricular activities are becoming "co-curricular" ones. If you move away from the hierarchies (which political correctness demands) then you step from the vertical to the horizontal. As a result, everything becomes of equal significance—which renders everything insignificant. And so, why worry about depth? Just go for a lot of "connections" without meaning, depth or value judgment . . .

Lowell: I think he is right on this point, and I think we need to keep it in mind with the uses we make of e-mail. There is a time for broadening, but, in my opinion, it should come well after a child has developed some depth of understanding of his world, first through direct experience, and then through literature, art, music—the deeply expressive activities of humans that speak both to our minds and our souls. A high school student *should* be ready for broadening experiences, but I'm afraid that here in the US everything they do is broadening, even at an early age. So they end up being shallow, unable to be critical because there is no deep foundation from which to judge new experiences.

Buddy: (. . .) A final thought: there wouldn't be so much argument over the "canon of great literature" in American Universities if students read books outside of class, Lowell. That whole debate sounds silly to Europeans. Know why? Their kids still read more than they watch TV . . . so the "canon" isn't such a big deal to them. But you can see how that canon takes on greater importance in a post-literate society where the teachers and parents think: MY GOD, this might be the only 19th century novel the kids ever read . . . which ONE should it be?

Now take this same hysteria and apply it to e-mail. Perhaps this explains why I was defending the stuff while you were attacking. Sure, some of it's junk mail and you get boxes of that in print form every month. Here? I receive virtually none. And sure, e-mail is demanding, time-consuming and mainly about the here and now (like TV, radio and other media sources). . . . But remember: I have no TV, no radio, no answering machine, and virtually none of the media junk to deal with. So when I defended e-mail, Internet, distance learning, etc. I was coming from the vantage point of one involved with a community of readers/writers who will not suddenly abandon Dickens, Conrad, James for this stuff, but use this stuff to enrich their study of the former. And the moment I see them growing superficial I will address the issue, scold them for taking refuge in the shallow end of Life's swimming pool, and threaten to pull the plug. To pull it without first warning them of that consequence doesn't seem an "educational" practice as much as a tyrannical one. How are kids to learn about the life of the mind and the choice between superficial thought and wisdom unless we as educators show them the difference? I won't give up that fight. Not in handwritten journals, typed essays, or e-mailed reports. That's a promise . . .

Again we see that different situations require different responses. But what I think is important about this message in this context is the need for a commitment from the teacher to see that the learning that takes place through the wires has depth; that students are pulled down off that fast moving electronic tractor and forced to get a little dirt under their fingernails. As Buddy points out, this is not easy, for it flies in the face of a cultural trend that encourages us to accept all experiences as being of equal value, no matter how superficial. Given this philosophy of education, the 'Net becomes the ultimate learning resource simply by virtue of its endless supply of experiences, virtual though they be. This is what I have often seen described as the "democracy of information," unencumbered by the wise mediation of the pedagogical sage.

Unfortunately, anyone who traffics in telecollaborative projects should be prepared to deal with teachers as well as students who embrace this notion of education. Even though we have always been careful not to indiscriminately broadcast our projects but rather send notices about them through carefully selected channels, we have had to get used to teachers surfing our projects just as they and their students surf the rest of the 'Net (and, I suspect, life itself). Just to give one example, in the previous chapter Buddy wrote about the teacher in Hawaii who suddenly pulled her students from *The Media Matter* after the first round of exchanges. Here is the full text of her message to Buddy:

Our class has made the decision not to continue with the Media Matter online discussion group. It was fun while it lasted, but the kids wanted to move on to creating their own Web pages, so that's what we are doing. Perhaps we'll join up with you on another project. Thanks!

I haven't included here the reaction Buddy sent along to me when he forwarded the message. Suffice it to say that he wasn't impressed with her assessment that "It was fun while it lasted." This is the guide-on-the-side approach that leads to the shallowness of mind and purpose that those seeking educational reform justifiably rail against. It is student as tourist, with the same been-there-done-that mentality I noted before. It is the consumer approach to learning, in which the teacher's role is to secure the commodities that fulfill her clients' desires. In this case the students collected online experiences like trinkets—with about the same value attached to them.

Engaging Subjects Rather Than Using Objects

This consumer approach to learning inevitably leads to shallowness, but there is something even more distressing about this approach to telecollaboration, something that I think hearkens back to my earlier observations concerning empathy and detachment, and our responsibility to see the humans beyond the screen. When I received the message from Buddy concerning Hawaii's withdrawal, my reaction was a little like a victim of seduction, who, upon ushering the new lover to the door, gets a smile and a jovial, "Hey, it was fun. Let's do it again sometime." Though not so profoundly degrading, that message from Hawaii conveyed a callous disregard for the other members of this project who had spent considerable time communicating with the teachers' students. While we were trying to build a community of inquiry, she looked upon us as just another experience for her students, resources that required no more sensitivity than one gives an essay pulled down from a Web site.

Of course, this insensitivity isn't something the 'Net causes, but through its widening separation of the word from the person it tends to reinforce and encourage it. I suspect the teacher from Hawaii is a fine person, and would be aghast that her actions caused such strong feelings of betrayal. My guess is that she felt that we got as much from her students as they got from us. This is, in my experience, the most common attitude toward relating over the 'Net. Of course, mutual exploitation is still exploitation and it is this coarsened view of cooperative learning that is corrosive no matter how much information is passed over the wires. As Michael Lerner has written in *The Politics of Meaning*, "Many people intuit that treating the world and other human beings as resources to be exploited may lead Western societies to the brink of social and ecological disaster" (1996, 31). One doesn't have to share his apocalyptic vision to recognize the teacher's critical responsibility to assure that students working on the 'Net do not turn humans into objects of use. One of the best ways I know to prevent that from happening is to discourage skimming from site to site, contact to contact, seeking to engage other human beings solely in an effort to gather information for oneself. Rather we should demand that whenever possible our students get behind the objects on the screen to engage the subjects from whom they came. We should encourage cooperative pursuits of knowledge that not only develop in-depth understandings but also build a sense of community and personal responsibility to each other. Here, as elsewhere, we have to battle against education conceived as a commodity to be consumed rather than relationships to be developed.

Comprehending Context

The struggle to find the human behind the words can not only promote empathy and commitment, but it can help us push past the inevitable language problems of global communication. I learned enough Spanish to get along in Ecuador, but I embarrassed myself enough times while living there that I would be very hesitant to rely on it for communication in a telecollaborative project, especially with native Spanish speakers. In our projects we have discovered teachers and students who are less weak-kneed than I. Indeed, in *Utopian Visions '97* participants from several schools struggled mightily to express themselves in a language that required constant consultation with a dictionary. Consider this statement from a report on agriculture from a student in the Czech Republic: "A country–estate was more extend forest and lake property written down in the Provincial Plaques and it subjected to special rules concerning property and farming." I am sure that composing sentences like these was a laborious and frustrating effort. If my students had not been made aware of how much work these students put into communicating their ideas in a language different from their own they would surely have ridiculed such convoluted statements. Instead, they saw it as their part of a cooperative effort to finish the interpretation that these writers started. It was not always an easy task and seemed especially hard for those of my students who had no foreign language background. I often had to rephrase the faulty English for them, recognizing in the process that my own experience in learning a foreign language was a key factor in puzzling out what students were trying to say not only in Mexico, but central Europe as well. This effort brought back to mind the many misunderstandings that I had noticed in previous projects where the English skills of international school students were good enough to express basic ideas but not sophisticated enough to convey subtle nuances. This, I felt, had been the primary cause of hard feelings. Phrases that I understood as a terseness caused by a narrow vocabulary were misinterpreted by students as an intentional brusqueness and insensitivity.

By the end of *Utopian Visions '97* I realized that one of the responsibilities of teachers who engage their students in international communication should be the possession themselves of certain international skills—such as a foreign language. A good math teacher possesses a depth of knowledge about algebra that goes far beyond what any of her students will be expected to learn. Shouldn't a good teacher using global communications have a deeper knowledge of language in the international realm than her students? Otherwise how will she be able to see through the superficial problems of grammar that plague students for whom English is a second language?

But let's go beyond the language. We've already seen that language is tied to culture. I have argued that students who use telecommunication work out of contexts that are merely shades of a common techno-culture. Yet those shadings do indeed color the communications in ways that can cripple comprehension. Shouldn't a good teacher of global communications projects have some knowledge of the different orientations his students encounter on the 'Net, or at least some experience in dealing with cultural differences determined by place? It doesn't have to be experience with a particular place. When Buddy wrote to me of his stay in the Sarawak longhouse I could draw on my own travels in the Amazon basin in order to connect with what he was trying to tell me. I'm not sure this explains it entirely, but those who live for a time outside of their home country seem to develop a sixth sense for cultural nuances that, when it comes to global telecollaborative learning projects, becomes a critical teaching skill. One of the frustrations I experienced in our *Utopian Visions* projects came from the fact that three of the four teachers whose classes participated had never lived or traveled extensively outside the country. Whereas Mike Schaffer (who had lived all over the world) and I could read between the lines, helping students interpret contexts that grew out of particular national, regional, or ethnic backgrounds, the other three teachers rarely picked up on these subtleties, often leaving their students with superficial or even mistaken impressions of what their correspondents were trying to convey.

Let me hasten to add that these were excellent teachers, among the best teachers I have encountered in my twenty years of teaching. But the skills required for their normal work did not take into account the unique demands of telecollaboration: it explodes the limited focus of traditional curriculum, even as it hides the contexts from which that explosion originates. All of the troublesome pedagogical issues we have discussed in this book represent aspects of the explosion of responsibilities that a conscientious teacher must accept when entering the realm of global telecollaboration. It is one of the implications of Weizenbaum's observation that our responsibilities must be commensurate with our reach. Writing long before the Internet arrived on the scene, Weizenbaum recognized the opportunities that were on the horizon and was concerned that we not ignore the ethical obligations that accompanied them. As far as I can tell, very few educators have listened to him. Far too many have glibly seized the marvelous and seemingly easy opportunities that the new communications technologies have made available while remaining blissfully ignorant of the many subtle new skills and ethical sensitivities necessary to use them appropriately in the classroom. What is most discouraging is that neither the teachers nor those who prepare them seem even vaguely aware of the most important skills and attitudes they are lacking. Ironically, their global Internet connections are not likely to facilitate that awareness, for whatever damage they do is likely to be at a distance, out of sight, so they are spared witnessing the consequences to others of their "fun."

Does this mean that every teacher should be required to go live overseas before being licensed to shepherd his students through the 'Net? I suppose not. But I do think that every teacher undertaking this work has the responsibility to recognize her limitations and to seek out help, especially people, who can provide assistance in understanding the context from which others are writing. A good social studies teacher, for example, may have the historical and geographic background to help. Administrators, students, and parents who have extensive international experience can help point out subtle cultural nuances. They can provide the perspective that comes with having spent extensive amounts of time in another land. They can help get students and teachers out of the parochial box that, regardless of their best intentions and considerable skills, hampers their comprehension of communicating across national boundaries.

Even in this it may seem that I am demanding too much. After all, people from all over the world communicate with each other all the time via the 'Net without much trouble. But few of those people are trying to instruct others about themselves and their lives, or cooperate in a learning venture, where misunderstandings are almost sure to undermine the fundamental goals. Yes, students can share scientific data without any need for international expertise. In fact, many of the most popular 'Net learning activities are global science projects. But that very fact underscores my point—for mathematics, the language of science, is intentionally designed to eliminate all human nuances. As soon as the students start discussing what the data *mean* they confront the likelihood of misconceptions and missed intentions. The world is much larger than the 'Net makes it seem, and the common language we use on it masks differences that, however slight, create problems when we try to share human insights. If we are going to joyously seize the opportunities to "travel" all over the world via the 'Net, we also need to accept the responsibility to learn what those problems of communication are and do our best to prepare our students to recognize and respond appropriately to them. And if a teacher is not prepared to fulfill that responsibility, she must have the ethical sense and self-discipline to decline the opportunity, for one of the implications of Weizenbaum's charge is that the damage we can do through telecomputing is extended just as much as our reach.

Preparing for the Future

Regardless of the potholes on the Infobahn, we do have to prepare our students for dealing with it once they graduate into a world more and more connected with global business ventures. Whether they go to college or directly into the workforce our students will encounter pressures, if not outright demands, to use the 'Net—at least for the foreseeable future (which I would gauge to be about ten years, given the present rapid pace of technological change). Still, learning how to navigate the 'Net is a minor task and the downloading of information is becoming more and more automated. Designing Web pages is easy to learn in its basic form (my students needed about a week of instruction in order to make a presentable site) and a specialized area of programming in its more elaborate form. None of these tasks is worth dwelling on at any level of the K–12 curriculum if we are interested in more than teaching mechanical skills.

The potholes—those nontechnical areas of human communication that can get all tangled up in the machinations of the 'Net—*are* worth dwelling on. Our responsibility as good stewards is to shepherd our students around those potholes, examining and charting each in turn. Integrating technology into education should not concentrate on making computers an integral tool of learning, but rather on helping students explore the many and subtle ways that technologies influence their social and personal lives, the course of history and their perception of the world. Only when they are well versed in these issues can they, in turn, become good stewards of the earth, the powerful technologies at their disposal and the next generation of young people.

Responsibilities to Ourselves

Like any other aspect of teaching, our responsibilities with regard to the 'Net do not end with the student. However, we should always bear in mind that none of our other responsibilities are as extensive or as complex as those we carry for our students. This is reflected in the relatively short amount of attention I will be giving each of the other five responsibilities.

Many teachers have lost the habit of thinking about being responsible to themselves as professionals. The coming of the 'Net to the classroom should cause us to pay much more attention to this issue. Its effect on teacher status is certainly ambiguous. We have discussed the tension between agency and structure in the context of the struggle between our will and the societal forces around us. A similar view can be applied to the situation we confront using the 'Net within our classrooms. On the one hand, we can eagerly seize the responsibility to determine how this tool fits into our students' academic activities, but we must also be mindful that the school district, the vendors, the public, and the technological "system" all impinge on our freedom to carry out that responsibility.

Many of us staked our claims in cyberspace precisely because it provided a means of reasserting some vestige of autonomy in our teaching. With textbook publishers, software companies like Microsoft, and even Disney now eyeing the telecommunication field as new commercial entry points into education, I have no doubts that we will have to fight to keep any semblance of that autonomy in the future. For every Buddy Burniske using a laptop to break through his classroom walls there are scores of bureaucrats and companies hard at work erecting virtual boxes in which to confine teachers and their students—and just as many vendors willing to sell them the merchandise to do it. To believe that individuals with networked computers will somehow hold their own against those already vested with economic and political power is to buy into what Langdon Winner describes as the myth of "The Great Equalizer." The truth, thus far, is much less encouraging.

Current developments in the information age suggest an increase in power by those who already had a great deal of power, an enhanced centralization of control by those already prepared for control, an augmentation of wealth by the already wealthy. Far from demonstrating a revolution in patterns of social and political influence, empirical studies of computers and social change usually show powerful groups adapting computerized methods to retain control. (1986, 107)

Nothing I have experienced online leads me to believe that the situation has changed for the better since Winner wrote those words. Though the Internet holds out the promise to teachers of "empowerment," in general they have not gained more power *in relationship* to the bureaucratic and corporate interests that provide the mechanisms to access it. The drive to turn Internet-aided education into standardized techniques and lesson plans will continue to grow as long as teachers are unwilling or unable to take responsibility for the activities to which they lead their students. Three years ago a group of teachers—our building leadership committee—returned from a national conference buzzing about a speech given by an educational technology consultant who counted among his clients both Apple Computer and Disney. I don't have his exact words to verify what he said, but the message that the committee *heard* is probably more important anyway. They reported to the rest of the staff that this ed tech "visionary" (as he was introduced) "promised" them that if we teachers don't get our acts together, if we don't do a better job distinguishing what we do from merely providing students with information, Disney, Microsoft, Apple, and other information and entertainment companies will run us out of business.

I take this promise seriously. I also take seriously Postman's assertion that "schools are not now and have never been chiefly about getting information to children" (1995, 42). If we allow ourselves to be seduced by the hype of the information society and see ourselves as just part of a "delivery system," the prediction of teacher obsolescence probably will prove to be accurate—and justified. The teacher's role, no matter what the learning environment, is always more, always far deeper, always more personal, than just a guide to information. If we are going to use the special communications facilities proffered by the 'Net, it is crucial that we *collaborate* in designing and carrying out the projects in which our students participate. It is the only way I can see that the 'Net can truly contribute something meaningful to our profession. Indeed, if we aren't willing to accept this responsibility, the 'Net may very well facilitate our professional demise.

Responsibilities to Our Schools

The 'Net not only threatens the professional status of teachers, in much the same way it could contribute to the death of schools as we know them. Both technology critics (Postman 1995) and advocates (Papert 1993) have questioned the viability of schools in the age of the computer. Postman, for one, is not encouraged by teachers' reaction to this threat:

For four hundred years, school-teachers have been part of the knowledge monopoly created by printing, and they are now witnessing the breakup of that monopoly. It appears as if they can do little to prevent that breakup, but surely there is something perverse about school-teachers' being enthusiastic about what is happening. (1993, 10)

Postman was actually talking about the effect of television but certainly the Internet is no cause for renewed cheer. Information in the form of images and text is now piped through computers and TV directly to children, bypassing the evaluation and culling service that schools (along with parents) once performed. For both better and worse the schools' once substantial power to determine what information reaches young people has evaporated. Unless schools adapt to this new situation they may very well go the way of dinosaurs.

Unfortunately, most attempts to adapt have been of the me-too variety. If young people come to school saturated with images, we respond by teaching with images. If they can gain access to oceans of information elsewhere, we see to it that they can access it at school as well. Rather than establish schools as refuges where youth can come in out of the media rain and gather their own thoughts in the quiet company of caring sages, we throw open the doors and windows and welcome the deluge. If schools play along with this "information anytime, anywhere" approach to education, teachers have little choice but to adopt the guide-on-the-side approach of instruction and the information-as-knowledge paradigm of learning. But having forfeited their unique educational role, schools will have little to offer that offsets the enormous expense of all the facilities and personnel it employs. Information transfer no longer requires them, and there are too many who stand to gain financially and politically to let such an "inefficient" public institution stand unchallenged.

Those of us who understand the crucial role that teachers and schools play in the lives of children have a responsibility to transform the popular perception of 'Net aided learning. We must project a more meaningful vision of education than computers and the 'Net can provide on their own. This responsibility entails grasping the significance of Postman's call for a narrative that serves to give a higher purpose to education than merely the collection and manipulation of information. "Without a narrative," he writes, "life has no meaning. Without meaning, learning has no purpose. Without a purpose, schools are houses of detention, not attention" (1995, 7). If we are to make our schools houses of attention the first order of business is to establish a purpose of our own that gives credence to what we do.

Postman asserts wisely, and simply, that schools are not merely institutions designed to teach young people how to make a living, but how to make a life (1995). This fundamental view of education is open to widely diverse interpretations, as it should be if it is to serve such a large and diverse population. Yet it provides a focus for our sense of responsibilities that draws us deeper into the lives of the children we serve and away from the tools that may serve them.

In schools, as in society as a whole, we are in danger of allowing our technological means to switch places with our human goals. Technological training and experience is being elevated rapidly to an end in itself. This is no accident, according to Douglas Noble, who, in *The Classroom Arsenal* (1991), has documented the central and intense role of the military in computer-based learning and cognitive psychology research that has most heavily influenced the way computers are used in schools. Noble shows that the most powerful driving force behind computer-based education has never been a desire to provide a means for serving human ends, but rather in order to better engineer humans to fit into a man-machine system that more and more provides the structure of both military and business operations. The ultimate outcome of such an inversion of means and ends would be that:

Human beings, already reduced to the status of "human resources," or "personnel," defined in terms of their function within institutional systems, would thus be still further reduced to hardly animate, mental "materiel"—cognitive processing units within the interstices of large technological systems. (Noble 1991, 189)

Eight years ago I would have scoffed at anyone who suggested that such a view would penetrate deeply into the culture of K–12 education in this country. But that year I attended a state Computer Users in Education conference and discovered I was way behind the times. The pet term being tossed around in nearly every presentation I attended, by teachers, professors, and keynote speakers, was "liveware." I was astonished to hear this term used to refer to the human beings who make up, according to most of the speakers, the most unpredictable and, therefore, most troublesome component of the learning "system." Noble's prediction had come to life and it appears to have continued to work its way deeper into the mainstream educational psyche ever since.

It seems to me that for schools to adopt this view of education is to commit institutional suicide. Schools are not needed to fit liveware into the machinery of military or corporate life. That reduced learning task can be much more cheaply accomplished via the globally networked computer systems of which the 'Net is a part. If schools are to have a function in society, teachers who recognize that its primary role is helping young people learn how to make a life—especially a thoughtful life—will have to take the responsibility to show the public and their own students (and perhaps their own supervisors) how necessary and beneficial it is to deepen and discuss and humanize the decontextualized information provided by the new computer-based media.

Responsibility to the Community

Progressive education (in the pedagogical sense) has had a resurgence with the advent of the computer. Its principle proponent, John Dewey, is now being held up by technologists as the patriarch of practical, experience-based (which the technologists, in an outrageous but typical inversion of logic, view as synonymous with computer-based) education. I hear this oversimplified interpretation of Deweyian education most often associated with a call to better prepare students for entry into the real world—the real world of work, that is—by providing them with the skills needed to prosper in that very competitive environment. I don't think Dewey would be pleased. Though he certainly called for education to be grounded in real-life experience, he also saw a very different role for education in relation to the community at large.

Each generation is inclined to educate its young so as to get along in the present world instead of with a view to the proper end of education: the promotion of the best possible realization of humanity as humanity. (Dewey 1916, 95)

Dewey stressed what today's reformers tend to ignore, that society is much more than the businesses that operate in it and the role of education is to improve society, not just prepare students to fit like cogs into its economy.

When the school introduces and trains each child of society into membership within such a little community, saturating him with the spirit of service, and providing him with the instruments of effective self-direction, we shall have the deepest and best guarantee of a larger society which is worthy, lovely, and harmonious. (1899, 44)

I think these words from a century ago, amid at least as large a technical transformation of society as we are witnessing today, can serve as an excellent guide in helping us understand our responsibilities as teacher to the larger community as we engage our students in online work.

First, all of our efforts should, in some way, help our students focus on the improvement of their society. We should thus design and participate in 'Net projects that serve this purpose. And what if our students cannot agree on what will improve society? Then I would say that attending to that disagreement becomes the most important educational task.

Second, the "instruments of effective self-direction" should not be viewed as solely for promoting the students' own welfare in that society, but to make it a better place for all. If we as public educators are obliged to equip our students with these powerful tools before sending them out into the community, I think we are also obliged to help them to view those tools as social tools, to be used to create a more "worthy, lovely, and harmonious" community.

As with the school itself, I see nothing inherent in either computers or the 'Net that will foster such improvement. Indeed, it is more likely that the 'Net, by drawing people into virtual communities that have no physical place, that facilitates a narcissism that has no social conscience, will, in the long run, accelerate the dissolution of the sense of real community that we know television has contributed to for decades.

This is why our *Utopian Visions* projects have evolved more and more into efforts to reflect student interest back into their local communities. It seems to me that we will only be able to draw nearer to Dewey's vision of education's responsibility to society to the extent by which we are able to pull our students through that self-absorbing screen back into the communities in which they live.

Responsibilities to the World

Buddy has repeatedly framed the problem for us: Can we integrate without annihilating? He has used it in various contexts, but it is most appropriate when thought of in terms of our responsibility to the world.

Ecuador changed dramatically during the three years I lived there during the 1980s. Mechanized farming practices had already displaced tens of thousands of campesinos, who had no wage-earning skills and thus sank into abject poverty in the city—a common story in third world countries. Now satellite communication brought Quito, once relatively isolated high in the Andes, into constant, quick contact with the rest of the world. Ideas and images that had developed gradually from within American culture poured into the city and splashed out into a countryside still far removed from twentieth-century Western civilization.

The significance of the sudden impact of telecommunication hit home to me through an encounter high in the mountains one sunny Sunday afternoon. I had parked my jeep near the end of the road and had begun hiking up the narrowing path when I saw coming down the slope a young boy leading a donkey. There was a huge stack of kindling lashed to the donkey's back. My first impression was that this perhaps ten-year-old boy was undoubtedly heading for the thatched roofed hut I had passed just down the road, retracing the steps his people had taken for hundreds of years. But as I drew close I noticed something that was so incongruous it stopped me in my tracks. The boy's poncho was pulled open in the front and showing boldly on the white background of his T-shirt was a picture of Rambo, machine gun blazing. I spent much of my hike thinking about that boy; what kind of confusion must be present in his mind; what kind of future he and his culture would face. Technologically he and his culture were being propelled from the seventeenth to the twentieth century with no sense of developmental continuity or historical context to help make sense of it. I could find little to be optimistic about.

Many times I have sat in my high-tech classroom proudly contemplating the work my students and I have done over the 'Net when the image of that Ecuadorian boy has popped into my mind. I take it as my conscience reminding me of a responsibility to the world that I really don't know how to fulfill.

We in education seem to be plunging headlong into the same technological trap that has snared society in general: confusing what can be done with what ought to be done. Doing what can be done requires only technical proficiency and unfettered technical development. Doing what ought to be done requires ethical proficiency and the development of a sense of responsibility that accepts self-denial when the range of our actions may bring harm to others. This is something we seem to be growing less and less willing to do in our schools and less aware that it needs to be done as our communication reach extends around the globe. It is a trend that must be reversed if we are to have any hope of using the 'Net in a globally responsible manner.

Yes, we can integrate—we will integrate. It is almost impossible to imagine the technology bandwagon suddenly being detoured around schools. However, it will take a mighty and concerted effort not to annihilate in the process. I doubt that it will happen. But we owe it to those whose cultures are rapidly succumbing to the pressures of technology to at least keep their images before us so as to remind us that this "revolution" is not taking place without casualties.

Our Responsibilities to the Truth

Woven through the fabric of all of our other responsibilities is the calling to seek the truth. This doesn't have to be construed as Truth in some single Platonic ideal state. I'm talking about the responsibility to search out the truth of our own situations with regard to this new learning activity; or, as Buddy put it at the very beginning, to discover things the way they really are, not as we wish them to be. It is unfortunate that this even has to be mentioned, and I'm certainly not saying that most teachers don't care about the truth. But I think it is necessary to speak specifically to the issue because the conjunction of two trends have conspired to inhibit the amount of attention teachers give it in their work: (1) the loss of teacher control over what resources are used in the classroom; and (2) the intense propagandizing of high-tech corporations and advocates. When it comes to the use of computers and telecomputing, teachers have been encouraged to "leave the driving to us"; to abdicate thoughtful deliberation over the deeper consequences of these complex pedagogical tools; to concentrate solely on the "how" questions, not the "why." As we have tried to show throughout this book, it is the "why" questions that are the crucial ones, and the answers offered by the Microsofts and Disneys and Classroom Connects, and even most of the principals and curriculum supervisors I have encountered, are superficial at best, and almost always condescending. Given this state of affairs, it seems to me that teachers have an ethical responsibility to pursue those more complex "why" questions to their source. I suspect the conclusions we all reach will vary widely—a good thing, I think. It isn't so important that we come to the same truths, but that we take responsibility to search for them.

This chapter has been, in a sense, an attempt to draw together some of the many routes Buddy and I have taken in our search for the truth in this learning arena. As I bring it to a close, it seems appropriate to try to establish where I see telecollaboration fitting into the larger responsibility we have for educating our youth. Once again, I will draw on Douglas Noble, who gives his own view at the end of *The Classroom Arsenal* of what education should be about:

The goal of education is neither the engineering of learning as an end in itself nor the production of cognitive components or technical skills for the technological infrastructure of the information age; rather it is the cultivation of human beings, through an encouragement of a deep self-understanding along with an understanding of and participation in the world. The best schools are those that are personalized, that are organized as communities of teachers, students and parents who are fully engaged, who understand why they are learning and teaching, and who together construct a full, rich interdisciplinary curriculum, a nurturing, attentive pedagogy, and a sense of worldly commitment and care. (Noble 1991, 190)

I hear the ring of truth in that statement. It contains most of the elements crucial to developing a thoughtful, fulfilling life. I think it articulates the general educational goals Buddy and I have been trying to push to the foreground of the discussion about educational telecollaboration. The truths we have found in the pursuit of those goals have been very different from those currently promoted. This is why we put such a stress on dialectic. It is why the book began with an assertion by Paulo Freire, an assertion—slightly expanded—that I think is worth revisiting at the end. Discovering what is—or even if there is— an appropriate place for telecollaboration in the classroom requires truly critical thinking, something Freire reminds us is bound up with dialogue:

Only dialogue, which requires critical thinking, is also capable of generating critical thinking. Without dialogue there is no communication, and without communication there can be no true education. (1996, 73–74)

Only genius can hold to the path of truth for very long without the corrective of dialogue with others. Those of us who stumble and bumble our way along must rely on the educative power of communication with others of differing views to help us steer through the fog toward wisdom. In its essence this is what dialectic is designed to do and Buddy and I have used the collision of ideas it facilitates to educate ourselves as well as our students.

I think there is an even more profound implication to Freire's claim, one that is especially important in our dealings with educational technology. For Freire, the entire process of education, including the dialogue within it, is dialectical. There is no simple, linear cause and effect in "true education," but a continual interdependent cycle of communication, critical thinking, and insight growing toward the light of truth. Critical thinking not only facilitates dialogue but needs it. Education isn't just the goal of communication it is also the means of improving communication. The whole process promises to reveal ever more fully the glow of truth, and, in turn, the truth nourishes this process.

Churning under the argumentative surface of dialectic lies an assumption that may seem strange to those possessed of a mechanical view of the world but fully in line with the real world of human learning: that there are no ends independent of the means used to attain them, no multitude of vehicles that can be selected to cruise down a one-way street to a single educational destination. Our pedagogical ends circle back as means, part of a complex, paradoxical interdependence of the learning process, a process in which the final goal is at least partly determined by the means used to get there. This is what ultimately sets dialectic apart from the linear cause-and-effect model of mechanics and places it squarely within the life process itself. I think this is why Parker J. Palmer chooses to view truth as a process rather than an object:

I understand truth as the passionate and disciplined process of inquiry and dialogue itself, as the dynamic conversation of a community that keeps testing old conclusions and coming into new ones. (1998, 104)

This dynamic, dialogical understanding of truth escapes any attempts to formalize it, to transform it into some object or systematic procedure that can stand apart from the humans who pursue it.

If all of that is too abstract, let me try to contrast the dialectic pursuit of truth with the typical technological approach through an example. Anyone who has worked with computers for a good length of time in schools has encountered the "Data to Wisdom Chain," a technological hierarchy of learning that seeks to connect computer processing with human insight:

Data
   organized is
Information
   made meaningful is
Knowledge
   linked to other knowledge is
Intelligence
   granted experience is
Wisdom

Notice the straight-line progression from data to wisdom, as if it is some assembly-line manufacturing process. As Talbott observes, in this system "data and information are the raw materials of wisdom" (1995, 200). And this, he says, is "the lie" of the technological view of learning.

Given the most extensive data set imaginable, I cannot reconstruct the world from it. First, I have to know what the data are about, and this forces me inexorably back toward a new starting point in wisdom. Data that contained their own meaning would not be data. (Talbott 1995, 200)

We are confronted here with the fundamentally paradoxical nature of learning. Information cannot generate its own meaning for our students—they have to have a prior capacity to find meaning in that information. Where does that capacity come from? From the very end to which information is supposedly the means. In this sense, the Data to Wisdom chain runs backwards. But this isn't quite adequate either. In reality it seems to flow both ways, in a constant dialectical dance that can never be put into mechanical terms, for it is, ultimately, a living process. It is, in fact, the hallmark of mental growth, the basic chicken-and-egg paradox of learning, which can only be applied to, and fully embraced by, the human mind.

Perhaps this is why the Elizabethan dramatists through which Buddy introduced dialectic in chapter 1 refused to bring their plays to resolution. The human condition is never really resolved. In his scathing critique of American education,

Allan Bloom notes that dialectic as originally conceived by Plato through Socrates "takes place in speech and, although drawn forward by the search for synthesis, always culminates in doubt" (1986, 229). Doubt is an essential element in the pursuit of truth; it is the rain that fills Buddy's Sea of Questions. But you will have to search long and hard to find anyone advocating the introduction of doubt within our mechanical learning models today. It is the administrator's Land of Answers that too often governs learning today. The goal is to solve problems, not embrace them as valuable features of the learning landscape. Bloom recognizes the poverty of this situation, for he quickly reminds us, "[M]an is not just a problem-solving being, as behaviorists would wish us to believe, but a problem-recognizing and accepting being" (Bloom 1986, 229). In one of those strange, compelling convergences of the educational "left" and "right," Bloom seems to endorse the "problem-posing" orientation to learning that is central to Freire's methodology—and so foreign to mainstream American education.

The ability to recognize and leave open the contradictions, paradoxes, and uncertainties presented to us by the world is one capability that distinguishes the mind from the machine and makes dialectic a particularly suitable approach to human learning. It does not preclude the computer from being used to enhance that process. But we have to recognize that by inserting this deterministic machine into that dialectic course we alter the ecology of learning. Perhaps that wouldn't be a problem if we worked diligently to maintain limits on the computer's use. But as I write there is little interest in seeking limits, only opportunities, and the more we rely on the machine for learning, the more we will be drawn into the mechanical worldview it epitomizes, to the point that the means will likely swallow the end and education as a living, growing, dialectical struggle toward truth will retreat further toward extinction, replaced by the assembly of a marketable product stamped with a label called "success."

The roaring of the lion in this book is, ultimately, a roaring against that trend—a warning that this ultimate machine, so often used to enliven classroom work, could finally suffocate the real living process of learning. It is not a plea to get rid of computers, but rather a wounded cry to remember what and who learning is really about; to comprehend that e-mail exchanges do not constitute communication; that the accumulation of data does not lead to wisdom; that pursuing information is not the same as pursuing truth; that educating is a loving art, not a mechanical procedure.

Ironically, it is this very concern that keeps me studying and working at tele-collaborative projects. For as the world becomes more and more enmeshed in the electronic grid, it seems to me that no educational task will be as critical to the well-being of future generations as helping them *understand the difference* between the narrow knowledge attained through information processing and the ever expanding truth that waits to be revealed through the dialogue of human beings.

9

The Drama of Dialectics

R. W. Burniske and Lowell Monke

Everything in this book springs from argument.

This is not to say that we enjoy shouting matches or the irrational confrontations that an impoverished definition of argument suggests. The aim of such hostile discourse is the conquest or humiliation of those who hold opposing views. Such arguments may please an ego, but they rarely discover a satisfying truth. For that, we're better served by argument as both the means and end of exploratory discourse (Kinneavy 1980). Our collaborative efforts, from the design and coordination of online learning activities to the composition of this book, result from such a discourse. In effect, we argue on behalf of argument, drawing upon dialectical tensions to place exploratory discourse at the core of our telecollaborative endeavors. By doing so, we refrain from the reductive, hostile debates that inspire a power struggle, adopting a more open-ended approach to difficult questions. Thus, we employ a modern medium to fulfill an ancient, educational purpose: the pursuit of truth and wisdom.

The following electronic mail exchange, which took place over a five-week period after we had written the previous chapters, illustrates the method to our madness. It seems appropriate for this book, an extended dialectical discussion, to end with the convergence of our voices. We offer it to demonstrate how we engage our differences, rather than flee from them, to inspire the "drama of dialectics" that shapes our thoughts and pedagogy. As is our custom, we allow each other time and space to compose a thoughtful response, embracing the spirit of ancient discourse rather than modern sound bites.

Monke:

OK, if we are to remain true to our method, we need to work toward closing this discussion, but without the usual attempt to bring a nice neat closure to the issues we've raised. That shouldn't really be hard to do, since we're dealing with an historical phenomenon in telecollaboration that's way too big and too new for anyone to get a complete handle on at this point, if ever. But maybe we can raise the level of discourse yet another notch by addressing one last time a few of the most vexing issues we've raised in this examination.

I think it would be a good idea, since you've agreed to let me have the first word (which I suppose you will use to claim the right to have the last one), to start this dialogue by bringing it up to the here-and-now. Much of what you have written about in this book grew out of the context of your experiences in Malaysia. You've commented often about how much of a struggle it was not really having a feel for the situation here and I've stressed throughout the book that I think much of the disparity between the way we viewed the value of tele-collaboration hinged on our different environments.

Well, now that you've been back in the States for a few years, coordinating the *Utopian Visions* project from here, how has your change in place shifted your perspective? We've talked about it a little over the phone and you've alluded to it in e-mail, but it's still not quite clear to me either the extent or really the full nature of the difference in the way you view telecollaboration in the classroom now that you've done it from both sides of the planet.

Burniske:

Great place to begin. It takes us back to the origins of our friendship and collaboration, doesn't it? As you've pointed out, one must contextualize rather than generalize, but I don't think my views on telecollaboration have shifted as dramatically as my place of residence. More than anything, physical relocation has reinforced one of the primary lessons I've learned from telecollaborative activities: the greatest threat to education is the death of dialectics. In Malaysia, the government thwarts debate; in America, corporations achieve the same. What's so distressing for me, perhaps because I grew up in an argumentative family in the 1960s, is the public's acquiescence.

How does this manifest itself? One of the defining cultural metaphors in Malaysia is the "shadow play." To understand Malay politics you need to be familiar with this form of entertainment, but you must watch the audience rather than the performance. People in front of the screen are mesmerized by the shadows playing upon it; those on the periphery, however, are less susceptible to the illusion. They see the shadows, hear the music and narrative, but also observe the puppetmaster behind the screen, deftly manipulating the puppets *and his audience.* How different is that from the theater of American politics, which exploits a national obsession with television to mesmerize its audience?

In both cases, infatuation with shadows playing upon a screen distracts people from the substance, and motives, of the puppetmaster. For example, in the midst of "The Media Matter," as you may recall, Disney purchased ABC television. My students in Malaysia were surprised to find their counterparts in Iowa, the ones self-righteously attacking the evils of government censorship, apathetic about this "business merger." The ISKL students questioned the journalistic integrity of an ABC news program such as "Nightline" if it chose to interview Disney's CEO, Michael Eisner. Wouldn't the interviewer feel awkward interrogating his boss? Might it not jeopardize objectivity or cause the interviewer to shy away from difficult questions? Amazingly, this didn't cause much of a stir among the students in Des Moines. Half a decade later, how many American viewers of the ABC Evening News realize that it is owned and operated by the Magic Kingdom? How many would even see a problem with that? It's ironic that people shrug at corporate-controlled media yet rail against state-controlled media. Don't both lead to the censorship of opposing viewpoints? How can a society teach its young to seek "Truth" if it tolerates the daily deceptions of its government and media? That's one trend that scares the hell out of me because it really *could* signal "the end of education."

What have I learned about telecollaboration by moving from one side of the globe to the other? I've spoken enough about the opportunities and responsibilities, but perhaps it's necessary to emphasize one of the principal dangers at this point. So I'll say this: global telecomputing could present the same threat as global broadcasting. Both have the potential to homogenize thought, effectively destroying dialectics within our schools. Another medium that shares this potential is a school curriculum. By marginalizing classroom teachers, depriving them of a voice in essential debates or treating them like automatons, we make our schools a place of censorship rather than enlightenment. Censorship doesn't protect students as much as it deprives them of learning opportunities, as demonstrated by that sad episode at the conclusion of "The Media Matter." The prevalence of censorship and administrative hegemony in our schools merely conditions faculty to refrain from challenging the status quo. And if they shy away from difficult questions in faculty meetings, or passively embrace curricular mandates, what are the chances that teachers will inspire dialectical discourse in their classrooms or telecollaborative activities?

We've argued a great many things through this medium, Lowell, but one topic we've neglected is the significance of this medium itself in renewing our dialectic. I was fairly miserable in Kuala Lumpur, but given the tyranny of the majority—within that school as well as the surrounding culture—where do you suppose I would've located a forum as stimulating as the one I found here?

And is it such a terrible thing to admit that the medium itself not only facili-tated the dialogue, but often stimulated it, calling attention to itself as we strug-gled to bend it to our will? As technologies mature they become less visible, but if we foreground telecollaboration for the moment, and you step back from your reservations to ponder something you've often been reluctant to admit, what would you say are the prerequisites for this medium to inspire dialectics in the classroom?

Monke:

I remember your students reporting on the "shadow plays" in one of the UV projects. It's interesting that you compare it to TV in this country. Remember the cave allegory in Plato's *The Republic* (1968)? The most famous educational metaphor of all time uses shadows on the back wall of the cave to describe how far away most people are from understanding reality. Plato thought that images were the lowest level of knowledge and that the task of the teacher was to un-bind the student and lead him or her up out of the cave into the light. To me, TV is a modern day counterpart to the shadows on the cave wall, but it's more in-sidious because the images are so much sharper and the content so manipula-tive. I'm not actually so concerned about ABC being censored by Disney—no news program dependent on advertising can question fundamental corporate values—as I am the fact that Disney and other big-time commercial entertain-ment corporations are determining all the cultural icons we see on that big screen cave wall. That's the kind of total censorship you allude to later in your message and you're right—it truly stifles meaningful dialogue.

But now along comes the computer, which may be, as you have suggested, a modern day Narcissus pond, but can also be seen as making the images on the cave wall all the more transfixing and definitive by allowing the cave dwellers to shine their own images up there as well, thus participating in the shadow play. This interactive power deepens the illusion that the images are reality, and makes it even more difficult for teachers to pull students' heads away from that hypnotic shadow play out into the light.

OK, enough metaphor. The important thing is that I think my students in-tuitively understand these are mere illusions—sort of. On the one hand they seem to know they are being manipulated by images and are deeply cynical of all content. But at the same time, they seem unaware how much their behavior is affected by the form and the ideology of the source.

This just reinforces the validity of your main assertion: Neither cynicism nor naivete evokes much demand for dialogue. Rather, the response is to choose sides and seek victory. Since few really value, or even believe there is a truth, what else is left but winning? And more and more it is total victory, a vanquishing of the enemy in which there is simply no tolerance of ambiguity or room for civil discourse that seeks to bring the two poles together.

I don't see how the Internet is going to help change this in the long run. Yeah, I know it helped you get out from under a repressive curriculum. But I see this as just another example of what Ellul calls "the ambiguity of technical progress" (Ellul 1990, 35)—it tends to support opposing goals at the same time. While it liberates you individually, it also furthers the trend toward technologizing teaching. The Internet, unlike textbooks and district-wide lesson plans, benefits the innovative teacher because its use in schools hasn't been standardized—yet. But look at the trend: all the how-to books, all the plug-and-play programs, all the universities' and corporations' mass offerings. In the long run, the Internet is allied to the very administrator you battled in Malaysia. Once he understands its abilities to rationalize the educational process he will be more than willing to get troublesome teachers like you out of the way and turn instruction over to technicians who will obediently plug students into the automaton teacher provided by Internet vendors. Long ago he turned education into a mechanical process in his own mind. He just hasn't recognized yet that he now has the tool to complete the process in the classroom.

So, while you and a few other energetic teachers are allowed to feel the bit between your teeth, the Internet will be used to rein in the vast majority of teachers to an even tighter pedagogical and ideological homogeneity—global in scope and technological in orientation. I admire your faith in individual agency, and recognize the value of trying to bend this tool to our purposes, but I don't like our chances against a censorship-by-financial-clout structure built by the likes of Microsoft and Disney.

As for our own use of this medium in "renewing our dialectic," I think the key word is "renewing." Keep in mind that we had a full year of face-to-face contact before resorting to the 'Net. Personally, I much preferred the lunches at The Manabi Hut to e-mail messages from Malaysia. And what made e-mail contact so valuable anyway? Your isolation? I too was a newcomer to Des Moines, and in this TV culture I found it difficult to locate the kind of stimulating, supportive community that we both experienced in Ecuador.

In fact, think for a moment about that community of teachers at Academia Cotopaxi—all those folks who worked together, played together, traveled together, suffered together, and cared for one another? Did we need the Internet in Ecuador? Or to put it another way: would that community have developed if we'd all had the Internet when we moved there?

Maybe the virtual community of the Internet is more a symptom, an indication of what is missing from our physical communities today than boon to our dialectical discourse. If so, then it seems that our efforts may be misplaced, which leads me to that last question of yours: it seems to me that you have already described the prerequisites for this medium to inspire dialectics in the classroom: (1) A real community (family, peer group, early learning environment) that nurtures curiosity and open discussion of the meaning of experience at an early age; (2) Experience with face-to-face discourse that goes deeper than the exchange of information or the development of communication skills; (3) A classroom environment that has already developed a community atmosphere based on the members' concern for each other and with pursuing the deeper meanings of their experiences. Given that, I think the Internet might serve as a pretty good tool for the kind of discourse we seek. But look at those prerequisites for a moment and ask yourself, If those conditions existed in the classroom, would you even care to use the 'Net?

But that begs another question: How do you justify the enormous expenditure of funds, resources, time, and energies to put this technology into the classroom in the first place? And how do you reallocate all those resources into the technical realm without impinging on those efforts at developing the prerequisite attitudes and conditions needed to use it appropriately?

Burniske:

I like your prerequisites for dialectical discourse, but don't wish to leave that topic just yet. So let's approach your question about the allocation of resources for "technology in the classroom" as it relates to this concern.

We both know that developing dialectics, whether face-to-face or in cyberspace, is no simple matter. What's more, the classroom environment suffers considerably if your first two prerequisites—community and discursive practices—are neglected. So let's think about the present generation of students, weaned on the "boob tube," imbibing a crass ideology that says, "Don't think; consume!" The kids didn't invent this ideology, but they quickly absorb it. A few years back a national brewing company had the temerity to sell its product with the flippant query, "Why ask why?" Implicit in that advertising campaign, like many others, was a dismissal of critical thinking. Imagine the impact of that dismissal upon kids, then consider the plight of a teacher attempting the Socratic method in a classroom by asking, "Are there any questions?" Kids often lack the desire and skills necessary for dialectics and little in popular culture encourages them to cultivate either. That's the way advertising agencies want it, but it doesn't bode well for democracy. As the rhetoricians tell us,

Persuasion is concerned primarily with influencing the way people think or act, whereas argument is concerned with discovering and conveying our best judgments about the truth of things through an appeal to reason. All arguments involve persuasion, but all persuasive acts do not involve arguments. (Ramage & Bean 1995, 3)

Is the Internet going to help us overcome the "power of persuasion"? It won't if it encourages more channel-surfing, a definite possibility with the advent of WebTV. Unfortunately, the initial hype and hysteria have distracted us from more substantial discussions, ones that I hope this book resurrects. We're overwhelmed with "persuasive acts," most of them exploiting fundamental anxieties, but seldom do we hear rational argument. How else can we explain the reversal of politicians, the ones who squeezed public education in the 1980s with the claim that we "can't fix what's wrong with education by throwing money at it," but now cry for expenditures enabling access to the Internet in every classroom? In both instances they've delivered emotional appeals—preying upon public concerns about children, job opportunities, and national interests—rather than sound argument.

As an educator I'd like to ask those elected officials why they prefer investing in machines rather than people. Are they aware that they're confusing job training with education? I doubt it, but what they do know is that the "boxes and wires" of telecomputing are manufactured by Big Business. And we all know Big Business pays those campaign finances we keep hearing about. So if we keep Big Business happy, investing in their gadgets, then they'll keep the politicians happy, spreading largesse and occasionally donating hardware and software to schools and libraries. This, in turn, will get kids "hooked" early, oiling the machine that paves the "Information Superhighway." Unfortunately, there's one significant casualty along the way: public debate. As government of the people, by the people succumbs to government of the corporation, by the corporation, the dialectics of democracy yield to the spreadsheets of plutocracy.

Perhaps this explains my sensitivity to the rhetoric of the "Education President" who presided over this experiment. Consider the following excerpt from his second inaugural address:

> Now, for the third time, a new century is upon us, and another time to choose. We began the nineteenth century with a choice, to spread our nation from coast to coast. We began the twentieth century with a choice, to harness the Industrial Revolution to our values of free enterprise, conservation, and human decency. Those choices made all the difference. At the dawn of the twenty-first century a free people must now choose to shape the forces of the Information Age and the global society, to unleash the limitless potential of all our people, and, yes, to form a more perfect union. (Clinton 1997)

As I understand it, implicit in the idea of "choice" is that we have at least two options from which to choose. And yet, the president made no mention of alternatives to these choices. Note, too, the amoral quality, the business-like detachment of the phrase: "Those choices made all the difference." Yes, Mr. President, they most certainly did. But could we stop to consider if they made positive or negative differences? Could we hear a rational argument, instead of emotional rhetoric, about how this choice will help us "form a more perfect union?" What these statements reveal is how little "choice" the common person has had at the start of these new centuries and movements. What are the chances of creating "a more perfect union" when the leader of it declares that "a free people must now choose to shape the forces of the Information Age"? If we're told what to choose, then how free are we? If there is no alternative, no opposing view, where's the dialectical tension necessary to discover Truth?

So while I like your prerequisites, Lowell, I also realize how far we are from satisfying them. This makes your most compelling question a rhetorical one: "If those conditions existed in the classroom, would you even care to use the 'Net?" My answer may be less enthusiastic now than it was a few years ago, when I suffered censorship rather than information overload, but it remains affirmative. Why? Because I want students, particularly those constrained by provincial settings and limited resources, to know that there's a world out there, one that they can explore through more than broadcast media. However, not for a moment do I believe the Internet alone will revive dialectical discourse, invigorating what Neil Postman calls "public discourse in the age of show business." Can we really expect kids who spend thirty-five hours a week in front of televisions showering them with "persuasive acts" to suddenly develop critical thinking skills, engaging in healthy online discourse the moment they log on? Hardly. Rather than wring our hands, however, we must take the outrageous allocation of resources as a challenge. It's no longer a question of "Should we introduce computer technology to our classrooms?" I'm afraid that "choice" has already been made for us. The question now is "How should we integrate this technology for educational purposes?"

You and I have assumed dialectical discourse is fundamental to the answer of that last question. Let's step back from our own work, though, and ask what "the end of education" ought to be—in the positive, rather than apocalyptic, sense of that phrase. What can be done to promote that end? Citing obstacles isn't good enough. The technology is marching into the classroom whether we like it or not. So let's ponder what's to be done with it before all the "choices" are made for educators. What advice do you have for the classroom teacher who is committed to students and educational ideals, but new to the technology? Imagine a colleague comes to you for help because the principal is breathing down his neck, telling him to "get with the program" and try this new technology that the district has pumped so much money into. Your colleague fears for his job, but also his integrity. He has strong convictions about what constitutes "good teaching" and a "good education." He can't see a place for "surfing the Web" within that philosophy, yet confesses he's not aware of anything else that teachers can do with the Internet in their classroom. So, how do you advise this individual? How would you suggest he integrate computer technology without annihilating his educational principles?

Monke:

I'd start by telling him to read this book. Yeah, I know that comes across as self-serving. But if I recall correctly, you posed much the same questions to me when the idea of this book first came up. We were sitting together in a restaurant in Baltimore when you asked me to think about a mutual friend of ours, a particularly thoughtful, conscientious teacher and Luddite, and how we would help him if the time came that he felt compelled to do this. It's his image I've kept in front of me as we've stitched this book together. I would sure like to think that what we've said would be valuable to him and others like him.

Still, I sense you are looking for more specific nuts-and-bolts advice here, so I'll try to give some guidance based on the experiences I've had with the four excellent but apprehensive teachers I've worked with at Central Campus. I'll give it a shot, but let me lead into it by responding to a couple points you made concerning dialectical discourse.

For a long time I would just shake my head when I read that CEOs were pushing for schools to teach "critical thinking skills." How could they be serious? Did they know what might happen? Did they really think we could teach people to be critical thinkers for eight hours a day and yet have them turn into perfectly gullible consumers when they go home and sit down in front of the television at night?

But now I know what they were getting at. I've seen how the computer can be used to produce a sort of encapsulated high-level thinking ability that is great for solving well-defined problems but useless in judging the merit of emotional appeals. It's an example of how "critical thinking" can be constrained—applied inside a box. I know that's not the way you are using the term; you want to develop critical thinking skills as a means to achieve good judgment. But as I see it used by school reformers, "critical thinking" is nothing more than "problem-solving" dressed up in fancy cognitive clothes—techniques that can be focused consciously and narrowly on a particular task, leaving the fragmented mind still vulnerable to propaganda of all kinds. Good judgment, on the other hand, is an all-encompassing human trait. It connotes donning exactly the protective mental clothing needed to resist this kind of manipulation.

Postman and Weingartner (1969) tackled this particular issue thirty years ago (long before there were computers in schools) when they suggested that one of the most important goals of education was to help students develop good "crap detectors." I think the motto "Why ask why"—along with the motto of my favorite global sweatshop company: "Just Do It!"—is the absolute antithesis of this goal. So it really doesn't matter whether we are telecollaborating or not. The dialectical approach, so far as it furthers the development of good crap detectors in our kids, provides an antidote to what now seems to have become a conscious effort by the advertising establishment to promote mindlessness.

Schools haven't escaped this campaign, either. "Why ask why" and "Just do it" are pretty much the promotional lines for using the Internet in schools too. Yeah, I know the party line: "They're going to need it when they get out; it's a great research tool; blah, blah. . . ." But how many other learning tools can cost a district like mine millions of dollars a year and get by on that kind of superficial justification? When it gets right down to it the argument degenerates to this: the public thinks we have to have it, the suburbs have it, we'll get behind if we don't have it, so don't worry that nobody can find evidence that it does any good: just do it! Mindless keep-up-with-the-Joneses consumerism in the one place it should be resisted. This is what I mean by the problem with "critical thinking." We have all kinds of talented people in my district busting their brains critically thinking about *how* to get the district wired for the 'Net, without paying any attention whatsoever to why we should or shouldn't be doing it. They're all in the box.

Which leads me to that not so hypothetical teacher you conjured for me who isn't sure he wants to get into the box with all those techies but has no choice. How do I help him? Let me be as specific as I can:

1. Resist—I'm serious. Few administrators in this climate are going to "ask why" unless someone steps up and says, "I protest." The only thing is, you can't "Just say no." That promotes as mindless an attitude as those catch phrases we have been criticizing. You have to be able to explain why not because we habitually approach technology with the attitude "if it exists, we have to use it," leaving the burden of proof on the resisting teacher. I think a good many teachers in a good many situations can and should make a case against having to integrate the Internet into their curriculum. It may not get them off the hook, but it may at least force a deeper discussion about the appropriate place of computers and telecollaboration in the school. The most powerful enemy of the wise use of computers in education is the uncritical use of them. And let's give administrators their due. Few of the ones I have encountered failed to take a more critical attitude toward computer use after teachers explained the pedagogical rationale behind their resistance. It has always resulted in a healthy change in technology policy. We've been arguing the benefits of dialectic all along. This is certainly one of them. In this case it's resistance that is needed to establish it.

But OK, let's assume that resistance doesn't lead to rejection. Now what?

2. Get help—what did you do when you decided to go online? You looked up Dan LoCasio, ISKL's computer coordinator. You and I both know how crazy the technical end of this stuff can get. I don't think any teacher should have to possess the full technical know-how of getting the machines to work. In fact, that's one thing I would hope teachers as a group would demand of anyone forcing this on them—provide the technical support for us so we don't have to sacrifice our teaching and/or personal time and skills to become technicians. If our teacher finds himself fussing with wires and TCP/IP addresses, he's being

abused and in turn is cheating his students. Worse, it might drive him out of teaching because he knows that's not what being a teacher is about.

The same goes for training in the use of the Internet. Our teacher has to become proficient with the 'Net, which takes a lot of time. He should demand some release time to learn the ropes. Administrators tend to treat learning to use the Internet like learning to use a new textbook, then they wonder why teachers have bags under their eyes. The great irony in those terrible training statistics you cited in chapter 1 is that educational leaders allocate funds according to the belief that educating staff about the machines isn't as important as getting more of them. I talked to a principal recently who told me that when they got their new computers many of her teachers started staying until 6 P.M. to teach themselves how to use them. Given that most of the teachers I know grade papers at night, the cost of learning to use this new tool is coming right out of their already limited family lives—and that's neither healthy nor fair. Nor is it a good precedent, for unlike textbooks, computer technology changes very quickly and keeping up can easily become an endless retraining process. Our colleague shouldn't be expected to do it all on his own time.

3. Find a partner—Two people may be necessary for dialogue but it isn't sufficient. You also need trust and commitment. These are, unfortunately, rare qualities in cyberspace. I would advise our teacher to team up with someone he can trust to follow through with the same kind of quality he demands of his own students. And having someone to commiserate and strategize with is so important when the communication galaxy turns into a black hole.

4. Look for ways to use the Internet to go deep, not far—I think this is the real crux of the matter. Every time this teacher came to me with an idea I would ask him two questions: "Will it drive your students into a deeper understanding of the issue you are concerned with? Does it have the potential to generate an argument or intense discourse among your own students?" An answer of "No" to either of those questions and I would advise him to keep thinking and keep looking.

5. Figure out what curricular activities you are going to drop—This will require some hard decisions, but I am convinced that one of the keys to successful integration is the ability to replace other activities. My experience with the teachers at Central Campus tells me that trying to load telecollaboration on top of an already full curriculum seriously diminishes the quality of that experience and causes turmoil for everything else. And whatever our teacher does, he should not sacrifice what he judges to be a higher quality learning experience just to get his students online.

6. Try to become an apprentice—if everyone did what you and I did, there wouldn't be any teachers out there joining projects, they would all be designing their own. That may be how you get the most out of a project, but most people aren't going to feel comfortable starting like we did. I think about the teacher in

Budapest who joined us on three different *Utopian Vision* projects. The last time around she became a real driving force and confident leader of her own students. In a sense she apprenticed herself to us. She could put together a strong project by herself or with another experienced teacher now. And look at the Lithuanians. They *are* running their own projects now, after very tentatively getting started with us three years ago.

Another route to apprenticeship is within the teacher's own school. If you were at Central Campus I would surely send the teacher down to you to ask if he could at least monitor your next project, even if it was outside his own subject area. My guess is that if this happened, you, or another teacher so approached, would take that as an opportunity to break down a few curricular walls and find a way to work with our teacher to design something suitable to both.

7. The medium matters—by this I mean that whatever project he does he should always strive to have his students reflect on both the content and the form of the communication. I'm convinced that all projects should have an element of The Media Matter in them. Our teacher should be constantly *aware*, fully conscious, of the way in which this medium shapes the information flowing through it, and try to foster that same awareness in his students. Almost any project can be deemed at least partially successful no matter how bad the content, if a deeper understanding of the medium itself is achieved.

This is, of course, exactly the opposite of what most Internet advisors advocate—to make the medium *invisible,* thus assuring that neither the teacher nor the students notice how it influences the way they think and communicate.

8. Compensate—I would remind our teacher that while the Internet will help bring your students certain benefits, you will have to compensate for its costs by yourself. That's why it is so important to stand outside the box and constantly examine what is going on. That can be accomplished to a great extent by maintaining a very strong personal and professional presence among the students. Don't let yourself fade into the background behind the electronic screen. The more time your students spend in cyberspace the more time they need with you to bring their minds back down to earth.

OK, that's it: advice to a wary new 'Net teacher from a wary old 'Net teacher. Long on preventing annihilation of good learning (and annihilation of the teacher himself), but short on integration, I'm afraid. For that I'm going to do just what I said I'd do—send him down the hall to examine the scars on someone who has tried to do it several times. What advice would you give him for working it into the curriculum? And while you're at it, I would be curious to hear how our aspiring teacher, who may be laboring in a typical urban public high school or a poor rural school, is going to extend this learning opportunity to all of his students, not just the more intellectually inclined? How do you engage students in dialectics whose preferred method of settling arguments is with their fists, or worse? How do you integrate this text dependent approach to Internet communication into a curriculum that serves students who can barely write, much less form cogent written arguments? In other words, just who is this approach designed for? An elite corps of international students? How do you suggest our teacher's less able students fit into this use of the 'Net?

Burniske:

To begin with, the idea of taking things deeply instead of "out far" struck a resonant chord. Perhaps you'll recall the Malay student who, in the midst of *The Media Matter,* offered the insight that "tele-vision" literally meant "far-seeing." He didn't know what to make of that initially, happening upon it during an exercise in which I asked students to investigate the origins of news media, including the etymology of terms used to describe them. What that student eventually understood, though, was that the inventors of television conceived of it as an instrument that helped viewers "see far," but not necessarily plumb great depths. I used that observation to introduce a Robert Frost poem called "Neither Out Far, Nor in Deep," which describes people on a beach looking out at the sea. The poem concludes with the following quatrain:

> They cannot look out far.
> They cannot look in deep.
> When was that ever a bar,
> To any watch they keep?
> (Frost 1983, 1181)

Your counsel is wise, Lowell, but doesn't it apply to most media in the classroom? I've seen teachers use the chalkboard brilliantly; I've seen others make a mess of it. I've watched teachers use videotapes to show various interpretations of a scene from Shakespeare; I've seen others press "Play" at the beginning of class and "Stop" at the end. Should we ban the chalkboard, television, or VCR from the classroom because certain teachers misuse or abuse such tools? Of course not. What we should do, however, is discuss how to use these media for educational rather than recreational purpose. This is where I temper my criticism of the computer. I'm not convinced there is something wrong with the tool itself, though I wince at misguided and excessive uses of it in the classroom. What's important is that teachers investigate a variety of pedagogical tools, making choices rather than having choices made for them. Subsequently, they must ask if those tools, and the methods accompanying them, will help students "look out far" or "look in deep," justifying "any watch they keep."

Your questions take me back to chapter 5, where I offered an analogy while pondering the metaphysical concerns that inform instructional practices. I'd ask the "wary new 'Net teacher" to consider that analogy, asking the same questions of educational telecollaboration that a traveler asks before making a journey by car:

- What's the destination?
- Who are the passengers?
- What kind of vehicle will I be driving?
- What's the best route to get everyone safely there—and back?

My use of computer technology in a humanities classroom is shaped by these questions. The Internet is clearly a powerful vehicle, one that both affords and constrains learning activities. However, I think of that Frost poem in much the same terms. I would NOT prescribe using either vehicle at all times or with all groups. Yet, that's the kind of nonsense that's common in our schools, depriving both students and teachers the opportunity for intellectual adventure. All too often we must follow a curricular itinerary: if it's Tuesday, this must be chapter 4. I bridle at such prescription because it is demeaning and demoralizing. It denies students and teachers the opportunity to create, to act spontaneously and intuitively. In a word, it denies us our humanity. The art of teaching issues from an individual teacher's vision and the personal expression of that vision. This is not to say that the pedagogy must be entirely new, or the methods unique, just that it must emanate naturally from the teacher who gives thought to the destination, passengers, vehicle, and route.

Now before you jump me for describing students as "passengers," placing them in a passive role akin to television viewers—numbed by a passing landscape viewed through a screen—allow me to suggest that a good passenger can and should take an active part in the journey. Not only is the passenger a second set of eyes, ones that may assist the driver looking for road signs, but also someone who reminds that driver to slow down on the curves, be patient with slow moving vehicles, and beware erratic behavior that endangers lives. Your critique of computer technology is especially important for novices who may become so concerned with the vehicle that they lose sight of the destination, passengers, and alternative routes.

Incidentally, this idea of the Internet as a "vehicle" has caused us to lock horns more often than any other issue concerning telecollaboration. There are many explanations for this, including my entry to the telecollaborative dance through the back door of Humanities and your entry through the front door of Sciences, which helps explain my perception of the machine as a rhetorical tool and your understanding of it as a computational device. I don't think we can fully resolve the dialectical tensions that arise from such differences, any more than we can resolve the differences in our personalities or pedagogical styles. What's most important though, and the reason I felt we had to write this book, is to acknowledge that such differences exist and investigate them through *dialogue*. To resolve this dispute, as I observed in the very first chapter, would require an act of violence that would harm not only the discourse, but also the people engaged in it.

Indeed, what all of these conversations have helped me understand—and something that I believe you should give more credit to the medium for enabling—is that we need to help teachers discover more robust approaches to "telecollaborative learning." If we unpack the term, we find that it literally means "two people sharing labor at a distance." Done well, that means the people involved will look out for one another, help one another with the labors, and do far more than simply exchange information. Clearly, though, this is not the case when teachers fail to make a commitment to a project or allow their students to approach telecollaborative work in superficial and selfish ways. This, I think, is one of the reasons why it's important to "find a partner" and "apprentice" during one's initiation to telecollaborative learning activities. That way, the novice will have at least one reliable collaborator, a faithful colleague who will make a strong commitment to both the work and dialogue that must accompany it.

So while there's little I can say that will persuade you to think differently about the "vehicle" we've employed for our telecollaborative work—including the composition of this book—I would hope that our argument helps us both gain a better understanding of this vehicle's affordances and constraints. You've pointed out its limitations and reminded me repeatedly of its systemic dangers; however, I hope our collaboration has helped you consider possibilities that you couldn't imagine before, ones that could only be realized through extraordinary experiences like *The South African Elections '94 Internet Project, The Media Matter,* and *Utopian Visions*. I'll concede that those projects suffered flaws in both design and execution, but I'd also argue that they acted upon a genuine desire to create new opportunities for learning, and in many ways they succeeded, exciting our imagination while providing intellectual challenge and substance for the students and teachers who engaged in the dialectics they inspired.

What does all of this say about the "vehicle" in question? By extending the metaphor, I'd say this: I do not love my car, but I do appreciate the places it enables me to visit. This applies to networked computers, particularly when I consider the isolation and censorship I suffered in Kuala Lumpur at a time when I wished to engage in thoughtful, open-ended discussions. And yes, I do think that isolation is critically important, because it is a fact of life for many educators suffocated by a dominant discourse in their school, community, or culture.

The public discourse I encountered at an international school in Malaysia may have been diametrically opposed to the one you wrestled with inside a public school in Iowa, but the effect was the same. It made me question assumptions that were terribly limited and limiting. Those assumptions set blinders over the eyes of all who recited a well-rehearsed, unexamined chorus. Few citizens would openly question or criticize the Malaysian prime minister; just as few of my colleagues felt safe questioning their administrators or school policies. What you and I wanted, really, was an intelligent conversation about the place of technology in education, one that would restore the significance of dialectical discourse *about* and *within* telecollaborative learning activities.

Upon return to my homeland I discovered an environment in which few people were questioning the prudence of investing in computer technology while neglecting the professional development of educators. This helped me understand, and empathize, with your struggle within that discourse. However, it also motivated me to enter a doctoral program in "Computers and English Studies" and teach in the Computer Writing and Research Lab at the University of Texas. I wanted to conduct research and experiment with computer technology before experts and policymakers devised programs—replete with cookie-cutter objectives, prefabricated learning activities, and standardized methods for evaluation—that would turn all of this into one more tedious, technical piece of the educational equation. I wanted to cut through both the hype and hysteria to see what, if anything, new technologies and communication tools might offer innovative, classroom teachers. In essence, we were both trying to subvert from within. You were railing against the vehicle as a deterministic villain, trying to help people see the outlines of the box that circumscribed their free will, while I was trying to figure out ways to fly outside the box, making the vehicle suit my purposes rather than those of educational bureaucracies. Ultimately, what we've accomplished, despite this fundamental difference with respect to the vehicle itself, is the one thing that matters most: *dialogue.*

If our only contribution to the question of telecollaboration in the classroom is to remind educators that online activities must encourage thoughtful dialogue and critical inquiry, not simply the collection of information or the solution of simplistic problems, then we will have helped our hypothetical and real colleagues far more than we could by resolving our present dispute over this vehicle. Meanwhile, the best way to counsel that novice you sent my way is not to show him the scars—that'd scare him away from teaching altogether—but to help him ask better questions about teaching and learning. As one friend observed, "You can tell a pioneer from the arrows in his back." This is nothing new, of course, nor is it confined to the use of computers. The math teacher who asks students to keep a reading journal, the physical education teacher who assigns an essay, and the humanities teacher who asks students to create a database for the study of a novel are all pioneering, challenging conventions by introducing methods from other disciplines. Each of them will encounter resistance from members of the school community.

What I'd say to your novice, to lessen his anxiety and encourage him to experiment with various technologies—from chalkboard to LCD panel—is to ask the four questions I've outlined. If any of those questions should receive privileged treatment, it's the second one: "Who are the passengers?" That's the one that reminds us no single tool or methodology is universally "right." I've suffered enough dogma disguised as pedagogy, including that of an English department infatuated with "graphic representation," a euphemism for students drawing pictures to illustrate poems, stories, dramas, and novels. Such activities have value, but not in every class, with every group, every day, regardless of the topic. That's where pedagogy ends and dogma begins—with a deadening, "one-size-fits-all" approach. So let me confess once more what should be patently obvious: I'm a pedagogical dilettante, continually tinkering, experimenting to create the right vehicle for a particular group and destination.

While your questions are difficult, I'd resist the bias that there is something inherently wrong—or right—about a particular medium or method. You ask: "Just who is this approach designed for?" I'd answer that question with another: "Which approach?" Not all telecollaborative projects are alike, nor does a given subject dictate a particular "approach." When I teach Shakespeare's drama I refuse to show students a video adaptation until after they have read the entire play at least once, enacted it in class scene by scene, and fully engaged it as a "text" meant to be performed, not simply read or critiqued in a modern sense. I have heard colleagues advocate video viewing prior to studying those dramas because "you can't expect ESL students to read Shakespeare." That reasoning is as suspect as it is condescending. It fails to consider how cinematic representations might overwhelm the imagination of students who need to construct mental images of characters and events before a television does all the work for them. The same applies to computers. Before becoming a slave to educational objectives, obsessing over available vehicles, we should ask who the "passengers" are and make certain we're not forcing them all inside a compact car heading up a steep mountain road.

I'd also argue that telecollaboration isn't an "approach" designed for "an elite corps of international students" rather than "less able students." Telecollaboration, in all its forms, will become what we make of it. So while I can't deny that the machinery reached private schools first, implying economic elitism and privileged opportunity, I would take exception with the idea that telecollaboration will remain "elitist" methodology. Yes, my students in Malaysia were from privileged families, but they were not exceptionally gifted or talented. The majority were ESL students who had significant language barriers; a fair number of the native speakers, meanwhile, were jaded, apathetic students. Their only claim to "elite" status was socioeconomic, but I wouldn't say this primed them for telecomputing or dialectical discourse. As far as they were concerned the social system "worked" just fine. What reason had they to protest or argue, to engage in dialectics in telecollaborative activities or anywhere else?

Marginalized communities, however, do have reasons to protest, which may explain why I've seen some of the most inspiring and meaningful uses of computers within such communities. Volunteers at the Nelson Mandela Township (NEMATO) in Port Alfred, South Africa, which received a donation of four computers prior to my visit in 1995, were thrilled with the way their students, poorly educated blacks who had been denied a fair education during the apartheid regime, responded to the electronic mail exchanges during the *Nadine Gordimer Internet Project.* For students formerly deprived of educational opportunities, cut off from a world sanctioning their government for its racist policies, correspondence with peers in Malaysia felt like a miracle, and inspired them to commit more time and effort to communication than they ever had before. For the first time, they felt there was a reason to care about education, to learn about a world beyond the township, the Eastern Cape, and the Republic of South Africa. They suddenly had a chance to correspond with people "out there," beginning with an informal "keypal exchange" that became a thoughtful discussion of social concerns.

In the mixed race townships of the Cape Flats, meanwhile, I witnessed one of the most remarkable teachers I've ever seen, a dynamo who taught fifty children in a classroom built for half that number. In the back of her room she had five donated computers lined against a wall. How on earth could she make use of five computers with fifty kids? Like this: create five groups with ten students per group and have them rotate through five work stations, one of which was the computer station, where each group split into pairs working with one terminal. I'm sure the teacher had her share of struggles before devising this scheme, but what impressed me was how fluidly she integrated this into a classroom in addition to other activities, not in lieu of them. Even more impressive was her students' critique of this new medium. They complained that some of the software wasn't right for them, such as a reading exercise that asked them to identify, among other things, the "wardrobe" and "bureau" in an illustration. None of them had ever seen such furniture.

One could interpret this, I suppose, as evidence of "cultural imperialism" in the computer industry, but it felt more like corporate ignorance to me. And who knows, perhaps one of those Cape Flat students will one day write software that is more appropriate for township kids, something that helps them participate more fully in a society, and an economy, that marginalized them and their families for much too long. It's worth noting, however, that the students I observed didn't feel marginalized by those computers or software. Instead, they felt included, fortunate to have tools that were denied their predecessors, including books and software in languages other than Afrikaans. They took advantage of that opportunity to ask questions about this strange new machine and the world from which it came, a world from which they had previously been denied access.

Now, here in Texas, I've witnessed similar developments. The Austin Learning Academy (ALA) in East Austin established an adult literacy program several years ago. They, too, acquired a limited number of computers, but felt it important for the adults pursuing a GED to develop basic computing skills, including familiarity with e-mail and Web browsers. Unfortunately, none of the instructors had ever used the Internet as a teaching tool, so they couldn't ask the questions identified earlier to help them "think through" this medium. So I offered to help, meeting with students and teachers to learn more about what they wanted and needed. The result? "East to East: Letters to / from East Austin and the Eastern Cape." Here's a message I received from one of the ALA's coordinators after the first exchange of letters:

Date: Fri, 4 Jul 1997
Subject: Re: 1st letter from South Africa!

Hi Buddy,

You'll be happy to know that we sent messages off to SA on Tuesday and had a blast. Four women in Mr. W's GED class came that day [. . .] One student was so excited that she tossed all night before and came to class early since she had never had the intro to the net. I made copies of the letters but I didn't clear it with them to share outside of the class so I'll have to check. I'm sure it'll be ok (I'm not always clear about what would be private in a class setting re email!). They also fussed at me for not allowing enough time to read the whole blurb on Nemato so, I slowed down, let them set the pace and, yes, we did indeed have time to tap out the letters and send all but one on the way. We had a glitch with one of the terminals or the teachnet so I sent that one just a little after they left, then printed all of them out to give to the teacher. Otherwise, it was smooth. He will return them to the students after making copies. (Sisnett 1997)

As we both know, Lowell, telecollaboration is not about computers. It's about people learning to communicate and share the labors through a new medium. The design of this project, the "idea" of e-mail exchanges between Texas and South Africa, is not what made "East to East" meaningful to those students. It was human interest, compassion, and enthusiasm. However, if telecollaboration were the vehicle that enabled and inspired this, motivating participants to learn, providing them with just a glimmer of hope, then what's wrong with that? Why toss the proverbial baby out with the bath water? Perhaps the most important reminder for educators introducing computers to their classroom is contained in one phrase from the preceding message: "I slowed down, let them set the pace." Great teachers have an innate sense of the proper pace and learning environment for a particular group. Without that kind of wisdom, that sensitivity to students and their environment, the latest hardware and software, the most exotic cyberdestinations, are useless.

What's more, as we've observed from the beginning, if we want our telecollaborative projects to be universally accessible, then we ought to resist the seductions of the latest technology. At more than one conference presentation I've heard someone voice concern over equity and access in one breath, then use the next to direct their audience to visit an "interactive Web site." Lost upon them, perhaps because they enjoy privileged circumstances on a North American university campus, is the idea that someone in an impoverished community in this country or a developing country might not have access to anything more than electronic mail. Fortunately, organizations such as the Alliance for Global Learning <http://www.global-learning.org> have recognized this problem, taking steps to assist teachers with limited access to networked technology and professional development opportunities. We need to build upon such efforts to ensure that marginalized groups in technology-poor schools, districts, and countries have a voice in global discussions. This means designing and facilitating projects that employ electronic mail as the lowest common denominator rather than forcing participants to visit Java-scripted Websites that require high-end hardware and software to open audio and video files.

Which brings me, finally, to the last bits of advice you offered: "The medium matters" and "compensate." I'm weary of my own voice, though. Would you care to address these issues more specifically? You once mentioned a classroom exercise that fascinated me, perhaps because of my interest in languages and ignorance of how computers actually work. As I recall, the exercise enabled you to foreground "the media matter" as well as "compensate" for the binary qualities of the computer. In it, you demonstrated how a computer "thinks," and the impact of that understanding upon your students. I wonder if you could describe that more fully, as a way of illustrating how you compensate for all those hours that your students sit before illuminated screens. How, essentially, do you try to reach a healthy equilibrium between humanity and machinery? What recommendations would you offer the unsuspecting new 'Net teacher to mitigate the seduction of that electronic pond, building resistance to images that can both mesmerize and paralyze?

Monke:

That the medium matters and that we have to compensate for the dominant form, pretty much go together for me. The former focuses attention on what I think has to become a more central concern in our curriculum while the latter expresses the way I think we need to deal with it. The idea of compensation comes, again, from Postman and Weingartner (1969), who claim that within society as a whole we tend toward an imbalance, swinging from one extreme to another in our cultural orientation. A good educational system is one that attempts to balance the scales by pointing out (using our good crap detectors) what society at large is leaving out or misrepresenting and giving the missing aspects added weight in school so that the next generation will emerge as more whole human beings. That makes a lot of sense to me, and in a society that has swung to the technological extreme it would seem that we need a much more humanistic approach in schools right now to compensate for it.

That's the theory in a nutshell. But you insist on pulling me back into the classroom to talk about practice. Fortunately, you've given me a juicy example to work with. If you visit my class around December and say, "You demonstrated how a computer thinks," you will be verbally assaulted by at least a dozen students, derisively calling you to task for anthropomorphizing the computer. Someone will surely shout "Computers can't think!" and you will be severely scolded for equating what happens in a machine with what takes place in the human mind.

You and I both care deeply about language. We know that not only do our thoughts give shape to our words, but our words tend to shape our thoughts. One of the ways in which I compensate for the effects of the computer is to help students become very conscious of the words they use to refer to what the computer does. Rarely will you hear in my classroom any human qualities attributed to the computer. It's not easy, given that the terminology developed for the computer was intentionally built on the metaphor of the mind. And it's getting harder now that some cognitive scientists have flipped the metaphor around, having decided that the computer can serve as an adequate model of the mind (we also do not let anyone get by with referring to themselves in computer terms).

Of course, this self-conscious approach toward the computer only comes about if the students decide that the mind and the computer really are different from each other—and that's where the exercises you mention come in. I generally start by explaining (and demonstrating) to the students that the computer is a digital, binary machine, meaning that its operations are based on combinations of two discrete electrical states: on and off. Symbolically those electrical switches can be thought of, interchangeably, as true/false, yes/no, stop/go, 0/1—any number of binary relationships. To give the students an idea of how a computer can actually work in this way, I have them do simple mental activities. For example: I write eight numbers on cards, throw them on the table and have my students sort them. How long does it take? I ask them to describe how they did it? Then I give them a large board with eight pockets on it, into which they slip the numbered cards so the numbers can't be seen. I tell the students they now have to rearrange the cards in the pockets so they are in order, but they can only take two cards out of the pockets at a time and the only way they can move a card is to switch the two they have out at any given time (oh yes, they must also "forget" the number on any card when it is put back into a pocket). The students see quickly how difficult and tedious it is to sort the cards that way. Well, that's how a computer does it—essentially two cards at a time.

These kinds of activities give my students a sense of the incredibly complex and powerful but totally mindless quality of the computer. We talk about what it means that the computer can only operate in this way in everything it does. What the students generally come to realize is that the underlying process of computing would be considered infantile in terms of human thought. What makes the computer so powerful is, along with its speed, our ability to combine the binary switches in the machine in such a way that we can apply a lot of very sophisticated mathematical rules to manipulate those o's and 1's. And for this reason, the computer truly is a marvel—the embodiment of a formal mathematical system of thought.

Still, it doesn't exhaust all of human thought—once they discover it's all based on math most of my students are convinced of that—and we spend a good deal of time considering ways it may fail to account for all human cognition (for a long time leading Artificial Intelligence researchers like Marvin Minsky and Seymour Papert believed that this binary formalism *could* account for all human thought; of course, Papert went on to develop Logo and is a major advocate of computer-centered learning—while Minsky now works for Disney.)

There's more that we do. I occasionally do a lecture in the form of the common children's game Twenty Questions. The yes/no nature of my responses help students recognize how this form of processing constrains and shapes the way we think and communicate with a computer—that there is this quality called ambiguity that we humans can contend with but the computer cannot. All of these kinds of compensatory activities are just a matter of demystifying the technology. I think that's very important, as you can't really control what you don't understand. And any technology we don't control, controls us. One of the monumental failures of our current educational system is our willingness to send students all the way through college without helping them understand how the most ubiquitous tools surrounding them actually work. Is it any wonder that technological development seems beyond our control? Or that our students feel they have so little control over their own lives?

What I've been describing here is merely consciousness raising, a very important element for young people consigned to spending long hours staring into that screen. But I've come to believe it's not nearly enough. It provides the intellectual awareness but not the kind of inoculation against the computer's damaging effects that I think we need to work harder to achieve.

I realized this after I had my students read *Brave New World* for *Utopian Vision '97*. *Brave New World* is very much about the conflict between technology and the human spirit. And like any good novel it set off discussions whose effects on some of my students seemed to sink deep down into the core of their being—to the point that they weren't just aware mentally of the conflict, they actually began to feel it. They began to sense, not just think, that what is really missing from this magical logic machine is the human spirit.

It is just that human spirit that we have to concentrate on protecting and strengthening if we are to fully compensate for the effects of computer technology in the classroom and society at large. If you want a model for how to achieve that, I think you could just look at the path of your own experience, coming as you do out of an education steeped in the humanities. In a message I sent you long ago—saved because you included the passage in your reply (yes, isn't this form of communication wonderful)—I brought to your attention your own ability to compensate:

Your defenses against the dehumanizing tendencies of technology are so deep you hardly notice the attacks. This is the real irony of this whole issue: it is people like yourself who are psychologically best equipped to cope with high technology. Yet our schools are determined to blast the human-centered foundations to smithereens, never even letting young people encounter the Romantic poets or the Victorian novelists, not to mention the Greek gods. My concern is not that we prevent young humanists from using technology, but that we try to make sure that before they use the technology they know what it is to be human.

Just before I sent that to you I had attended a district in-service where an educational "futurist" had made the case (with Powerpoint graphs, of course) that we should dump Literature as a requirement in high school and replace it with Technical Reading—that is, how to read manuals. It's this de-emphasis of learning to know oneself and the world in favor of concentrating on learning to know the machine that I object to, because it feeds on itself—the more we use this mental machinery the more the cold, instrumental, mechanical view of learning lodges itself in educators', and students', minds. It becomes so much their world that eventually these kinds of insane suggestions become "visionary." And then you and I are faced with a serious problem: Having more or less learned how to steer this telecollaborative vehicle we find that there are no roads left that pass through the minds of our students leading toward self-discovery and revelation of the world in its wholeness. This is what I meant when I said the means of learning influence the end.

If we want those roads to remain open, we really do have to consciously compensate for the computer's inherent qualities. I've heard it said many times that computers are neither good, nor bad, nor neutral. I think it might be more appropriate to say that they are both good and bad because they are not neutral. Part of that tension you so rightly promote as beneficial grows out of our having to cope with this ambiguous character of technology. I am more than willing to acknowledge and celebrate all the benefits of our work that the computer has facilitated. What I so strenuously object to is the willingness of so many of our educational leaders to ignore the troublesome aspects that adhere to those benefits—their giddy embrace of technological development as inherently and solely good, to be applied indiscriminately at all levels and for all purposes in schools without a thought for the deeper consequences of the "revolution" they enable. That's why I tend to focus on the critical. Somebody has to point out the other end of the dialectic.

It's clear to me that if we want to cultivate whole human beings who have the wherewithal to cope with life to a large degree on their own terms (and comprehend the ideas of others who seek the same wisdom), we have to work hard at developing the uniquely human inner resources of our children *before* we let them lean on unfathomable tools. How can we "integrate" such technology into a human-centered learning environment when that center has not already been well developed? In contrast to public schools, which are dropping music and art programs to buy more computers, Waldorf schools, to give one example, not only provide strong arts, music, and nature programs in the elementary schools but actually use art, music, and nature as means of instruction in all areas. I think this is compensation—and inoculation—at the deepest level of learning. Given that preparation, the use of computers and telecollaboration at the high school level becomes less problematic for me. But even there it just seems common sense that if we want to expand young people's budding wisdom, then we should concentrate even harder on applying these tools toward helping them grapple with the insights of those who had a genius for understanding our inner and relational lives—dead white European males like Homer, Shakespeare, Blake, Mozart, and Van Gogh, but also the Nadine Gordimers, James Baldwins, Thich Nhat Hanhs, and dozens of other more recent explorers of the human condition that you could name much more easily than I.

Now I'm wandering into your bailiwick. Am I off-base here? Out to lunch? Slipped a cog? Loosened a screw? Exceeded my RAM? Fried my motherboard? You keep asking me how to integrate without annihilating. Now I'm going to press you. You've described how to integrate this technology without sacrificing Gordimer's insights into the human condition, but at the expense of becoming an archery target. And as I have just noted, I have also seen plenty of teachers integrate the technology happily while protecting their backsides, but at the cost of turning the activities into tasteless tapioca that advances understanding of the machinery more than the human condition. Do you see some way that our hypothetical teacher can integrate this technology without having to choose between sacrificing intellectual rigor on the one hand, and sacrificing his own blood on the other? In other words, just what is your closest to utopian yet realistic vision of telecollaboration in the classroom?

Burniske:

You weren't off base until you began referring to yourself in computer terms.

The concern you've raised, though, is the one that brought me back to the States after nearly a decade abroad: the desire to preserve a holistic, liberal arts education. The educator's mission is to inspire young minds to hope and dream, introducing them to new ideas without forcing premature conclusions. Telecollaboration could prove an ally, but only if it allows us to knock down classroom walls without making the educational roof collapse. You ask for my "utopian yet realistic vision of telecomputing in the classroom" and I'd say it is one in which students learn how to both "look at" and "look through" the medium, as suggested by Richard Lanham, Jay David Bolter, and Christina Haas, among others. That's the only way we can achieve an awareness of both the medium and its messages, overcoming McLuhan's oft-quoted, though inaccurate claim that "the medium is the message." As we've seen, the medium shapes the message, but the content of a speech delivered through radio, television, newspaper and Internet remains the same. It is in the impact of the speech, its persuasiveness through sensory stimuli, that the respective media differ.

Terminology has similar influence, yet we often embrace new terms without considering how they shape our thinking. As you'll recall, when we began this work I referred to our online activities as "telecommunication" projects. I was surprised to hear you refer to it as "telecomputing." That term, I thought, privileged the computers too much, since we designed activities not for the sake of computers or computing, but human communication and learning. It wasn't until we encountered the term "telecollaboration," which sums up this type of work most accurately, that we settled upon a satisfactory description. Yet, how many educators continue to use these terms synonymously, without considering their connotations and classroom ramifications? Anyone can create a "telecomputing" project, since it demands little more than a one-way transaction between students and machines. If I ask students to create Web pages and upload them to a server we would fulfill "telecomputing" at a basic level. It's far more difficult to arrange for "telecommunication" via electronic mail, newsgroups, or Web-based discussion forums. Finally, "telecollaboration" proves the most challenging of all, demanding elements from these first two genres along with a commitment to distribute the labors of research, inquiry and dialogue among distant peers.

I'd like that hypothetical teacher of ours to be mindful of this, and find ways to help students "look through" the *telecomputing* lens to explore ideas, while periodically "looking at" *telecomputing* to ask how it shapes their thoughts. Ideally, the teacher should follow her own Muse, calling upon a variety of interests and passions, experience and intuition, to inspire *telecommunication* activities. It's my hope that school administrators, meanwhile, will learn to distinguish between holding people accountable and regulating their every move. I'm not advocating more testing or evaluations, just classroom visits that help the administrator get a feel for the environment a teacher has cultivated, asking how *telecollaboration* and other pedagogical strategies influence the learning environment. To do this, the administrator must check personal bias at the door, allowing teachers to express themselves through a wide range of methods, from conventional to experimental, without compelling them to become technological or curricular specialists.

Unfortunately, this is easier said than done, for ours is an age of specialization.

I first realized this, as a child, when American League pitchers stopped coming to bat and football players became "nickel backs." I relearned it as an adolescent working at McDonald's, where every crew member was assigned a particular task and work station (for the record, I specialized as the "bun man," preparing countless trays of buns for sizzling burgers). Years later, I drew upon these insights to investigate the theme of "specialization" while teaching "Baseball Literature" at an all-boys prep school. I asked students to read an essay by Bartlett Giammatti, then president of Yale and soon to be commissioner of major league baseball. Giammatti (1985) believed the designated hitter deprived baseball of a time-honored tradition: the "skilled generalist." He feared this development, along with the emphasis on relief pitching, would fragment the game, creating specialists instead of generalists. Players would no longer be encouraged to hit, run, and throw to the best of their ability. They'd become specialists of a designated order: designated hitter, designated runner, designated fielder, and so on. What the game would gain in specialization it would lose in fragmentation. The same, I think, applies to education.

Our society's respect for specialists discourages teachers from becoming skilled generalists. The result is intellectual impoverishment of our schools and children. It's absurd to suggest that telecomputing started this trend, but foolish to ignore its ability to further it. While I was putting together that baseball course, in fact, a colleague asked if I had studied "baseball in literature" at the university level. When I said I had not he shook his head and told me it wasn't a good idea to move away from "your specialties." This belief was seconded by colleagues outside my department, people who frowned upon "dilettantes." The goal as a professional educator, they implied, was not to broaden our interests, but to narrow the scope of one's investigations.

The prevalence of such thinking became painfully apparent while I was working on an M.A. at Oxford a few years later. There in Lincoln College's library, adjacent to the works of and about Geoffrey Chaucer, was a book entitled, "Dialects of Southern London in the Latter 14th Century." I thought this a rather narrow topic, but when I jokingly offered it to a fellow student he grew defensive. My friend declared that as one "advanced" through higher education one had to learn more and more about less and less. When I asked why this was so I was told that the only way to become a professional is by becoming a specialist. "A specialist," I was told, "is considered an expert, and with expertise comes authority." Ultimately, then, specialization transforms the amateur into a professional by investing him or her with authority.

I wondered about this a great deal. I wondered why educators should value specialization when the greatest challenge is encouraging students to think in holistic terms, breaking down the walls of Discipline. The problem with much of secondary education is that it is frightfully compartmentalized. Faculty are fragmented because they belong to the citadels of Discipline first, the faculty of a school second. Students, particularly those in a secondary school, are seldom encouraged to think in interdisciplinary terms. Their teachers, rather than exploring ideas that could unite disparate subjects, tell them to settle down, stop thinking about the history or science test they just took, and open their books to discuss the next bit of compartmentalized data. While this makes one sympathize with students, it does not mean the solution to such problems is for teachers to become more specialized. The schoolteacher's desire for more public esteem, by way of expertise and authority, could have pernicious consequences:

For if specialization wins for teachers the public regard and economic standing they have historically lacked, it may do so at the risk of falling into the same traps of technological dependency and public apathy that have been associated with expert relations in other fields. Teaching also could come to be seen in a more technical light rather than as a field particularly dependent on decisions made about the social ends of education (Welker 1992, 8)

If telecomputing furthers such trends, I definitely *will* say there's something inherently evil in the machinery. Specialization serves the purposes of researchers, but not classroom teachers. Like most teachers I aspire to learn more about my field, but I am also interested in learning more about other fields. We need to value the "skilled generalists," and applaud them for making associations that "specialists" often cannot make. To encourage greater specialization is to lead a culture astray, isolating people rather than uniting them as a community. This has, of course, been the cry of humanist educators for centuries, but it bears repeating when fanatics suggest replacing the study of poetry and fiction with computer manuals. Perhaps the cautionary note of a modern, educational philosopher brings this point home:

... we can and should do something to mitigate the barbarism of intense specialization, which threatens to be as destructive in its own way as the abandonment of specialization would be . . . for the sake of our cultural traditions, our democratic institutions, and our individual well-being, our specialists must also be generalists; that is, generally educated human beings. (Adler 1982, 72)

The world needs good "skilled generalists," as Bart Giammatti put it, or "Renaissance men," as we formerly described them. After all, the pitcher must still know how to use a glove. No designated fielder can rescue him when the ball shoots out on a line, like Truth itself, taking aim at his skull. Likewise, someone, somewhere, needs to examine relationships between disciplines and ideas, genres and time periods. Without such people, how will the specialist of Northern London dialects speak to the specialist of Southern London? How might the fourteenth century speak to the twenty-first? How might telecomputing speak to humanity?

Perhaps the key to such communication is a broader definition of our terms. I know you're as annoyed by the label "Computer teacher" as I am by the term "English teacher." You don't "teach computers" and I don't "teach English." We both teach human beings. Labeling teachers by discipline may assist school bureaucracies, but it fragments student perceptions of the world. While I was "teaching English" in Kuala Lumpur, I was also introducing high school sophomores to the *Utopian Visions* project, asking them to consider the intersection of art, history, government, education, transportation, and more. Initially, some students protested that this wasn't their idea of "English class," but eventually they realized the discipline was a liquid that assumed the shape of its container. I believed then, as I do now, that challenging the status quo was good for them. It broadened their definitions and understanding of "English class." The same must be done for definitions of "telecomputing." Students ought to examine far more than computers while "telecomputing." In this manner, "looking at" the computer technology could lead to a more holistic examination of human inventions, ones that lost visibility as societies grew more accustomed to them. In *Writing Space: The Computer, Hypertext, and the History of Writing,* Jay David Bolter discusses "writing as a state of mind," challenging conventional definitions of technology itself:

There is good etymological reason to broaden our definition of technology to include skills as well as machines. The Greek root of "technology" is *techne,* and for the Greeks a techne could be an art or a craft, "a set of rules, system or method of making or doing, whether of the useful arts, or of the fine arts" (Liddell and Scott 1973, 1785). In the ancient world physical technology was simpler, and the ancients put a correspondingly greater emphasis on the skill of the craftsman—the potter, the stone-mason, or the carpenter. In his dialogue the Phaedrus, Plato calls the alphabet itself a techne. He would also have called the ancient book composed of ink on papyrus a techne; Homeric epic poetry was also a techne, as was Greek tragedy. All the ancient arts and crafts have this in common: that the craftsman must develop a skill, a technical state of mind in using tools and materials. Ancient and modern writing is a technology in just this sense. It is a method for arranging verbal thoughts in a visual space. The writer always needs a surface upon which to make his or her marks and a tool with which to make them, and these materials help to define the nature of the writing. Writing with quill and parchment is a different skill from writing with a printing press, which in turn differs from writing with a computer. (Bolter 1991, 35)

You ask for my "utopian yet realistic vision of telecomputing." I say let me use it as a tool, examining both the medium and the messages it shapes, but let me also treat it as a subject of study with my students. As a skilled generalist I want the freedom to decide when it's best for students in my class to "look through" telecollaborative activities, "look at" telecollaboration, or ignore it altogether. Meanwhile, I'll know we've turned a corner when people stop talking about "technology" as though it began with the creation of computers. Better yet, the time will come—though you may not believe it—when people will grow bored with this new fad as well. Which makes me wonder what you'd like to see *after* the Internet Revolution has run its course? When that pendulum swings, once again, what shift in paradigm would you embrace? What would you like to see happen in "post-modem" schools?

Monke:

I'm glad you've brought us back around to what it means to be educated (as opposed to merely trained). I think it's important that we bring our discussion to a close by focusing on how telecollaboration fits into the purpose of education, rather than make the mistake so many educational "seers" make—trying to determine how education should respond to new technological demands. But it's not just the futurists who are making that mistake these days. I've been spending a lot of time recently interviewing the leaders of my own school concerning the massive infusion of technology into the district. The most common justification I have heard for all the changes we are going to have to make to accommodate it is that we have to change the way "we do business" in order to make this incredibly expensive investment pay off.

This inversion of means and ends is perfectly understandable, but it puts us right back in the wagon with my poor uncle Virgil, doing the best we can to hold on as the rampaging technology takes us where it will. We've already discussed the ambiguity of this structural determinism set against your desire for individual initiative, but one more swipe at it is necessary in order to get at the questions you ask.

Even the most diehard Luddite has to admit that the computer has been the catalyst for accomplishing something neither Dewey nor Montessori nor all the radical reformers of the sixties could do: actually convince the general public that a curriculum taught by poorly prepared teachers, working in physical and categorical isolation out of dull textbooks, makes for boring, irrelevant learning. This is perhaps the computer's greatest contribution to education. In that sense it has been a godsend. It has allowed people like you to sneak around some heavily fortified curricular walls. It has reinvigorated thousands of teachers and administrators and set them to thinking again about what it means to be educated. By "reconstitut[ing] the conditions of survival" (Postman 1993, 18), it forced a discourse on what the purpose of education should be that was long overdue. This is all to the good. But the structure and ideology that have accompanied the computer into the schools, if not yet the classroom, are erecting new walls (cognitive ones this time) that just as surely separate people from each other and from a meaningful exploration of their world. If telecollaboration is ever to be a primarily beneficial tool in our pedagogical repertoire, we have to alter the way we relate to technology in the larger sense.

It's in viewing technology in this larger sense that I'm going to betray an uncharacteristic, if perverse, optimism. The technological bandwagon may be accelerating across the field of education, but in society at large there are signs that the horses are beginning to stumble, the wheels are beginning to shimmy, the number of people pulling on the reins beginning to swell. Certainly the carnage left in its wake is becoming more noticeable. Books like *Silicon Snake Oil* (1995), *Data Smog* (1997) and *Why Things Bite Back* (1997) have found a receptive audience that more incisive books like Roszak's *The Cult of Information* (1986) didn't reach a decade ago. Look at Michael Lerner's best seller *The Politics of Meaning* (1996): Disillusionment with technocratic ideology is a major theme. I encounter more and more people who are now less enamored with their relationship to high technology than they are aggravated by it. The sheer speed and complexity of high-tech development is beginning to noticeably stress human culture. Our civilization's emphasis on technological development over the last two centuries has brought us an abundance of benefits, but it appears to have taken human welfare about as far as it can without creating very serious and obvious crises in both ecology and psychology. I think it is beginning to dawn on people that it's about time to give the technological horses a breather (not shoot them), while we hitch human development to a different team and head down a different path.

That doesn't mean that "post-modem" schools will be computer free, but it may mean that an opportunity will arise soon to slowly begin reestablishing the human being at the center of education. I think Roszak may have given us a clue as to what we should do in his updating of Thoreau's famous maxim that new technologies are just "improved means to an unimproved end:"

... we live in a time when the technology of human communication has advanced at blinding speed; but what people have to say to one another by way of that technology shows no comparable development. (1986, 16)

We now have magnificent means for communication in place. We have more information than we can deal with. In the post-Internet era I would hope that we would finally decide to concentrate on that "comparable development," improving what we have to say to one another, rather than the channels through which it is said. If we set that as our goal, I think it would result in a very different kind of shift in the way "we do business" in schools.

First, it would focus our attention on ideas rather than information. Whether it is the idea of utopia, the Golden Rule, the Second Law of Thermodynamics, or the Pythagorean Theorem, profound ideas, openly and deeply explored, naturally transcend any artificial curricular boundaries [the Dewey school was doing this with elementary school children forty years before the computer was invented (Mayhew & Edwards 1936)].

Second, in order to find meaning in those ideas students would have to be able to relate them to their own experiences. This would require a much stronger concern for the context of their daily lives. My vision would have this context gradually, over the course of the academic career, emanate out, like the ripples in a pond, from the sandbox to the village green, to the Capital Mall, to the global grid. That kind of gradually expanding world, filled with meaning at each stage before moving on, will require an enormous shift in culture, both in and out of school. It's really pretty hard to fault a teacher for "plugging kids into the 'Net" when the only safe or inviting exploratory environment available in the community is the shopping mall. If we are going to make learning deeply meaningful, we have to give kids a more richly convivial community to live in and the opportunities and security to engage it.

The same principles of gradual expansion can be applied to communicating these ideas and experiences: Start with the most fundamental, most natural, most transparent medium, speech, and gradually work our way to the most opaque, mechanical, and constrained medium, the Internet. Eventually students would explore all the various ways to make themselves understood and to understand in each medium. Certainly, this would involve both "looking at" and "looking through" every form of communication as they learn to comprehend the power and limitations of each.

One more ingredient is essential to this post-modem school, I think; something hardly anyone even considers in the security-conscious school environment today. I don't think we will get anywhere with any methods of education unless we can instill in our schools an atmosphere of love and respect for our students, their struggles, their concerns, their judgments, their capabilities, their very lives. This is the one ingredient no machine can provide. I'll take it as a sign we are headed in the right direction when I go a month without hearing some community or national leader refer to students as "products" or "national resources."

Wisdom, good judgment, a compassionate understanding of the human condition might just emerge from such an educational environment. Telecollaboration could certainly be a part, a late part to be sure, of such an environment. In fact, the projects we've been doing would seem to provide one pretty good example of an attempt to implement the utopian educational vision I've just described. In such an environment the Internet might actually serve exceptionally well.

Of course, you and I both know that this kind of education is fraught with dangers. Education that centers on the exploration of ideas inevitably leads to ideals and ideals lead students to do a lot of real, unrestricted critical thinking—in other words, criticism. Whether their criticism is justified or not (our task would be to help them sort that out), it's sure to make life uncomfortable at times for both the schools and society at large. It's the kind of education that got Socrates hemlocked (of course, the Greeks took ideas much more seriously than we do). The point is that this form of education is not just warm and fuzzy "values clarification"—it is truly revolutionary because it tends to generate new and passionately held ideas about how to conduct our lives.

I know this kind of idealism is dangerous—it can sprout all kinds of nasty activities. But idealism is what also gives nourishment to hope, inspires sacrifice and refocuses attention away from self towards others, precisely the kind of compensation we should be trying to foster to offset the consumeristic/narcissistic effects of the current uses of computer technology. I think it is a terrible tragedy that the idealism of our youth has been replaced by such deep cynicism. How can we hope for a better world if the next generation has no vision of such a possibility or a passion for working toward it? It is idealism that could generate a social consciousness on the back side of the Internet/Technology revolution. In fact, it represents the antithesis of the totally instrumental, amoral technological ideology in vogue today. It is how we can address the responsibility for creating a better world—incomparably more effective, in my opinion, than any multicultural keypal program.

I'm glad you made the case for "generalists," because it is within those ranks that I think idealism still has a chance. I hear some mention of "general knowledge" when technologists talk about integrating the curriculum through telecomputing. But I think in their case it is usually insincere, coupled as it is with a much stronger drive, led by Tech Prep and School to Work, to get students to focus on a specialized vocational area at younger and younger ages. A sixteen-year-old girl told me the other day that one of her teachers informed her that even though she is an extraordinary musician, her drive toward success will be badly damaged if she drops one of her music classes this year in order to volunteer in a classroom for severely disabled students. His assessment may be accurate, but what she wants to do is right, and any educator who can't step out of his specialized area long enough to recognize the difference has no place in my post-modem school.

I don't think society's most crucial needs right now are scientists, mathematicians, computer programmers, Web masters, or even professional musicians. It needs better husbands, wives, parents, neighbors, community activists, educators, politicians, statesmen, and stateswomen. It's no coincidence that all of these roles have traditionally been considered generalist roles. It is in these roles that we have not had that "comparable development." It is, therefore, precisely where we need to concentrate our energies in school now—to improve the ability of young people to succeed at those generalist roles in a far more complex social environment than we have ever had to deal with before. It's going to be a lot more difficult, a lot messier, a lot more turbulent, a lot less certain, and a lot more fun teaching youth how to make a life rather than just how to make a living.

I see the Internet having a very limited role once this kind of education is established. And I remain, obviously, somewhat skeptical that we can use it now to help us move in that direction. Still, one of the benefits of engaging in dialectic is discovering that one is rarely wholly right or wholly wrong. Maybe we, or others, *can* find ways in which the 'Net helps move us along the path we're pointing. Maybe it *can* be "just" another pedagogical tool, shaped by us solely as a means to accomplish the human goals we establish. Maybe we *can* transcend the machine that both serves and threatens us.

Or maybe not.

In any event, it's time to get up from this virtual table for awhile. I know you will have a few last words that will once and for all resolve all these issues. I'll just close by saying that after nearly a decade of working together almost exclusively through the 'Net, it will be nice to sit down with you at a real table over a real bowl of *ceviche* and talk face-to-face once again.

Or maybe not?

Burniske:

That depends on whether or not you're buying.

Actually, I'm sure it'll be the usual Dutch treat. Isn't that what we expect of dialectics? The best ones resist closure. Like the playwrights who inspired me to think of my classroom and telecollaborative activities in dialectical terms, I'd encourage the reader to step from the theater of this book to argue about the role of telecomputing in general, and telecollaboration in particular, within their own school community. I'm familiar with the urgency of those discussions from the perspective of a student, teacher, and parent—three roles that I've played simultaneously in recent years.

In fact, a new school year began just as I turned to this final epistle. At the end of the first day, my thirteen-year-old son came home with his school's "Acceptable Use Policy for Technology." He asked me to sign the form, a five-page, single-spaced document. I asked if he understood what it said.

"Yeah, I can't look at porn," he replied, "and if I do whatever the teacher says then I won't get in trouble." This is what my son, a bright, perceptive adolescent learned at school on his first day. He didn't speak of a song he'd heard, a poem he'd read, or a funny story his teacher told. Instead, he came home talking about an "Acceptable Use Policy for Technology."

I asked what the consequences were if I didn't sign the form.

"Mom can sign it," he said.

"Oh, of course," I said. "And what if she refuses?"

"Then I can't use the Internet at school."

I wondered if that would be such a bad thing.

Then I went through the form with him, asking if he understood terms like "innocuous" and "objectionable" or "defamatory."

"Not really," he said.

I tried to explain.

Eventually, like many parents, I signed the form despite misgivings. I signed, hoping this would help my child, not hurt him. However, I didn't like signing a document that referred to him as a "user" instead of a "student." Nor did I appreciate the litigious prose threatening to "terminate access" for ill-defined transgressions that could force users to "indemnify" the school "for any losses, costs, or damages, including reasonable attorneys' fees" incurred due to "any breach of this agreement." What sort of message did this document send to a thirteen-year-old? My son, who has seen twice as many countries as years, just shrugged in response to such questions. He didn't understand all the fuss, but it was equally apparent that he didn't understand this policy statement.

I wondered how other parents across the city, state, and country reacted when presented with this new species of parent-permission form known as an "AUP" (Acceptable Use Policy). How many of them could decipher the language of such a document, let alone weigh its social and legal implications? Here I was, a graduate student at a research university, working in computer labs equipped with the latest network technology, and I was having a hard time with it. I didn't like supporting a policy that warned of "disciplinary action" against "users" who "solicit the performance of any activity which is prohibited by law," particularly when my son confessed that he didn't know what it meant to "solicit" performances. Was I making too much of this? Perhaps, but I think it wise to at least pause before endorsing a document that states the following: "Although drawing and painting have legitimate academic use, those activities are prohibited when done for recreational purposes."

As student, teacher, and parent I know why school officials included that statement in their AUP. I have seen adolescents abuse privileges. I know how skilled they are at turning educational tools into recreational toys. Pause for a moment, though, and think about that sentence. Consider what it implies. Imagine reading it to a group of children. Don't think about it in relation to computer technology; think of it as part of a school's curriculum. Think of it, finally, as an "educational" statement. Now then, care to endorse it? If so, please sign here_____

After wrestling with policy statements I turned to my other son, a feisty seven-year old, and asked how his first day of school had gone. I was eager to hear his first impressions upon joining a mixed-age class (2nd–3rd grade) in our neighborhood's public school. Happily, he didn't mention computers, though I imagine it's just a matter of time. He did allow, however, that he'd learned a new word: "Procedure." I asked how he had learned that word. "I musta heard it two hundred times!" he said. Then he offered in that mocking, BIG VOICE of a little person imitating adults: "Class, it's VERY IMPORTANT that you follow these PROCEDURES!"

There was something providential about these stories. Their coincidence brought back memories of this book's genesis. Our dialectical exchange didn't begin with the idea of breaking down the digital walls of telecomputing. It began as a conversation between two teachers trying to find more effective ways to teach. It's appropriate that it should end that way. It's also appropriate to admit that we've had a few difficult moments along the way, occasionally touching a nerve or saying something that was just a little too sharp, a little too close to the bone. Yet, we've learned how to argue, how to empathize even when we disagree. Eventually, we stopped trying to win those "binary" debates and learn from each other.

Not about policies.

Nor procedures.

But about teaching.

And kids.

And about the end of education.

And "not-learning."

"Not-learning?" Yes, not-learning, a far more common practice in our schools than we care to admit, though seldom acknowledged and rarely understood. Educators often misinterpret "not-learning" as a disability or lack of skills when it actually has more to do with personal desire and determination. I've borrowed the term from Herbert Kohl, who has this to say about the origins of the behavior it describes:

Not learning tends to take place when someone has to deal with unavoidable challenges to her or his personal and family loyalties, integrity and identity. In such situations there are forced choices and no apparent middle ground. To agree to learn from a stranger who does not respect your integrity causes a major loss of self. The only alternative is to not-learn and reject the stranger's world. (Kohl 1994, 6)

I can empathize with this behavior. A few summers ago I chose to "not-learn" a computer programming language. To qualify as a doctoral candidate in a Computers and English Studies program, I was required to pass a foreign language requirement: three years of a conventional language or two years of that language plus two years of a programming language. I gave the computer programming a try. After two weeks, I had had enough. I simply didn't want to learn PASCAL, a moribund programming language that had more to do with codes and syntax than creativity and pedagogy. Don't get me wrong. We need people with specialized skills, which is why I've learned to teach in a networked computer classroom, introducing students to hypertext and a variety of online learning tools. However, we also need "skilled generalists." In this instance, becoming the former would've jeopardized the latter.

After two weeks of cryptic lectures, a rapid succession of overhead transparencies offered to 200 students in a cramped auditorium, and programming sessions in equally cramped computer labs with teaching assistants more comfortable with computers than people, I chose not to continue. It was a hostile, dehumanizing environment. To succeed in it would mean changing who I am, acquiring the language and customs of a culture that I didn't find appealing. While I wasn't fully aware of it at the time, I now see my decision as a choice of literacies. Choosing to "not learn" a programming language meant rejecting that part of a culture that routinely strips language of emotion, reducing it to purely grammatical constructions. Quite frankly, I wasn't willing to go that far to acquire computer literacy.

This may sound like the dull rationalizations of a misguided romantic, but I can assure you it was a painful ordeal, one that forced me to look closely at who I am and what I wish to become. By choosing to "not-learn" that programming language I resisted its influence; I refused to let it alter the way I see the world and my place in it. Instead, I chose to learn more Spanish, reacquainting myself with a language and culture that I happily embraced while living and working abroad. This meant reading *The Labyrinth of Solitude* by Octavio Paz to prepare for translation of a selection from that text. It also meant reflecting upon travels in Spain and Latin America, a nostalgic return to people and places that shaped my life—places liked Ecuador and The Manabi Hut. Good fortune has allowed me to choose what to learn and often where to learn it. This I knew. What I hadn't realized, however, was that fortune also allowed me to choose what to "not-learn."

I was conscious of this choice after reading Ludwik Fleck's monograph, *Genesis and Development of a Scientific Fact*. Half a century ago, Fleck admonished scientists to examine the "thought style" of their community's "thought collective," lest an obsession with objectivity and scientific methods should blind them to a "fact" of human existence:

The concept of absolutely emotionless thinking is meaningless. There is no emotionless state as such nor pure rationality as such. (1979, 49)

What I value about reading, writing, speaking, and listening—all of which rely upon the "technology" of an alphabet and grammatical structures—is the way these activities enable us to explore and express our humanity. An obsession with technology as an end in itself threatens such exploration and expression. Thus, while it's important to choose what forms of literacy we wish to learn, it's equally important to choose what forms we will "not learn." Every student should have the right to "not-learn." A humane, public educational system would respect that right as much as the right to learn. Yet, after the extraordinary expenditure of time and resources—on state and national levels—one can easily imagine an educator's response to the student brave enough to raise her hand and say, "I'd rather not work with a computer today."

Perhaps this explains why, as a teacher, I feel so anxious at the start of a school year. It's not because of the material I'll be teaching, or my methods for teaching it. It's because I don't know how the students will respond. I'm uncertain of the values and beliefs they carry with them, what they're prepared to learn, and what they'll choose to "not-learn." How could I have known that while teaching in Egypt, Ecuador, and Malaysia—or even the United States? The moment students enter my classroom I confront myriad questions, many of which they can't answer themselves. Who are these children? What do they have in common with each other, or with me? How can I earn their trust? How might I inspire them to think critically? How can I awaken their curiosity, helping them enjoy learning, without turning the class into an "edutainment" center? How might I help them grow beyond their own expectations, compelling them to examine their assumptions while respecting their choice to "not-learn" ideas that threaten a "loss of self"?

These are difficult questions, but ones that deserve attention before we turn to policies and procedures. This is why I admire people like Herbert Kohl, the ones who commit themselves to helping others learn yet respect their right to "not-learn." I admire people like Lowell Monke, too, the peaceful resistance fighters who fight the good fight, ironically challenging the value of computers in education even while teaching in computer-networked classrooms. Such educators have taught me how to evaluate teachers, reducing my criteria to a single question: "Would I want this person to teach my own child?" Happily, I can say that I'd be delighted to have my children learn from a number of colleagues, including Lowell Monke. And it's not merely because of what those people would "teach," but because of what they would "not-teach." For starters, I'm confident that they would "not-teach" my child to "just do it." Instead, they'd adopt what Kohl describes as "creative maladjustment," invoking the words and spirit of Martin Luther King:

Now we all should seek to live a well-adjusted life in order to avoid neurotic and schizo-phrenic personalities. But there are some things within our social order to which I am proud to be maladjusted and to which I call upon you to be maladjusted. I never intend to adjust myself to segregation and discrimination. I never intend to adjust myself to mob rule. I never intend to adjust myself to the tragic effects of the methods of physical violence and to tragic militarism. I call upon you to be maladjusted to such things. (King, quoted in Kohl 1994, 129)

We know what happens to maladjusted individuals. Society ostracizes them. If they fail to conform, or at least remain quiet, society often punishes them. For this reason Kohl points out that "adjustment is not to be abandoned lightly: It is wonderful to fit comfortably within a family, at work, in culture, or society" (1994, 129)." He then borrows a definition of this elusive term, claiming that:

...."adjustment" means "the ability of an individual to live harmoniously with his environ-ment—physical, social, intellectual and moral—and with himself, keeping intact his per-sonal integrity."... Adjustment is not an end in itself; rather, it is a description of the relation between an individual and ... (his or her)... environment. (Redl and Wattenberg 1951, 185)

This is why educators must wrestle with their conscience. We wish to adjust, to belong, but at what price? Can we really live harmoniously with both envi-ronment and self if we forfeit our convictions and compromise our integrity? Who among us has not worked within a school or district that was hostile to the learning environment they wished to create? When confronted with such envi-ronments we may choose to conform, resist, or flee. Unfortunately, we often conform or flee when we ought to choose "maladjustment," preserving that which we cultivated and nurtured, that which we cherish:

When it is impossible to remain in harmony with one's environment without giving up deeply held moral values, creative maladjustment becomes a sane alternative to giving up altogether. Creative maladjustment consists of breaking social patterns that are mo-rally reprehensible, taking conscious control of one's place in the environment, and readjusting the world one lives in based on personal integrity and honesty—that is, it consists of learning to survive with minimal moral and personal compromise in a thoroughly compromised world and of not being afraid of planned and willed conflict, if necessary. It also means searching for ways of not being alone in a society where the mythology of individualism negates integrity and leads to isolation and self-mutilation. It means small everyday acts of maladjustment as well as occasional major reconstruc-tion, and it requires will, determination, faith that people can be wonderful, conscious planning, and an unshakable sense of humor. (Kohl 1994, 130)

I know why we often fail to resist. I know why we compromise. And yet, when seven-year-olds are overwhelmed with "procedures" and thirteen-year-olds forced to sign acceptable use policies that they don't understand, why shouldn't parents offer a little resistance and encourage "creative maladjustment" in their children? It's hard to get an education when you're preoccupied with procedures. It's even harder to think critically about technology when your introduction to it is an authoritative policy statement. Ultimately, this smothers a child's curiosity, stifling opportunities to raise questions. Are we so keen on technology that we're willing to tell children what that AUP told my son: "Although drawing and painting have legitimate academic use, those activities are prohibited when done for recreational purposes?" I will understand if my son chooses to "not-learn" that rule. I will support him if he resists it. Indeed, I would be proud to learn that his computer privileges were suspended because he was caught drawing and painting for recreational purposes. At least I'd know he still has spirit, as well as the courage to follow his creative Muse.

I hope this book prompts a similar, spirited response, for I believe it had more to do with courage than computer technology. For that matter, it had more to do with teaching. And learning. And reviving public discourse. It had more to do with creative maladjustment and the subversive activity we call "learning." The Internet served as our shibboleth, but not our focus. That was, and must continue to be, the issue of teaching children how to think for themselves and the good of their communities. We must debate the use of computer technology—and all technology—in our classrooms. One way to invigorate the debate is to improve teacher education. A teacher's professional development should not come in addition to other tasks, but in lieu of some. Why not lessen the class loads, establishing new precedents, as a starting point? If politicians want to throw money at education let them set a maximum class size of twenty students in public schools. Let's not assign secondary school teachers more than four sections and eighty children per day. Let's throw money at the human beings for a change. Let's make their work environment as humane as possible, improving the chances that our children will receive humane treatment as well. If school boards fear that teachers will abuse such freedom, they ought to provide in-service programs during the school day. Establish professional development centers within schools, where teachers may go to learn at their own pace about the Internet and telecollaborative learning activities.

As mentioned previously, the National Center for Education Statistics reported that Internet access in K–12 schools increased from 35% in 1994 to 89% in 1998 (NCES 1999) while only a small fraction of schools surveyed had provided professional development opportunities for the faculty charged with using this technology for instructional purposes (NCES 1999). Something's obviously wrong with this picture. Why are politicians hell-bent on throwing money at schools for Internet connectivity, yet neglecting the teachers? I think we know why, yet we allow that topic to remain notably absent from public discourse on technology in education. And yet, isn't the professional development of our teachers essential for dynamic schools and healthy democracies? Our best hope resides with individuals brave enough to discuss the net effect of telecollaboration, educators like the head of the National Association of Elementary School Principals who placed human concerns before technological ones when he made the following observation:

I have not the slightest doubt about the value of computers in our society. But I question whether we have learned to apply this technology to ᴋ–8 instruction. . . . If computers make a difference, it has yet to show up in achievement. We must have the courage to resist the public enthusiasm for sexy hardware and argue for the funds necessary to train our teachers. We cannot send them into the computer room with nothing but a user's manual. If you've ever read one of those things . . . they give new meaning to the phrase, "English as a second language." (Henry 1997)

We should, indeed, "argue for the funds necessary to train our teachers." I would go further, though, and say that we need to "argue for the funds necessary to teach our children." Every student, teacher, and parent should have an opportunity to contribute to those discussions. Let's revive dialectical discourse and apply it to far more than computers when we talk about schools. One of the chief lessons I learned while teaching in ᴋ–12 classrooms from the Middle East to North America, South America to Asia, was this: *Schools will never be good places for students until they are good places for teachers.* The legacy of the Internet gold rush at the end of the twentieth century, I fear, is that our schools have become good places for machines, but not necessarily good places for human beings.

Our present climate, which finds educators so immersed in the technology "thought collective" that they cannot imagine its potential harm, makes it all but impossible for students to "not-learn" keyboarding skills and computer applications. Yet, as you've pointed out several times, Lowell, before we adapt to new learning environments we must consider the potentially harmful effects of that adaptation. Perhaps "computer illiteracy," and the "creative maladjustment" that supports it, could prove a virtue in response to dehumanizing forces. Ultimately, we need to cultivate more critical awareness of the culture that computer literacy and telecollaboration generate. My own ambivalence enables me to think, read, speak, and listen as both a believer and skeptic. It also sustains my conviction that human emotions are a prerequisite for investigations of topics such as "Computers and English Studies." I should hope that I never lose such convictions, nor the ability to understand students who refuse to prostrate themselves before Technology's altar.

The "end of education," in the positive sense of that phrase, is inspiration and enlightenment. Yet, how can we inspire or enlighten children if we fail to present meaningful questions or alternative viewpoints? We must teach our children, and ourselves, to cultivate the "salutary anxiety" that I spoke of in the first chapter of this book. Remember that old wooden bridge I described, the one sustained by the "opposition" of wooden beams? I often refer to it while teaching students about argument and persuasion. They think me a lunatic when I offer the paradoxical claim that "opposition is support." However, my sanity is less suspect when I use athletics for my analogy; bitter rivals like the Boston Red Sox and New York Yankees need one another. To make my point I'll ask: "What's the worst thing that could happen to one of those teams?" Someone usually replies: "Lose the game." I shake my head and say: "Lose the opponent." After all, it's the opponent who gives meaning to an otherwise meaningless activity: hitting a leather ball with a wooden bat. Similarly, politicians need opposition to give meaning to their ideas, to help them seek better solutions to social problems. When our elected officials creep to the middle of the road they may improve their chances for election yet endanger the dialectics necessary for a healthy democracy. We can no sooner discover Truth without opposing views compelling us to think more deeply than a wooden bridge may stand without the dialectical tension of its materials.

Above all, we must endow our children with hope, encouraging them to examine difficult issues while dreaming of a better society. That is what I have enjoyed most about the *Utopian Visions* project. The dialectics that we cultivated in that telecollaborative project have a deep resonance to them. In several instances, the discussions became an end in themselves, encouraging a better understanding of ourselves and the world we've inherited. Asking students to describe a more perfect society and look forward to a time beyond their own lives is a wonderful, rewarding experience. If telecollaboration helps us dream of that "brave new world," fashioning better people, societies, and institutions, then we will have much to celebrate. However, technology cannot accomplish such things on its own; it needs the human spirit and imagination. We should have learned, long ago, to have faith in people, not technology, and to exploit technology, not people. Somehow, we got it the other way around. Perhaps if we teach them well, drawing lessons from our own mistakes, the next generation will get it right?

Let us hope so.

NOTES

Chapter 4

1. Until I stopped teaching math courses a couple of years ago I was still not fully immune to this mind-numbing subservience. At the beginning of each year I received not only the district adopted textbook and its massive bulk of supplemental material, but also a full set of daily lesson plans covering the entire year's curriculum. I was always assured that I was free to deviate from this structure, that it was designed for those teachers who weren't so able to think for themselves. Pity the poor teachers so labeled—and their students.

2. This includes not only the cost of hardware and software but also support, training, administrative, and "end-user operations" costs. Des Moines Schools certainly doesn't pay this much, but that is because much of the support costs are absorbed by personnel (including students) who shift or add to their workload in order to keep the machines running. For a more detailed discussion on the hidden costs of educational computing in public schools, see Monke (1999).

Chapter 6

1. I must say that I find this reasoning chauvinistic and utilitarian (McDonaldized?). Surely these cultures need not justify their existence according to how they may assist our learning, or whether they are well suited to the kind of world we are spreading through our technological might. This brand of social Darwinism conveniently relieves us of taking responsibility for their destruction. Still, I have heard this line of reasoning so many times I feel compelled to address it on its own terms.

Chapter 8

1. See Perelman (1992), for an enthusiastic exploration of this ethos.

2. See Borgmann (1984), for a discussion on technology's role in commodifying experience.

BIBLIOGRAPHY

Adler, Mortimer. 1982. *The Paideia Proposal: An Educational Manifesto*. New York: Macmillan.

Altman, Joel. 1978. *The Tudor Play of Mind: Rhetorical Inquiry and the Development of Elizabethan Drama*. Berkeley: University of California Press.

Apple, Michael. 1982. *Education and Power*. Boston: Routledge & Kegan Paul.

Apple, Michael. 1990. *Ideology and Curriculum*. New York: Routledge.

Bach, Richard. 1977. *Illusions: The Adventures of a Reluctant Messiah*. New York: Delacorte Press.

Bakhtin, M.M. 1986. *Speech Genres and Other Late Essays*. Translated by Vern W. McGee. Austin: University of Texas Press.

Berry, Thomas. 1988. *The Dream of the Earth*. San Fransisco: Sierra Club Books.

Betley, Thaddeus. 1951. "Analysis of Accidents of Teen-Age Drivers in Texas." Unpublished M.A. thesis. University of Texas at Austin.

Birkerts, Sven. 1994. *The Gutenberg Elegies: The Fate of Reading in an Electronic Age*. New York: Faber and Faber.

Bloom, Allan. 1986. *The Closing of the American Mind*. New York: Simon & Schuster.

Bolter, Jay David. 1991. *Writing Space: The Computer, Hypertext, and the History of Writing*. Hillsdale: Lawrence Erlbaum Associates.

Borgmann, Albert. 1984. *Technology and the Character of Contemporary Life*. Chicago: University of Chicago Press.

Bowers, C.A. 1988. *The Cultural Dimensions of Educational Computing: Understanding the Non-neutrality of Technology*. New York: Teachers College Press.

Bronowski, Jacob. 1973. *The Ascent of Man*. Boston: Little, Brown and Company.

Burbules, Nicholas. 1993. *Dialogue in Teaching: Theory and Practice*. New York: Teachers College Press.

Burniske, R. W. 2000. *CyberPilot's License*. Available online: http://www.cwrl.utexas.edu/~burniske/cpl.

Burniske, R. W. 8 April 1997. Dialogues: Kuala Lumpur/Personal Visions/Communications. Online Posting. http://uv.cwrl.utexas.edu

Burniske, R. W. and Lowell Monke. Utopian Visions. Available online: http://uv.cwrl.utexas.edu

Callahan, Raymond. 1962. *Education and the Cult of Efficiency*. Chicago: University of Chicago Press.

Cappuccio, D., W. Kirwin, L. Pawlick, & S. Namasivayam, 1996. Total Cost of Ownership: Reducing PC/LAN Costs in the Enterprise. Gartner Interactive, February 9. Available online: http://garner12.gartnerweb.com/en/...12.garnerweb.com%2fggbin%-2fggquery.

Carroll, Lewis. 1983. *Through the Looking-Glass and What Alice Found There*. Berkeley: University of California Press.

Censors through the Ages. 1992. *The Economist,* December 26–January 8.

Ciardi, John. 1960. *How Does a Poem Mean?* Boston: Houghton Mifflin.

Clinton, William Jefferson. 1997. "Inaugural Address of President William J. Clinton." Washington, D.C.: Available online: http://www.pub.whitehouse.gov/white-house-publications/1997/01/1997–01–20-presidents-inaugural-address.text.

Cyberspace, 24 Hours in. Building Bridges: South African Township's Computer Lab Teaches English and Internet Skills. Available online: http://www.cyber24.com/htm2/4_37.htm, May 10, 1999.

Cyberspace, 24 Hours in. Opening Pandora's Box: Muslim Students in Malaysia Journey by Internet to Hollywood and Beyond. Available online: http://www.cyber24.com/htm2/4_287.htm, May 10, 1999.

Dertouzos, Michael. 1997. *What Will Be*. New York: HarperCollins.

Dewey, John. 1899. *The School and Society*. Chicago.

Dewey, John. 1916. *Democracy and Education*. New York: The Free Press.

Dickens, Charles. 1965. *Great Expectations*. London: Penguin.

Dickens, Charles. 1967. *Hard Times*. New York: E. P. Dutton.

Duffy, Thomas M., and Donald J. Cunningham. 1996. "Constructivism: Implications for the Design and Delivery of Instruction." In *Handbook of Research for Educational Communications and Technology,* edited by D. H. Jonassen. New York: Simon and Schuster.

Education, U.S. Department of. "Getting America's Students Ready for the 21st Century: Meeting the Technology Literacy Challenge." Washington, D.C.: Available online: http://www.ed.gov/Technology/Plan/NatTechPlan/index.html, 1996. March 7, 1999.

Eisner, Elliot. 1985. *The Educational Imagination*. New York: Macmillan.

Eliot, T. S. 1963. "Choruses from The Rock." In *Collected Poems 1909–1962.* New York: Harcourt, Brace and World.

Ellul, Jacques. 1964. *The Technological Society*. Translated by Robert Merton. New York: Vintage Books.

Ellul, Jacques. 1990. *The Technological Bluff*. Grand Rapids: William B. Eerdmans Publishing Company.

Faigley, Lester. 1992. *Fragments of Rationality: Postmodernity and the Subject of Composition, Composition, Literacy and Culture*. Pittsburgh: University of Pittsburgh.

Felsen, Henry Gregor. 1950. *Hot Rod*. New York: Dutton.

Fitzgerald, F. Scott. 1979. *The Great Gatsby*. New York: Scribner's.

Freire, Paulo. 1997. *Pedagogy of the Oppressed*. New York: Continuum.

Frost, Robert. 1973. "Mending Wall." In *The Norton Anthology of Modern Poetry*. New York: W. W. Norton and Company.

Frost, Robert. 1983. "Neither Out Far Nor in Deep." In *To Read Literature*. Edited by D. Hall. Second ed. New York: Holt, Rinehart and Winston.

Frye, Northrop. 1964. *The Educated Imagination*. Bloomington: Indiana University Press.

Getzels, J. W. 1982. "The Problem of the Problem." In *Question Framing and Response Consistency,* edited by Robin M. Hogarth, 37–49. San Francisco: Jossey-Bass.

Giamatti, A. Bartlett. 1985. "Baseball and the American Character." Boston: Massachusetts Historical Society.

Gordimer, Nadine. 1975. Introduction. In *Selected Stories*. London: Penguin.

Gordimer, Nadine. 1995. To the scholars at the International School of Kuala Lumpur.

Greenblatt, Stephen. 1980. *Renaissance Self-Fashioning: From More to Shakespeare*. Chicago: University of Chicago Press.

Gurr, Andrew. 1987. *The Shakespearean Stage, 1574–1642*. 2nd ed. Cambridge: Cambridge University Press.

Haas, Christina. 1996. *Writing Technology: Studies on the Materiality of Literacy*. Mahwah: Lawrence Erlbaum Associates.

Hale, Constance. 1996. *Wired Style: Principles of English Usage in the Digital Age*. New York: HardWired.

Harris, Judi. 1998. *Virtual Architecture: Designing and Directing Curriculum-Based Telecomputing*. Eugene: International Society for Technology in Education.

Henry, Tamara. "Questioning Computers." *USA Today*. 25 July 1997. p. 4-D.

Hill, Stephen. 1988. *The Tragedy of Technology: Human Liberation Versus Domination in the Late Twentieth Century*. London: Pluto.

Hirsch, E. D. 1987. *Cultural Literacy: What Every American Needs to Know*. Boston: Houghton Mifflin.

Hutchins, Edwin. 1996. *Cognition in the Wild*. Cambridge: The MIT Press.

Ihde, Don. 1990. *Technology and the Life World*. Bloomington: Indiana University Press.

Innis, Harold. 1951. *The Bias of Communication*. Toronto: University of Toronto Press.

ISKL. 1995. School Profile: 1995–1996. Kuala Lumpur: International School of Kuala Lumpur.

Jacobs, Joseph. 1984. *Aesop's Fables*. New York: Capricorn Press.

Kinneavy, James L. 1980. *A Theory of Discourse*. New York: W. W. Norton.

Kohl, Herbert. 1994. *I Won't Learn from You: and Other Thoughts on Creative Maladjustment*. New York: New Press.

Lanham, Richard. 1993. *The Electronic Word: Democracy, Technology and the Arts*. Chicago: University of Chicago Press.

Lanier, Jaron. 1995. "Agents of Alienation." *Interactions*, July, 66–72.

Lasch, Christopher. 1979. *The Culture of Narcissism*. New York: Warner Books.

Lerner, Michael. 1996. *The Politics of Meaning: Restoring Hope and Possibility in an Age of Cynicism*. New York: Addison-Wesley.

Levin, James A., Al Rogers, Michael L. Waugh, and Kathleen Smith. "Observations on educational electronic networks: The importance of appropriate activities for learning." *The Computing Teacher* 16. Available online: http://lrs.ed.uiuc.edu/Guidelines/LRWS.html (1989). March 7, 1999.

Liddell, Henry George, and Robert Scott. 1973. *A Greek-English Lexicon*. Oxford: Oxford University Press.

Lindfors, Judith Wells. 1999. *Listening to Children's Inquiry*. New York: Teachers College Press.

Lipman, Matthew. 1991. *Thinking in Education*. New York: Cambridge University Press.

Lippmann, Walter. 1984. "The Indispensable Opposition." In *The Norton Reader: An Anthology of Expository Prose*, edited by Arthur M. Eastman. New York: W. W. Norton & Company.

Mander, Jerry. 1991. *In the Absence of the Sacred: The Failure of Technology and the Survival of the Indian Nations.* San Fransisco: Sierra Club Books.

Mayhew, Katherine, and Anna Edwards. 1936. *The Dewey School.* New York: D. Appleton-Century.

McLuhan, Marshall. 1964. *Understanding Media: The Extensions of Man.* New York: Signet Books.

McLuhan, Marshall, and Bruce Powers. 1989. *The Gobal Village: Transformations in World Life and Media in the 21st Century.* New York: Oxford University Press.

McLuhan, Marshall. 1995. "The Gutenberg Galaxy." In *Essential McLuhan,* edited by E. M. a. F. Zingrone. New York: Basic Books.

Monke, Lowell. 1994. Damn Tests. May 4. E-mail to R. W. Burniske.

Monke, Lowell. 1999. "Infusing Technology into a School: Tracking the Unintended Consequences." *Bulletin of Science, Technology & Society* 19 (Feb): 5–10.

Noble, David. 1997. "Digital Diploma Mills: The Automation of Higher Education." *Monthly Review* 49 (9):38–52.

Noble, Douglas. 1991. *The Classroom Arsenal.* New York: The Falmer Press.

Organisation, International Baccalaureate. 1998. Diploma Programme. Available online: http://www.ibo.org/.

Ovid. 1985. *The Metamorphoses.* Translated by Mary M. Innes. Hammondsworth: Penguin.

Palmer, Parker. 1998. *The Courage to Teach: Exploring the Inner Landscape of a Teacher's Life.* San Fransisco: Jossey-Bass.

Papert, Seymour. 1993. *The Children's Machine.* New York: Basic Books.

Papert, Seymour. 1996. "Literacy and Letteracy in the Media Ages." Available online: http://www.wired.com/wired/1.2/departments/idees.fortes/papert.html: Hot-Wired, 1996. March 7, 1999.

Pascal, Blaise. 1958. *Pascal's Pensées.* New York: E. P. Dutton.

"Pedagogue." *The New Shorter Oxford English Dictionary.* Volume 2. 1993.

Perelman, Lewis. 1992. *School's Out.* New York: Avon Books.

Philosophy, University of Bristol Department of. 1995. Message to Ethic-l listserv.

Plato. 1952. "The Paedrus." *The Dialogues of Plato.* Translated by Benjamin Jowett, pp. 115–141. Great Books of the Western World. Edited by Robert Hutchins. Chicago: William Bennett.

Plato. 1968. *The Republic.* Translated by Allan Bloom. New York: Basic Books.

Postman, Neil, and Charles Weingartner. 1969. *Teaching as a Subversive Activity.* New York: Dell.

Postman, Neil. 1985. *Amusing Ourselves to Death: Public Discourse in the Age of Show Business.* New York: Penguin.

Postman, Neil. 1986. *Amusing Ourselves to Death.* New York: Penguin.

Postman, Neil. 1988a. "The Disappearance of Childhood." In *Conscientious Objections.* New York: A. A. Knopf Inc.

Postman, Neil. 1988b. "Defending Against the Indefensible." In *Conscientious Objections.* New York: A. A. Knopf Inc.

Postman, Neil. 1993. *Technopoly: The Surrender of Culture to Technology.* New York: Vintage Books.

Postman, Neil. 1995. *The End of Education.* New York: Knopf.

Ramage, John D., and James C. Bean. 1995. *Writing Arguments: A Rhetoric with Readings.* 3rd ed. Boston: Allyn and Bacon.

Redl, Fritz, and William Wattenberg. 1951. *Mental Hygiene in Teaching.* New York: Harcourt Brace and World.

Ritzer, George. 1996. *The McDonaldization of Society.* Thousand Oaks: Pine Forge Press.

Rogers, Everett M. 1995. *Diffusion of Innovations.* 4th ed. New York: Free Press.

Rose, Mike. 1989. *Lives on the Boundary.* New York: Penguin.

Roszak, Theodore. 1969. *The Making of a Counter Culture.* Garden City: Doubleday.

Roszak, Theodore. 1986. *The Cult of Information: A Neo-Luddite Treatise on High Tech, Artificial Intelligence, and the True Art of Thinking.* Berkeley: University of California Press.

Schon, Donald. 1995. "Knowing-in-Action: The New Scholarship Requires a New Epistemology." *Change,* November/December: 27–34.

Shakespeare, William. 1969a. "Hamlet." In *William Shakespeare: The Complete Works,* ed. Alfred Harbage. New York: Viking Press.

Shakespeare, William. 1969b. "The Tempest." In *William Shakespeare: The Complete Works,* ed. Alfred Harbage. New York: Viking Press.

Shaw, George Bernard. 1965. *Man and Superman.* New York: Airmont.

Shawn, Wallace, Andre Gregory, and Louis Malle. 1982. *My Dinner with Andre.* Carmel, California: Pacific Arts Video Records.

Shenk, David. 1997. *Data Smog.* New York: HarperCollins.

Sisnett, Ana. 4 July 1997. Re: 1st letter from South Africa! Email to R. W. Burniske.

Sizer, Theodore. 1996. *Horace's Hope—What Works for the American High School.* Boston: Houghton Mifflin.

Smith, Richard, and Edwin Taylor. 1995. "Teaching Physics On Line." *American Journal of Physics* 63 (12):1090–96.

Solnit, Rebecca. 1995. "The Garden of Merging Paths." In *Resisting the Virtual Life: The Culture and Politics of Information,* edited by I. Boal and J. Brooks. San Fransisco: City Lights.

Spinoza, Benedictus de. 1994. *A Spinoza Reader: The Ethics and Other Works.* Translated by Edwin Curley. Princeton: Princeton University Press.

Statistics, National Center for Educational. 1999. "Internet Access in Public Schools and Classrooms: 1994–98." March 7. Washington, D.C.: Available online: http://nces.ed.gov/pubs99/1999017.html.

Stoll, Clifford. 1995. *Silicon Snake Oil.* New York: Doubleday.

Stone, Allucquere Rosanne. 1996. *The War of Desire and Technology at the Close of the Mechanical Age.* Cambridge: MIT Press.

Strunk, William, Jr., and E. B. White. 1979. *The Elements of Style.* 3rd Ed. New York: Macmillan.

Talbott, Stephen. 1995. *The Future Does Not Compute: Transcending the Machine in Our Midst.* Sebastopol: O'Reilly & Assoc.

Tenner, Edward. 1997. *Why Things Bite Back: Technology and the Revenge of Unintended Consequences.* New York: Alfred A. Knopf.

Tupper, Martin Farquhar. 1980. "Of Reading." In *Familiar Quotations,* ed. John Bartlett. Boston: Little, Brown and Company.

Turkle, Sherry. 1995. *Life on the Screen: Identity in the Age of the Internet.* New York: Simon and Schuster.

Tx2K: The Texas 2000 Living Museum. 1999. Institute for Technology and Learning. Available online: http://www.ital.utexas.edu/tx2k.

Tyack, David. 1974. *The One Best System: A History of American Urban Education.* Cambridge: Harvard University Press.

Weizenbaum, Joseph. 1976. *Computer Power and Human Reason: From Judgment to Calculation.* New York: W. H. Freeman and Company.

Welker, R. 1992. *The Teacher as Expert: A Theoretical and Historical Examination.* Albany: State University of New York Press.

Whitehead, Alfred North. 1929. *The Aims of Education.* New York: Mentor.

Wilde, Oscar. 1973. *Lady Windermere's Fan and The Importance of Being Earnest.* London: J. Roberts Press.

Winner, Langdon. 1977. *Autonomous Technology.* Cambridge: MIT Press.

Winner, Langdon. 1986. *The Whale and the Reactor: A Search for Limits in an Age of High Technology.* Chicago: University of Chicago Press.

Wolk, Ronald, ed. 1997. *Quality Counts: A Report Card on the Condition of Public Education in the 50 States.* Washington, D.C.: Education Week.

Young, Cynthia A. 1997. Internet Curriculum Planning System. Lancaster: Classroom Connect.

INDEX